STRANGE
SKIES

STRANGE SKIES

Pilot Encounters with UFOs

JEROME CLARK

CITADEL PRESS
Kensington Publishing Corp.
www.kensingtonbooks.com

CITADEL PRESS BOOKS are published by

Kensington Publishing Corp.
850 Third Avenue
New York, NY 10022

All Kensington titles, imprints, and distributed lines are available at special
quantity discounts for bulk purchases for sales promotions, premiums, fund-
raising, educational, or institutional use. Special book excerpts or
customized printings can also be created to fit specific needs. For details,
write or phone the office of the Kensington special sales manager:
Kensington Publishing Corp., 850 Third Avenue, New York, NY 10022, attn:
Special Sales Department, phone 1-800-221-2647.

CITADEL PRESS and the Citadel logo are Reg. U.S. Pat. & TM Off.

First printing: June 2003

10 9 8 7 6 5 4 3 2 1

Printed in the United States of America

Library of Congress Control Number: 2002116694

Designed by Leonard Telesca

ISBN 0-8065-2299-2

FOR WENDY CONNORS

2003

CONTENTS

Contents

ACKNOWLEDGMENTS

Thanks to Janet Bord, Joel Carpenter, Wendy Connors, Loren E. Gross, Kevin D. Randle, Brad Sparks, and Thomas Tulien, and—of course, always—my wife, Helene Henderson, for materials, information, ideas, assistance, encouragement, and support. And to John White and Bob Shuman for their good humor and superhuman patience.

INTRODUCTION

FOR A MOMENT it seemed like old times.

In the early morning hours of July 26, 2002, on the fiftieth anniversary of a sensational series of sightings over Washington, D.C., and the surrounding area (see chapter 5), several persons called into a suburban radio station to report seeing a bright blue or orange light with jets in hot pursuit.

The next day the *Washington Post* ran the story, quoting Renny Rogers of Waldorf, Maryland. "This bright-blue object [was] traveling at a phenomenal rate of speed," he said. "This Air Force jet was right behind it, chasing it, but this object was just leaving it in the dust. I told my neighbor, 'I think those jets are chasing a UFO.'"

Andrews Air Force Base, near Washington, confirmed that it had dispatched two F-16 jets to check out what the Colorado-based North American Aerospace Defense Command (NORAD) called a "target of interest" which had registered on Andrews's radar. NORAD's Maj. Douglas Martin denied that the pilots had seen anything. "Everything was fine in the sky," he assured the *Post*, "so they returned home." Another NORAD representative, Army Maj. Barry Venable, offered a rather more ambiguous account: "There are any number of scenarios, but we don't know what it was." All anyone knew was that whatever the target was, it had disappeared during the attempted intercept.

Post reporter Steve Vogel reconstructed more of the story from military sources who insisted on anonymity. Andrews AFB picked up an unidentified target at one o'clock. When attempts to communicate with it by radio failed, Andrews notified NORAD. Soon thereafter, two F-16s bearing air-to-air missiles were sent out to investigate, but the target then vanished from the radar screen.

"It was a routine launch," Lt. Col. Steve Chase, of Andrews, insisted. Later, Maj. Mike Snyder, of NORAD, told ufologist Kenny Young that NORAD itself had not tracked anything out of the ordinary. "The radar return may have been caused by a small plane flying low," he suggested, "and sometimes that will cause them to drop on or off the radar. . . . Sometimes a plane will simply come down and land on a small airport in the area or on a grassy strip."

On August 2, in an interview with Young, Maj. Venable stated, "We do not plan on releasing any further information about this event. To date, we have acknowledged that we scrambled fighters to investigate an unknown aircraft detected by radar. The unknown aircraft faded from our radar screens before the fighters arrived. The fighters investigated the area where the unknown radar track was located, detected no other suspicious activity or aircraft, and returned to base."

Joan Chase, of the Fund for UFO Research, located ground witness Renny Rogers. She interviewed him at length, and the two reconstructed the incident at the sighting location. Rogers, a government employee, lived not far from Andrews and was used to aircraft noises. He would never have gone outside to look at a passing jet if this one had not flown so low that it rattled his house. Outside, he saw a military jet heading south-southeast. It was at about 3,000 feet and heading away from him. He went back indoors and all was quiet for the next three to five minutes.

Then jet noises, almost as loud as those that had attracted his attention initially, sounded, and again he stepped out to see what was happening.

He looked up but saw no jet. When he happened to glance to his left, however, he was taken aback by the sight of a pale blue light moving effortlessly at a high—but not, he would insist, meteoritic—rate of speed. It was at first about 35 degrees above the horizon in the northeast, just above the trees. It "dipped" slightly—Rogers compared it to a roller-coaster motion—then ascended to an 85-degree position. All of this in three to four seconds. Now a tree obscured the view.

Rogers dashed to the south until he could see the object again, now at 45 degrees in the southwest and heading away from him. Within seconds a military aircraft showed up from the north, heading straight toward the light. Five or six seconds later the light vanished, and 15 seconds or so later the jet was no longer visible. According to Chase's summary of the witness description of the apparent UFO:

> a constant pale blue in color and starlike, about two or three times the size of the red wing tip lights of the jet pursuing it. He could see no hard edge . . . any more than a hard edge could be seen on an airliner beacon light or radio tower light. The entire light . . . flickered on a cycle of about 1.5 seconds throughout the time it was visible. The brightness of the light was unchanging. He compared the flicker to a high flying airplane beacon light but with different timing. Rogers compared the quality (not the behavior) of the light to "blue" (rather than green) glow sticks held alight by a helium balloon.

I can't prove it, but if I were a betting man, I would put money on the likelihood that this incident has a mundane explanation, something either so unexciting as a passing balloon or so secretive as an experiment to test air defense over the nation's capital in a terror-spooked America. Had this incident not taken place while I was writing this book, it would not be here. It seems a pale echo of a now—it appears—bygone era when airplanes, civilian and military, encountered extraordinary flying objects with what sometimes feels like disconcerting regularity.

So, necessarily, this is a book about historical events: sightings by pilots of UFOs. It is also about a phenomenon that is both historical and current, the UFO phenomenon itself, of which pilot sightings are only a small part of the story. When I was approached to write this book, I had a hard time imagining how it would be possible to put together a volume on such sightings in isolation, removed from the larger—much larger, much richer—context of reports from observers on the ground. My multivolume UFO *Encyclopedia*[1] doesn't even have an individual entry for pilot sightings.

There is, of course, no radical disconnection between pilot sightings and other kinds of UFO sightings. UFOs seen from the air look pretty much like those seen from the ground. In other words, their shapes include discs, triangles, spheres, cigars, and boomerangs. Their sizes range from tiny to immense. Among the latter, there is the occasional "mothership," a bigger structure (usually cigar-shaped) reportedly housing much smaller ones (usually disc-shaped). UFOs that pilots see also sometimes interfere in odd and puzzling ways with mechanical and electronic functioning, just as they are reported to do with earthbound motor vehicles. The UFOs perform incredible, conventional-physics-defying maneuvers, usually while making very little or no sound. Radar figures more prominently in pilot sightings than in their ground-based counterparts—one of the two essential differences.

The other is the absence in pilot accounts of close encounters of the third kind (CE3)—reports in which UFO occupants figure. The only exception I know of—discussed later in these pages—is a piece of science fiction which, in the murky fashion in which folklore circulates, started appearing in early flying-saucer literature where it was treated as a true story. CE3s began as anecdotes of brief observations of (mostly) humanoid figures inside or near landed or hovering UFOs, then over the decades evolved into ever more complex, mind-boggling narratives in which humanoids abducted humans. Now, it appears, abduction reports are receding and growing less frequent, to be replaced by . . . well, I guess we'll see.

There is a narrative of sorts to the UFO story, if that story is taken in its entirety. There is, however, no particular narrative to any one part of it, even CE3s and abduction claims, many of which many ufologists would probably refuse to take seriously if they stood apart from all else. When they stand apart from all else, nearly all—or maybe *all*—UFO reports appear to be products of circumstance.[2] The witness happens to be at a particular place when he or she happens to see an unusual aerial phenomenon that happens to be passing by. Unless we are missing some huge but hidden truth (who knows?), a UFO sighting is an accident. Whatever it is, the UFO is not there for your benefit. You're glimpsing something that presumably has nothing to do with you and to which you are, at best, scenery.

Now rare and largely historical, pilot sightings in themselves have no particular story line. All they are about, generally speaking, is the perspective relative to the earth's surface that the witnesses chanced to be at the time they crossed paths with the unknown. True, pilots are better trained to observe and identify objects in the sky than most of us are; after all, their survival depends on it. In that sense, pilot sightings are more likely—though, as we shall see, not certain—to resist prosaic accounting. But in the end the sightings are discrete cases, so necessarily this is a casebook: a collection of what strike me as the more interesting, suggestive reports, most of them unexplained, perhaps (given current knowledge) inexplicable; the rest—the ones that turn out not to be actual UFO encounters after all—are significant for other reasons. The latter as much as the former have helped create and perpetuate the legends of the UFO age.

Each of the chapters that follow is written around a general theme and highlights reports defining a particular strain in pilot encounters. Where necessary, the chapters open with a few paragraphs placing the events in the greater framework of general UFO phenomena and history. Beyond that, except where clear answers or troubling ambiguities are present, the cases speak for themselves.

Which raises the question: What are they saying? In 2007 the UFO phenomenon introduced to the world by a pilot sighting—Kenneth Arnold's, on June 24, 1947—will be six decades old. It will still be mysterious, and it will still, sad to say, be neglected. It will still be a fringe concern, as it has been for most of its history. It will still be waiting for the day, which will not likely come soon, when it gets its proper due. When that occurs—as it will eventually, if for no other reason than that it is remarkably persistent (people, reliable, sensible people, continue to insist they have experienced it) and remarkably resistant to wholly persuasive debunking—it may well rock the world. If we—meaning those of us who over the years have paid relatively close and reasonably open-minded attention—have learned anything about the UFO phenomenon, it is, I think, that no non-extraordinary solution for the questions it raises is possible.

At least some UFOs are surely the product of technological intelligence. Many thousands of sightings from credible observers all over the world record structured objects—craft—which somebody had to have built. The phenomena also behave intelligently. In the case of pilot sightings, UFOs tend to approach civilian aircraft and flee military aircraft. Their movements and maneuvers do not appear random. If all this is so, meaning and purpose underlie their activity. Pilots and other witnesses glimpse moments of it, but far from enough to discern the whole of it.

Something is happening, but what? And how are we human beings related to it? Or does it have nothing at all to do with us?

If the latter, we need only lament our fellows' lack of curiosity about the fantastic and fascinating display going on around us. If the former, if ultimately this drama is about *us,* one day we may have occasion for some bitter regrets. The UFO phenomenon may turn out to be a great big cosmic shoe just waiting to drop on our heads. We may wish, too late, that the U.S. Air Force had heeded what two of the most important sightings—both by pilots (Arnold and Chiles-Whitted) in the early UFO era—may have been telling us: that this world is no longer ours alone.

1

The Mystery Begins

To EVERY AVAILABLE appearance, UFOs as we understand them have been around for approximately two centuries. That isn't to say that no one ever saw one before then, but if so, he or she left no clear record of it. Some writers have labored to give the UFO phenomenon a long pedigree, pointing to a range of wonders chronicled over the centuries and reinterpreting them—unconvincingly—as flying saucers. The searcher looks in vain for something that sounds, from the description, like something one might see today. Instead, one is regaled with visions of angels and armies in the skies, of ghost lights that supernaturally announce deaths, of trooping fairies, of ships sailing through the air, and of phenomena that are easily recognizable as auroras, meteors, comets, and the like. There are no discs, cigars, triangles, ellipses, flying wings. In short, UFOs.

That is, until the 19th century, when the occasional account in a newspaper or scientific journal mentions lights acting unlike anything in nature, or structured shapes such as the "saucer" seen in Texas in 1878, or the metallic doughnut observed off Cape Verde in 1870. In the last decade of the century, sightings of enigmatic "airships"—typically, though not always, said to be long and cylinder-shaped, able to move at great speeds against prevailing winds—filled newspapers in America and elsewhere. Airships and other odd aerial phenomena continued to be seen in the years and decades that followed. Most of these experiences, if we are to judge from letters early sighters wrote to the Air Force, national magazines, and UFO organizations after 1947, were not reported at the time. Enough made it into print, however, to cause one curious eccentric, Charles Fort (1874–1932), to note—as no one had before—that an actual worldwide phenomenon existed.

Fort ended up writing three books, the first published in 1919, the last in 1931, arguing that such sightings amounted to evidence that beings from other planets are visiting the earth. Not the first to suggest that such visitation may be occurring, he was the first to draw that conclusion from a wide body of evidence, and the first to write book-length expositions on the subject.

He deemed hilarious the human tendency to reject what it cannot explain and to try to drive the unacceptable, by whatever means necessary, from respectable conversation. In a letter published in the *New York Times* on September 5, 1926, he expressed an idea that seems almost eerily prophetic. If Martians were visiting the earth, he remarked, they would not have to go to any great lengths to conceal themselves. "If it is not the conventional or respectable thing upon this earth to believe in visitors from other worlds," he said, "most of us could watch them a week and declare that they were something else, and likely enough make things disagreeable for anyone who thought otherwise."

Terror and Mystery in the Sky

On January 19, 1915, in the first year of World War I, two German zeppelins dropped bombs on English soil, killing 4 civilians and injuring 16. It was the beginning of the first air war. By the time it was finished, approximately 50 raids later, there would be nearly 2,000 casualties, the British population would be traumatized, and the modern era of warfare would have begun.

By 1917 the British had worked out effective measures to stop at least some zeppelins. Military aircraft—biplanes—were fitted with newly invented weapons such as tracer bullets and machine guns, and these devices proved effective. The Germans were forced to develop what were called "superzeppelins," which, unfortunately for the Germans, flew at an altitiude of about 20,000 feet, significantly reducing the accuracy of the bombing. The last year or so of the air war was fought with airplanes, not powered airships.

During the two years they were used, however, zeppelins—with only a few exceptions—flew during periods of relatively moderate temperatures. When they did not, crews risked and sometimes succumbed to death by freezing in the frigid atmosphere. Thus, most zeppelin attacks took place between March and September. That does not in itself, of course, prove that what Flight Sub Lt. J. E. Morgan saw was *not* a zeppelin. What he encountered in the middle of the evening of January 13, 1916, does, however, seem a little odd.

He was flying at 5,000 feet over Rochford, England, when he saw a row of lights that looked like windows of a railroad carriage with the curtains drawn. With no other weapon at his disposal, Morgan pulled out a pistol and opened fire. The lights ascended and quickly disappeared.

This brief, somewhat cryptic report appears in a book published in 1925, Capt. Joseph Morris's *The German Air Raids on England, 1914–1918*. It may or may not be the first pilot sighting of an unidentified flying object. Sightings of what we today would call UFOs, characterized in the terminology of the time as "airships," began in the late 19th century.

The first known mention is in a Canadian newspaper, the *Ottawa Free Press,* which reported an incident that occurred in the early evening of July 12, 1891, when "a dark object apparently suspended in the air" was observed over a street in the city. Through binoculars the "object appeared somewhat in the shape of a huge cigar." A bright light shone from one end, while "lesser lights were visible at intervals in the center." Witnesses told a reporter that this was no balloon; it was far too large, and it just didn't look like a balloon. It moved from south to north and eventually went out of sight.

No dirigibles were flying in North America in the 19th century, but claimed sightings like the one above grew in volume. In November 1896 the California press covered stories, at least some of them obviously fanciful, about mysterious airships, and in April and May of the following year the Midwest and Texas logged many hundreds of stories. Again, much of what was claimed was not taken seriously—there were hoaxes, pranks, and journalistic inventions aplenty—but some of the reports seem genuinely puzzling. Comparable ones, though not occurring in wave proportions, would be noted in the next years. Another wave erupted in 1909, not only in the United States (especially the Northeast), but as far afield as the British Isles and New Zealand. To all available evidence, these were not airships or zeppelins. Even today, their exact nature—or, to skeptics, their very existence—is a topic of uncertainty and controversy. As tensions rose between England and Germany in 1912 and 1913, airship reports erupted again. Whatever their stimulus, it was not zeppelins, as popular belief held. Zeppelins, as already noted, did not cross over from Germany onto British soil until early 1915.

Shaky as the Rochford encounter claim to being the first pilot UFO sighting may be, the next claimant suffers from vague sourcing, usually listed simply as *"Sky Trails*, June 1933." No issue of this reported publication has surfaced. The alleged incident came to light on a UFO e-list in 1994 from someone—untraceable—who reported that it was "taken from a journal kept by Richard

West. Portions of it were serialized in 'Sky Trails' magazine, a small general aviation magazine."

These reservations stated, the story goes like this: At 2:30 in the afternoon of a day in late September 1926, airmail pilot Colin Murphy spotted a glowing, cylinder-shaped object in the sky over southern Utah. It had neither wings nor propellers, and it was three times as long as the DH-4 he was flying; in other words, it was 90 feet in length. It was 8 to 10 feet in diameter. The object approached him several times. Each time it got within 50 yards, the plane would experience engine trouble. Finally, Murphy grew sufficiently alarmed that he landed his aircraft in a sheep pasture. As he did so, the strange craft "took off like a shot out of a gun" and vanished toward the south in a few seconds.

A strange occurrence over the Tasman Sea (a part of the South Pacific between Australia and New Zealand) has a stronger claim to credibility, with a prominent witness, aviator, sailor, and author Francis (later, Sir Francis) Chichester. On June 10, 1931, Chichester was looking out from the cockpit of his Gypsy Moth aircraft when he spotted flashes of light, apparently coming from several nearby aircraft. A "dull, gray-white shape of an airship . . . nosed toward me," he would recall. It resembled an "oblong pearl." Flashes to his left momentarily distracted him. When he turned back to stare straight ahead, the "airship" was gone, but soon a similar-looking structure came out of the clouds to his right.

As Chichester would relate, the object "drew steadily closer until perhaps a mile away when, right under my gaze as it were, it suddenly vanished . . . But it reappeared close to where it had vanished . . . It drew closer. I could see the dim gleam of light on nose and back. It came on, but instead of increasing in size, it diminished as it approached! When quite near, it suddenly became its own ghost. For one second I could see clear through it and the next . . . it had vanished. A diminutive cloud formed perfectly to the shape of an airship and then dissolved."

Though Chichester's experience has obvious UFO-like features, it also has some that sound purely hallucinatory. At the time he had no idea what to make of it, but years later, when flying saucers became a subject of popular fascination and speculation, Chichester would remark that his 1931 observation tallied "with many things people have seen since."

A letter in the files of the defunct National Investigations Committee on Aerial Phenomena (NICAP) recounts an aerial encounter said to have occurred on January 1, 1937, over Virginia. Howard S. Behr, who would later become a lieutenant colonel in the Air Force, was flying to Raleigh, North Carolina, at 3,000 feet. It was noon and the sky was overcast, though visibility underneath it was excellent.

He suddenly saw something to his right and about 1,000 feet beneath his aircraft, a Curtiss-Wright Sedan. An object was heading across his flight path perhaps half a mile away. It looked like a gondola, gun metal in color, with both of its ends turned up. It had no visible windows or propellers. He estimated that it was 35 or 40 feet long, traveling 60 mph faster than his aircraft, whose speed was 90 mph. It flew off to his left and was lost to sight.

The sight was so bizarre and unexpected that Behr could only conclude that he had suffered a hallucination. He mentioned it to no one. It was years later that he realized he had seen something that people would call a "flying saucer."

Foo Fighters and Others

The expression "foo fighter" has its origins in a comic strip where the character Smokey Stover used to like to say, "Where there's foo, there's fire."[1] In the 1990s a popular rock band would take the name Foo Fighters, inspired not by the long-forgotten comic strip, but by a curious, still unexplained phenomenon from the 1940s.

Foo fighters were strange lights and shapes that pilots and other witnesses, military and civilian, began to report in the early years of World War II, at least by 1941. Both Allied and Axis combatants saw the things. If anybody thought they were something unearthly, he or she kept it to him- or herself. The all-but-universal view on both sides was that the other side had developed some weird new weapon, possibly to monitor air missions.

Among the first sightings was one made by a Royal Air Force bomber crew over Holland near midnight on March 25, 1942. The aircraft was on its way back from a raid on Essen, Germany, when the tail gunner spotted a luminous orange disc or sphere. It was following the plane and appeared to be getting closer. The tail gunner notified the pilot, who saw the light moving in to within 100 or 200 feet. At that point the gunner let loose with several rounds. He was certain that he had hit his target, but the object seemed unaffected. After a short period of time, it shot away at a speed that the startled and confused crew estimated to be close to 1,000 mph.

In recent years British ufologists David Clarke and Andy Roberts found a highly interesting report, long stamped SECRET, in the files of the Ministry of Defense. The witnesses to the event were the entire crew of a Royal Air Force Lancaster bomber. In the words of a cover letter from Air Vice Marshal of No. 5 Group, "The crew refuses to be shaken in their story in the face of the usual banter and ridicule."

Based at Syerston, Lincolnshire, the bomber, piloted by a man identified only as Capt. Lever, was assigned to a run on Turin, Italy, on a night in November 1942. Late in the evening, at 10:40, their mission completed, the bomber and its crew were flying in a northwesterly direction. They were 10 to 15 miles southwest of the city when a strange flying object, heading southeast, sailed into view, at the same altitude (11,000 feet) as, or slightly below, the aircraft. It disappeared from sight for a short time. Five minutes later it was seen again as the bomber approached the Alps.

The unknown object was passing on a west–southwest course up a valley and below the mountain peaks. "The lights appeared to go out," the official report states, "and the object disappeared from view."

The report states that the witnesses

> believe it to have been 200–300 feet in length and its width is estimated at 1/5th or 1/6th of its length. The speed was estimated at 500 m.p.h., and it had four pairs of red lights spaced at equal distance along its body. These lights did not appear in any way like exhaust flames; no trace was seen. The object kept a level course. . . .
>
> The Captain of the aircraft also reports that he has seen a similar object about three months ago north of Amsterdam. In this instance it appeared to be on the ground and later traveling at high speed at a lower level than the heights given above along the coast for about two seconds; the lights then went out for the same period of time and came on again, and the object was still seen to be traveling in the same direction.

On an evening in early December of the same year, an RAF Hurricane interceptor piloted by B. C. Lumsden departed from England on its way to the French coast. As he cruised at 7,000 feet over the mouth of the Somme River, Lumsden noticed flashes that he took to be tracer fire. On second look, he was less sure. For one thing, the lights were moving too slowly to be bullets. Besides that, they were getting bigger and bigger, and when they got to his altitude, they were no longer ascending but moving level with his airplane.

He made a sharp, full turn, but the objects kept pace with him from behind. He suddenly plummeted 3,000 feet, but the objects matched his movement and stayed at their usual distance to his rear, maintaining the same distance from each other, though occasionally varying in relative height. Finally, as his plane reached 260 mph, they moved a thousand feet beneath him, and soon they were gone.

"I found it hard to make other members of the squadron believe me when I told my story," Lumsden recalled. "But the following night one of the squadron flight commanders in the same area had a similar experience with a green light."

On October 14, 1943, B-17s from the 384th Bomb Group were on their way back from a mission over Schweinfurt, Germany, when objects the crews would characterize as "discs" appeared in a cluster in front of them. Fearing an imminent collision, one pilot tried to turn his aircraft, but he could not move it fast enough. He would tell debriefers that his "right wing went directly through a cluster with absolutely no effect on engines or plane surface." One disc scraped against the tail section, but as he and his crew determined later, it left no marks. Twenty feet from this particular disc was a "mass of black debris of varying sizes in clusters of three by four feet."

Late that same year a shimmering gold basketball-shaped object sailed toward the rear of a B-17 on a daylight run over Germany. Tail gunner Louis Kiss watched it hover over one wing, pass over the top of the bomber, then position itself above the other wing. After a short period it flew toward the rear and was gone.

On the evening of April 26, 1944, on the way back from a raid on Essen, Germany, Flight Lt. Arthur Horton, pilot of an RAF Lancaster bomber, took a radio message from his tail gunner, who worriedly reported that they were being followed by lights which had suddenly appeared. There were four of them, divided into pairs on either side of the plane. They looked like large, glowing soccer balls. Other crewmembers were also watching them.

Horton began a series of radical evasive maneuvers. They lasted for a good 10 minutes, well beyond anything the aircraft could safely sustain, while the objects kept their position. The gunners could not decide whether to fire or not. They feared that if they hit the objects, they might explode. Finally, Horton and they agreed that if the objects did nothing, they would do nothing. Eventually, as they reached the Dutch coast, the objects, a crewmember reported, "seemed to burn themselves out."

Horton recalled this incident in a 1987 interview with a British UFO researcher. In later years, examining the declassified Ministry of Defense records, Clarke and Roberts found references to the incident in the logbooks Horton and Bernard Dye, one of the gunners, had kept of the flight.

Between November 1944 and January 1945 members of the 415th Night Fighter Squadron had repeated sightings over the Rhine Valley. Lights, usually said to be orange, white, or red, appearing alone or in pairs, would pace interceptor aircraft, always at night. The lights or objects, which the pilots thought were intelligently controlled, performed fast-moving maneuvers and seemed to respond to the pilots' actions. In one instance, on seeing the objects a pilot headed right toward them, hoping for a clear look. As he passed them, he experienced what he thought was "prop wash," though ground radar personnel insisted there were no other aircraft on the screen.

Regretting his bold decision to approach them, the pilot decided that he needed to remove himself from the situation. He flew into a big cloud, then descended 2,000 feet and executed a 30-degree turn. He looked behind him, and the foo fighters were still there to his rear. They followed him for a short while before vanishing.

Years later William D. Leet, who had been a major with the 15th Air Force, 5th Wing, 2d Bomb Group, recalled his own unnerving experience. "My B-17 crew and I were kept company by a 'foo-fighter,' a small amber disc, all the way from Klagenfurt, Austria, to the Adriatic Sea. This occurred on a 'lone wolf' mission at night, as I recall, in December 1944. . . . The intelligence officer who debriefed us stated that it was a new German fighter but could not explain why it did not fire on us or, if it was reporting our heading, altitude, and airspeed, why we did not receive anti-aircraft fire."

In one of the very earliest press accounts to escape military censorship, the *New York Times* of January 2, 1945, quoted Lt. Donald Meiers: "A 'foo fighter'[2] picked me up recently at 700 feet and chased me 20 miles down the Rhine Valley. I turned to starboard, and two balls of fire turned with me. I turned to the port side, and they turned with me. We were going 260 miles an hour, and the balls were keeping right up with us."

Pilots in the Pacific theater were reporting no shortage of comparably enigmatic aerial phenomena. In June or July 1944 the crew of a Navy B-24D equipped with radar allegedly tracked a mysterious object as both flew over the Marshall Islands in the South Pacific. In 1967 William J. Martin, one of 11 men on the plane, remembered:

> This radar picked up a blip, which we tracked to within one mile. The only thing in sight on a perfectly clear day was one cloud ball which we circled with the radar still showing a sharp, firm blip. . . . We could see nothing around, over, or under the cloud. Whatever was there was motionless inside the cloud. We did not fly inside it; neither did we fire into it. The area was northeast of Truk. We were flying cover for [a] TF58 on its way to Guam. . . .
>
> This was reported in our debriefing as the radar at that time was something special, and the briefing personnel were very much interested in its results.

Another dramatic incident happened shortly after midnight on August 10, 1944, to a B-29 crew on its way home from a bombing run over Palembang, Sumatra. In a March 4, 1952, letter to retired Marine Corps Major and UFO author Donald E. Keyhoe, Alvah M. Reida related:

> My co-pilot reported a strange object pacing us at about 500 yards off the starboard wing. At that distance it appeared as a spherical object, probably five or six feet in diameter, of a very bright or intense red or orange in color. It seemed to have a halo effect.
>
> My gunner reported it coming in from about the five o'clock position at our level. It seemed to throb or vibrate constantly. Assuming it was some kind of radio-controlled object sent to pace us, I went into evasive action, changing direction constantly, as much as 90 degrees and altitude about 2,000 feet. It followed our every maneuver for about eight minutes, always holding a position about 500 yards out and about two o'clock in relation to the plane. When it left, it made an abrupt 90-degree turn; accelerating rapidly, it disappeared into the overcast.

A Weekly Intelligence Summary of the Headquarters Eastern Air Command, South East Asia, dated May 8, 1945, and classified SECRET, records an extraordinary event which took place in the early morning hours of the third:

> The B-24 first observed two red circles of light approaching the plane from below while still over the Truk atoll. One light was on the right and the other was seen on the left of the B-24. The light on the left side turned back after one and one half hours. The one on [the] right remained with the bomber until the B-24 was only 10 miles from Guam. From the time that the B-24 left the atoll, the light never left its position on the right side. It was reported by the crew

members as sometimes ahead, sometimes behind, and sometimes alongside the B-24 and always about 1200 to 1500 yds distant.

At daybreak, the crew reported that this light climbed to 15,000 ft and stayed in the sun. It was a short time afterward that the B-24 let down and went through a 300 foot undercast and lost sight of the light.

During the flight from Truk to Guam, the light was observed to change from an orange color to a bright yellow or white like electric light. The light was also described as sometimes looking like a phosphorous glow. This sequence of color changes occurred at regular intervals. The light appeared to be about one foot in diameter and the changes in color did not follow a pattern of acceleration or de-coloration.

The light followed the B-24 in dives from 11,000 ft to 3000 ft, through sharp course changes and even brief cloud cover, always keeping its same relative position and distance. At one time, the pilot turned into the light and he definitely reports no closure occurring. During the night high cirrus clouds masked the moonlight and a possible wing shape with a silver glow was noted by some members of the crew.

Guam radar units reported no bogies plotted at any time that this light was within its range. The crew members reported that the light finally left them when only 10 miles from Guam. The light was never close enough to the bomber to give a single blip on the radar and therefore should have been easily detected. Two blips with IFF were not reported at this time, the B-24 being the only plane on the scope.

The report from the Guam radar units plus the fact that the light was always seen on the right side of the B-24, and that even when the bomber turned into the light, no rate of closure was noted[,] tends to make the possibility of a jet powered or even a conventional type [of] aircraft a doubtful one.

A preliminary evaluation by the Assistant Chief of Air Staff Intelligence gives the following possibilities:

It is believed the lights observed were those of an unknown type mounted on Japanese aircraft . . . on an experimental or observation mission. While certain jet exhaust flame characteristics are apparent, the range and length of light greatly exceed the known capabilities of friendly or enemy jet aircraft. While observations vary considerably from characteristics of "Balls of Fire" recently seen over Japanese homeland, there is great need for intelligence on all air phenomena.

In May or June 1945, the crew of a Marine transport plane flying east of Okinawa noticed something unusual in the cloudless sky about a quarter of a mile away. On first impression the observers thought it was a large balloon. On second look they saw that behind the immense cylindrical-shaped structure were three much smaller metallic discs. The discs then entered the cylinder, giving witnesses the clear impression that it was a carrier vessel. The cylinder then shot off at a fantastic speed. In later years there would be no shortage of reports of comparable disc-carrying cylinders, which ufologists would call "motherships."

On August 28, 1945, a C-46 was en route to Atssgi Airdrome, near Tokyo, just prior to the proposed Allied invasion of the Japanese mainland when its engine faltered between Shoma and Iwo Jima. Among those on board was a soldier named Leonard H. Stringfield. As the plane began to lose altitude, a very nervous Stringfield happened to glance out the window, where he saw "three unidentifiable blobs of brilliant white light, each about the size of a dime held at arm's length." Moving in a straight line through the clouds, they stayed on a parallel course with the endangered transport plane.

Happily, the engine suddenly resumed normal functioning, and the C-46 resumed its previous altitude and course. The objects did not follow it, instead remaining beneath it, to disappear finally into a cloudbank.

Stringfield, who died in 1994, went on to become a well-known UFO investigator in the years after 1947, when flying saucers became recognized as a phenomenon. Like all ufologists, he became familiar with cases in which engine trouble or failure was associated with UFO appearances, and he wondered if the presence of the mystery lights had affected the plane's performance.

In January 1953, at a classified meeting of a CIA-sponsored conference on UFOs, called the Robertson panel after its head, physicist H. P. Robertson, the attendees took up the subject of foo fighters. A cryptic reference appears in the minutes:

> Instances of "Foo Fighters" were cited. These were unexplained phenomena sighted by aircraft pilots during World War II in both European and Far East theaters of operation wherein "balls of light" would fly near or with the aircraft and maneuver rapidly. They were believed to be electrostatic (similar to St. Elmo's fire) or electromagnetic phenomena or possibly light reflections from ice crystals in the air, but their exact cause or nature was never defined. Both Robertson and [physicist and fellow panel member Luis] Alvarez had been concerned in the investigation of these phenomena, but David T. Griggs (Professor of Geophysics at the University of California at Los Angeles) is believed to have been the most knowledgeable person on

this subject. If the term "flying saucers" had been popular in 1943-1945, these objects would have been so labeled.

Between the end of the war and the initial years of the UFO controversy, a rumor spread that as early as 1940 Nazi scientists had become convinced that extraterrestrials were visiting the earth. Sightings of their ships inspired German scientists and engineers to try to duplicate their extraordinary maneuverability, thus their work on rockets and (allegedly) disc-shaped aircraft. A pseudonymous "expert" told Donald Keyhoe, author of one of the very first UFO books (*The Flying Saucers Are Real* [1950]), "I think they realized these ships were using some great source of power we hadn't discovered on earth. I believe that's what they were after—that power secret. If they'd succeeded, they'd have owned the world. As it was, that space project caused them to leap ahead of everybody with rockets." There is, of course, no reason to believe this is true.

Ghost Rockets

In addition to amorphous lights and metallic-looking discs, pilots and others told of seeing "rockets." A February 8, 1944, report from RAF Air Intelligence's No. 5 Bomber Group, actually titled "Rocket Phenomena," notes, "Reports by aircrews suggesting the use by the enemy of some sort of anti-aircraft rocket projectile have been received many times during the past year, and with increasing frequency during recent months." These "rockets" followed aircraft, in formation, and were able to change direction—all beyond the technical capacity of Axis (or, for that matter, Allied) engineers to accomplish.

Such sightings anticipate the "ghost rockets," which superseded foo fighters to occupy a sort of transitional phase in UFO history between the foos and the flying saucers. Because relatively few of the sightings of this new phenomenon were from the air, a detailed examination of it is outside the scope of this book. Suffice it to say that the ghost rockets were usually described as wingless, silvery, and cigar-shaped, and spewing a fiery exhaust.[3] Given the tensions that would soon lead to the Cold War, they were quite naturally thought to be secret Soviet experiments, which we now know conclusively that they were not. The sightings occurred mostly, though not exclusively (some continued into the next year), in 1946 and in northern Europe, especially in the Scandinavian countries.

One sighting from Scandinavia took place in the spring of 1945. Among the witnesses was Albin Ahrenburg, a Swede well known in his country as a pioneer of aviation. Along with other accomplishments, he was a founder of Sweden's first airline company. At the time in question, Ahrenburg was working for the Geographical Survey Office and serving as a civilian employee of the Air Force. He and six crewmembers were flying over the central part of the country when they encountered what Ahrenburg would call an "aerial bus"—perhaps an oval- or cigar-shaped object. It was nearly 40 feet long, with a row of oval windows along its side. It paced the aircraft for an astonishing hour and a half, Ahrenburg would confide to a Stockholm ufologist years later.

Ghost rockets, however, were not typically described as having windows, and sightings were relatively brief in duration. What may have been the first sighting of a ghost rocket as such was made by the pilot of an American C-54 transport plane. Flying over rural France at 7,000-feet altitude late on the evening of January 18, 1946, he saw a brilliant light at 35 degrees above the eastern horizon. Since it was falling, he assumed it was a meteor, but when it suddenly changed direction and rose a short distance, he changed his mind. It is perfectly possible that the object was indeed a meteor and the brief ascension merely an optical illusion, but the sighting is mentioned here for whatever it may be worth.

Ghost rockets never went away entirely, even if no one called them by that name anymore. For example, two sightings—apparently of the same object—took place over the South Pacific on the morning of December 19, 1952. At 6:45, 130 miles from Guam, the pilot and copilot of a B-17, Majs. D. G. McDonald and R. E. McKnown, flying at 7,000 feet, spotted a silver-white cylinder. It was about 25 miles in the distance, and a blue flame three times the length of the object itself spewed out behind it.

Minutes later, at 6:50, members of the 54th Strategic Reconnaissance Squadron, at Anderson Air Force Base, in Guam, spotted a metallic cylinder, bright silver flame shooting from its rear as it passed between clouds. It was visible for no more than a few seconds.

"Ghost rocket" is as good a characterization as any for what a jet-pilot instructor saw over south Texas one day in April 1953. The witness, Lt. Edward B. Wilford III, was taking a T-33 trainer on a maintenance-test flight, passing through a clear blue sky with visibility stretching out 100 miles. At 20,000 feet he happened to glance southeast, toward Corpus Christi, when he saw a contrail from what he assumed was an approaching aircraft, perhaps a B-36. As he watched it, he rejected the B-36 identification on the grounds that the approaching aircraft was moving far too fast.

North of Laredo, the object suddenly took a 90-degree left turn. Wilford pushed his T-33 up to 37,000 feet, bringing him closer, though still not close, to the unknown interloper, at 60,000 feet. From this vantage, however, the pilot could discern the object's shape. It was a solid, sharply defined brown cigar, with no wings or tail. Behind it was a long contrail which began a ship length away from the object's rear, and from there extending some two-and-a-half ship lengths. The object streaked at an estimated 1,200 mph toward the northwest horizon and disappeared.

The phenomenon of pilot-observed ghost rockets would remain remarkably persistent. On July 27, 1984, at around 11:30 P.M., the pilot and copilot of a corporate Lear jet flying from upstate New York to Pittsburgh noticed something unusual out of their right windshield, toward the west. It was a bright streak of light descending at a 45-degree angle, then moving on a straight, horizontal path. After rejecting their first identification—a meteor—the crew grew ever more puzzled as it became apparent that the object was some sort of structure. It was cylinder- or rocket-shaped, black, between 40 and 50 feet in length. A bright orange-red discharge "like the flame of a torch" came out of the rear, bursting on and off three or four times, each burst lasting three to five seconds in the course of the two-minute sighting. In the wake of each burst, sparks were visible for several seconds before fading out.

The UFO paced the aircraft, even though it was moving in the opposite direction—a detail that baffled the pilots. During the sighting they heard another aircraft in the vicinity as it queried the Air Traffic Control Center in Cleveland to ask about the object. They were informed that no other aircraft—besides, of course, the Lear jet—were known to be in the area; nothing was showing up on radar. As the plane prepared to land, the UFO was lost to sight in the northwestern sky.

The following year, on August 18, four men aboard a Cessna were flying south along Sweden's eastern coast, near Soderhamn, when one of the passengers noticed something glistening in the sun above the woods ahead of them. They were flying at between 3,000 and 3,500 feet, and the object, though at a lesser altitude, was heading in their direction. As it got closer, Per Lundqvist, the pilot, reported, "we saw that it was a metallic missile with steering fins at the back. Now and then it changed its course according to the terrain, and I interpreted this [to mean] it was following the power lines below us."

Lundqvist descended and attempted to follow the strange-looking vehicle, but it moved too fast and soon rose above them and disappeared.

The witnesses were so disturbed by what they saw that they notified the Swedish military at first opportunity. For the next six months defense investigators tried to identify the object without success. No one thought to link the sighting with the ghost rockets of the mid-1940s, but the 1984 object looked exactly like some reported four decades earlier.

The Size of Three Aircraft Carriers

In a privately published book, *Living on Edge: An American War Hero's Daring Feats as a Navy Pilot, Civilian Test Pilot, and CIA Mercenary,* Byron D. Varner recounts the long career of Rolan D. Powell. The book tells the story of a remarkable UFO sighting from mid-July 1945. In 1996 ufologist Walter H. Andrus, Jr., interviewed Powell, then living in Texas, and secured further details.

At the time Powell was assigned to the Naval Air Station at Pasco, Washington. He had a dual mission. One was to help form a new air group which would conduct operations from carriers in the Pacific. The other was to protect the secret Hanford nuclear plant, some 60 miles away, from Japanese attack. At that stage of the war, which was only a month from ending, such an attack was unlikely. Still, security demanded such precaution, and Powell and his fellow pilots took their job seriously.

At noon one day an alert sounded. The pilots rushed to the briefing room, where they were informed of an ongoing radar tracking of an unidentified object. At first it had been moving at a high rate of speed. Now it was hovering over Hanford. Powell and five other pilots took off in F6F Hellcat interceptors. At first they saw nothing, but as they increased their altitude, they spotted it high in the sky, at about 65,000 feet.

The pilots, who had never seen anything like this, communicated their puzzlement and confusion to each other. The object was oval-shaped, with a streamlined appearance resembling a stretched-out egg. A pink color, it emitted a vapor from its outside edges, leading Powell to suspect that it was trying to create a cloud in which to hide itself. The sky was otherwise clear. (Large UFOs hiding inside clouds, sometimes called "cloud cigars," would become a phenomenon sometimes reported in the post-1947 UFO era.) The object was immense, perhaps as large as three aircraft carriers placed side by side.

Powell radioed the base to inform it of what they were seeing. He was ordered to fly higher, even after he protested, "If we go much higher, we can ruin these engines." The engines were not meant to go above 37,000 feet, but Powell and his companions pushed the Hellcats up to 42,000 before choosing caution over valor.

The UFO hovered for another 20 minutes until finally shooting straight up and disappearing even higher into the atmosphere.

The next day Powell found nothing about the curious incident in the local newspapers, despite indications from the briefing officer that witnesses on the ground had also seen it.

2

"There It Is"

IT ALL BEGAN, in a manner of speaking, over a conversation about $5,000.

Kenneth Arnold, of Boise, Idaho, had come to Chehalis, Washington, to install fire-fighting equipment at Central Air Service. Early that afternoon, June 24, 1947, a Tuesday, he was through with the work and chatting casually with Herb Critzer. Critzer and Arnold were both pilots, the former the chief flyer for the company, Arnold the owner of a specially designed mountain plane that took him to and from jobs throughout the Northwest.

The subject was a missing C-46 Marine transport. It had gone down somewhere in the vicinity, probably to the southwest of Mount Rainier, in the Cascade Range. That was as much as anyone knew; no one had been able to find it, even after repeated searches. Finally, in frustration, the authorities had put up a $5,000 reward—no small amount in 1947—to whoever could locate it. Given the probable location of the crash, that "whoever" was almost sure to be a pilot.[1]

As they talked, it occurred to Arnold that he might as well take a shot at being that pilot. He was due in Yakima later that afternoon, but if he delayed the trip for an hour, on the way he would have some time to linger around Rainier's high plateau, between 9,000 and 10,000 feet above sea level. There were hazards in such mountain flying, he knew, but his aircraft was a hardy one. He would also conduct a thorough inspection of wires, movable parts, and all else, to ensure that he and his plane did not join the C-46 and its crew.

He flew out of Chehalis at around two o'clock and commenced the search, sailing under a clear sky and through smooth, stable air conditions. Though the search was pleasant, it was also, as it had for so many other pilots, proving fruitless. As Arnold began to consider winding it down, he took a 180-degree turn over Mineral, Washington, at 9,200 feet. It was nearly three o'clock, and a strange new phenomenon was about to disturb the sleep of the twentieth century.

It announced its presence two or three minutes into the turn, in the form of what Arnold would characterize as a "tremendous flash." Startled and confused, he could only wonder if another aircraft, perhaps a hot-dogging lieutenant in a P-51 interceptor, had given him a "buzz job." As he looked around him in alarm for the next 20 to 30 seconds, all he could see was a DC-4, probably an airliner on the San Francisco-to-Seattle run, but it was far off to his rear and about 5,000 feet higher than his plane. Then another flash washed over him. This time Arnold was able to catch where it was coming from. In the distance to the north, to his left, he observed a formation of bright objects close, or so he judged, to the top of Mount Baker, 130 miles away. (Later analyses of the sighting would indicate that the objects were in Baker's direction, but much closer, perhaps as little as 50 miles from Arnold's position.) They were moving at a speed so extraordinary that Arnold could barely credit what he was seeing.

They were too far away for him to make out their shapes. "I could see," he would write, "that the formation was going to fly in front of me, as it was flying at approximately 170 degrees." They had to be jets, he thought, though he knew of none that could move so fast, or anywhere close to it. As they approached the north side of Rainier, Arnold counted nine of them, "flying diagonally in echelon formation with a larger gap in their echelon between the first four and last five." As their contours became ever more discernible, he wondered why he could see no tails on them, unless they were camouflaged in some way.

The objects "flipped and flashed against the snow and also against the sky," he recalled. "I discovered that this was where the reflections had come from, as two or three of them every few seconds would dip or change course slightly, just enough for the sun to strike them at an angle that reflected brightly on my plane." Their flight path was erratic, their motion "like speed boats on rough water" or "a saucer . . . skipped across the water." The echelon formation reversed the one practiced by the Air Force; here, the lead object was higher than the eight behind it. Arnold was also amazed at how close to the mountaintops they flew, snaking along the hogback and swerving in and out of the peaks as they moved on their diagonal south-to-southeast trajectory.

"Since this formation . . . was almost at right angles to me . . . I was in an excellent position to clock their speed," he would write. "I determined to make an attempt to do so. I had two definite points I could clock them by"—Mount Rainier and Mount Adams, about 47 miles to the south. The clock on his instrument panel was registering a few seconds before one minute to three when the first object flew over Rainier's southern edge. Arnold thought the objects were at 9,500 feet—"pretty much on the horizon to me"—but he was almost surely in error. The mountain peaks through which the objects darted are between 5,000 and 6,000 feet high.[2]

As they passed, Arnold watched them carefully. At one point he turned his plane sideways and opened a window, not only to get a better view, but to satisfy himself that he wasn't seeing reflections on glass. They weren't that, he quickly determined. There was no question that they were craft of some kind, with highly polished metal surfaces (sunlight reflecting off these resulted in the flashes which first attracted Arnold's attention to them). They were in a "big thin line . . . holding an almost constant elevation," he told the Air Force. Eight of the objects looked like pie pans with a smooth triangular shape at the rear. One was crescent-shaped, with a smaller, sharp-pointed triangle at its trailing edge. The entire chain, in his estimation, stretched over five miles.

Arnold then employed a standard method of judging the angular size of an object in the sky. He compared the object to a known object held at arm's length. "I knew they must be very large to observe their shape[s] at that distance, even on a clear day," he would recall. "In fact, I compared a zeus fastener or cowling tool I had in my pocket—holding it up to them and holding it up on the DC-4—that I could observe at quite a distance to my left, and they seemed smaller than the DC-4; but I should judge their span would have been as wide as the furtherest engines on each side of the DC-4."

The objects were, in Arnold's judgment, about 50 feet long, though one subsequent analyst, Bruce Maccabee, notes that Arnold was confused about the dimensions of a DC-4. Given Arnold's position, the objects must have been something like 80 feet long.

As the last object passed over Mount Adams, Arnold's clock-monitoring indicated that the formation's speed was a mind-boggling 1,700 mph. This could not possibly be correct, he decided arbitrarily, and he adjusted the figure to 1,200 mph or more—still far beyond the capacity of any aircraft of the period. (The following October legendary test pilot Chuck Yaeger would break the sound barrier when his experimental aircraft hit 700 mph.) If, however, the objects traveled 50 miles in 102 seconds, as Arnold reported, his original figure was indeed the correct one.

When last seen, over Mount Adams, the objects had begun to

ascend. After two-and-a-half to three minutes, the sighting was over. Arnold had observed their passage over 80 to 90 miles.

"It Seems Impossible"

The incident would never have taken place but for his interest in the $5000 reward for the missing C-46. But now, as he would write, "somehow the $5000 didn't seem important. I wanted to get on to Yakima and tell some of the boys [other pilots] what I had seen."

He landed at Yakima around four, went straight to see Al Baxter, general manager of Central Aircraft, and excitedly asked if they could talk in private. Inside Baxter's office Arnold recounted what he had seen. He drew pictures of the objects. Baxter seemed amused, but also puzzled almost as if in spite of himself, and soon he brought in other pilots. As Arnold repeated his story, one scoffed, "Ah, it's just a flight of those guided missiles from Moses Lake," a nearby Washington Army Air base then used as a testing facility.

Feeling somewhat deflated, Arnold proceeded on to Pendleton, Oregon. Thinking about what the skeptical pilot had said, he realized that he had forgotten to mention that he had clocked the objects' speed. If he was right about that speed, they were moving extraordinarily fast. But could he have been wrong? He pulled out a map and a ruler and tried to recalculate the speed—not easy to do while he was still trying to keep an airplane in the air. He put the map aside and decided to do the serious calculating as soon as he was back on the ground.

When he landed at Pendleton, however, he was surprised to see a group of people waiting for him. (He soon learned that they were there to attend an air show.) They didn't speak as he stepped out of the plane, just stared at him in curiosity. Finally someone broke the silence. It was quickly apparent that word had reached Pendleton about the mysterious "missiles." Everyone began peppering him with questions. This time Arnold mentioned the speed, detailing how he had tracked the objects' passage from Rainier to Adams. On the spot others proceeded to do their own calculations. When they came up with the same 1,700+ mph figure, Arnold suggested that perhaps they were all measuring from too high up on the two mountainsides. A recalculation from their respective bases—really a pointless exercise, since Arnold had seen the objects well above the bases—still yielded an unacceptable 1,350+ mph. As the conversation continued, there emerged a consensus view, with which Arnold concurred, that missiles were surely responsible for the sighting.

That night Arnold retired to his hotel, still mulling over the curious episode. In the morning a tri-state air fleet arrived at the Pendleton airport, and the initial curiosity over Arnold's sighting was forgotten as aviation buffs flocked to watch the show of aircraft more conventional than those he had seen. Just before noon, Arnold was walking alone on a Pendleton street when a man approached him to say that yesterday he, too, had seen "mystery missiles." They had flown over his home in nearby Ukiah.

The brief exchange persuaded Arnold that his sighting was indeed as remarkable as he had first believed. His only hope of reaching an explanation lay in publicizing it further, to find out if anyone else hearing of the sighting could explain it. So he showed up at the office of Pendleton's *East Oregonian,* where he related his story to columnist Nolan Skiff. Reporter Bill Bequette sat in and took notes. The conversation lasted no more than five minutes—the two journalists were putting the paper to bed and had little time to spare—but Skiff and Bequette agreed that the whole business was unusual and newsworthy. In a 1975 interview Bequette remembered, "Arnold never suggested that he had seen a spacecraft or anything like that. I believe he was just curious about what he had seen and wanted to know what it was. He was a sensible guy."

Shortly thereafter, Bequette wrote up a short account for the newspaper and a shorter one for the Associated Press wire. The latter reads in its entirety:

> PENDLETON, Ore., June 25 (AP)—Nine bright saucer-like objects flying at "incredible speed" at 10,000 feet altitude were reported here today by Kenneth Arnold, Boise, Idaho, pilot who said he could not hazard a guess as to what they were.
>
> Arnold, a United States Forest Service employee [sic][3] engaged in searching for a missing plane, said he sighted the mysterious objects yesterday at three p.m. They were flying between Mount Rainier and Mount Adams, in Washington State, he said, and appeared to weave in and out of formation. Arnold said he clocked and estimated their speed at 1200 miles an hour.
>
> Enquiries at Yakima last night brought only blank stares, he said, but he added he talked today with an unidentified man from Ukiah, south of here, who said he had seen similar objects over the mountains near Ukiah yesterday.
>
> "It seems impossible," Arnold said, "but there it is."

And it was only the beginning. Bequette would recall that when he returned to the office from lunch not long after he had put the story on the wires, a clearly rattled receptionist told him that the paper had been inundated with phone calls from all over the United States and Canada, all wanting more details. Becoming aware suddenly that he was on to a much bigger story than he had realized, Bequette picked up the phone and was relieved to get Arnold in his hotel room. The reporter interviewed him there for two hours and afterwards dashed off a 40-column story which he phoned in to Associated Press in Portland.

Saucers from Mars

The following day an International News Service (INS) dispatch, datelined McChord Field, Tacoma, Washington, took the sighting into an area that Arnold, or indeed any previous commentator, had never thought to enter. It opened with these words: "Nine 'saucer-shaped Martian planes,' reported seen over southwest Washington at 10,000 feet late Tuesday by a Boise, Idaho, airplane pilot, were 'out of this world.'" After recycling the canard that he worked for the Forest Service, it quoted Arnold as calling the objects "flying saucers."

Arnold would not have called the objects "flying saucers," the quotation marks notwithstanding. He had used the word "saucers" only in connection with their motion, as in "saucers skipping across water." Equally dubious are the quotation marks surrounding "saucer-shaped Martian planes." Apparently these are not anyone's specific words, only scare quotes intended to underscore the outlandishness of the speculation the anonymous reporter was employing to spice up the story. Yet the dispatch has considerable historical significance for two reasons. First, it is the first time anyone publicly suggested that Arnold had seen spacecraft, thus introducing the extraterrestrial hypothesis into the about-to-explode controversy over sightings of unidentified flying objects.[4] Second, it gave the new phenomenon a name: flying saucers.

Not, of course, that the phenomenon was "new" in any literal sense. The first book on what would become known as UFOs was published as early as 1919. Charles Fort's *The Book of the Damned* (this last word defined as enigmatic phenomena excluded from conventional scientific consideration) came out of its author's meticulous combing of archival material, from newspapers, scientific journals, and the like, concerning reports of odd lights and structures in the earth's atmosphere and beyond. Though such phenomena had been recorded since around the turn of the 19th century, only Fort understood that these were not isolated events, as witnesses and other writers had assumed them to be, but parts of a larger pattern. In Fort's opinion, offered up in eccentric, often jokey prose which sometimes disguised his underlying seriousness, such reports could only mean that unearthly others were watching the earth.

On June 24, 1947, Arnold had never heard of Fort. By his own admission not much of a reader, he was indifferent to science fiction and oblivious to the existence of *Amazing Stories* and *Fantastic Adventures,* two Ziff-Davis pulp magazines which, alongside the lurid space-opera and bug-eyed-monster fantasies for which both were notorious, regularly featured articles on "true mysteries" of widely varying credibility. The June issue of *Amazing* carried a piece by Fortean writer Vincent H. Gaddis. Titled "Visitors from the Void," it surveyed witness reports of enigmatic things in the sky and speculated about otherworldly intelligences. Arnold knew nothing of this, nor did he know that *Amazing* and *Fantastic* were edited by a colorful huckster named Ray Palmer.

On August 20 an Oregon man wrote the Air Force to assert that he had seen "the same flying saucers at about the same time" Arnold encountered his. The Air Force asked the FBI to interview him. The FBI account of the interview reads:

> Fred Johnson, resident of First Avenue, Portland, Oregon, reported without consulting any records that on June 24, 1947, while prospecting at a point in the Cascade Mountains approximately five thousand feet from sea level, during the afternoon he noticed a reflection, looked up, and saw a disc proceeding in a southeasterly direction. Immediately upon sighting this object he placed his telescope to his eye and observed the disc for approximately forty-five to sixty seconds. He remarked that it is possible for him to

pick up an object at a distance of ten miles with his telescope. At the time the disc was sighted by Johnson it was banking in the sun, and he observed five or six similar objects but only concentrated on one. He related that they did not fly in any particular formation and that he would estimate their height to be about one thousand feet from where he was standing. He saw the object was about thirty feet in diameter and appeared to have a tail. It made no noise.

According to Johnson, he remained in the vicinity of the Cascades for several days and then returned to Portland and noted an article in the local paper which stated in effect that a man in Boise, Idaho, had sighted a similar object but that authorities had disclaimed any knowledge of such an object. He said he communicated with the Army for the sole purpose of attempting to add credence to the story furnished by the man in Boise.

Johnson also related that on the occasion of his sighting the objects on June 24, 1947[,] he had in his possession a combination compass and watch. He noted particularly that immediately before he sighted the disc the compass acted very peculiar [sic], the hand waving from one side to the other, but that this condition corrected itself immediately after the discs had passed out of sight.

Informant appeared to be a very reliable individual who advised that he had been a prospector in the states of Montana, Washington and Oregon for the past forty years.

Johnson was at 5,000 feet altitude when he saw the objects. His estimate that they were about 1,000 feet above him would put them in the same altitude range Arnold's objects seem to have been in when they were moving between the peaks. Johnson saw only five or six objects, unlike the nine Arnold observed, but he may have missed the others as he concentrated on one, which he watched through a telescope for 30 to 45 seconds. He also estimated their size to be 30 feet in diameter, smaller than Arnold's estimate, but these figures are soft at best. Johnson was in the right place at the right time, and there seems little doubt that he saw—though with magnification and thus greater detail— what Arnold saw from his airplane. The Air Force took Johnson at his word and pronounced his sighting unexplained.

Little Green-Suited Men

Another sighting occurred not far away that same afternoon. It was not of an object like the one Arnold reported, but it anticipated a phenomenon that would become as much a part of the UFO controversy as sightings of strange craft in the air—namely, encounters with such things on the ground.

The witness, farmer Bill Schuening, was driving his pickup along a rural road 35 miles north of Pendleton. At the time he could not have heard of Arnold's experience, though of course he did later and was encouraged to report his own because of it. A humming sound alerted him to the presence of something out of the ordinary, but at first he could not detect its source. Then his truck went over a hill, and as it descended, Schuening happened to look out on a field. A shiny, spherical-shaped object unlike any aircraft he had ever seen hovered five or six feet above the ground. That was odd enough. Even worse, though, was what was beneath it: "two little guys in green suits with white helmets," in Schuening's words. By "little" he meant no more than three feet high. Moments later "they were gone. How they got into [the craft] I'll never know. They were just gone." The sphere rose and headed in an easterly direction toward the Walla Walla River, circled, and was lost to sight in the direction of the mountains.

It would be interesting to know, though we never will, how close to three o'clock in the afternoon this little drama was playing out.

Flights of the Pelicanists

Because of its importance in the UFO controversy, Arnold's sighting is still being "explained" by those whose implicit assumption seems to be that if this seminal report falls to mundane accounting, all that follows is similarly susceptible.

Besides Arnold, who thought he had seen some kind of experimental aircraft, the first to propose a conventional identification for the objects was United Air Lines Capt. Al Smith, who told the *San Francisco Chronicle* on June 27 that the so-called objects were merely "reflections of his instrument panel," presumably in the plane's Plexiglas canopy. The same article quoted meteorologist Elmer Fisher, who expressed the view that Arnold had suffered a "slight touch of snow blindness from the mountain peaks." University of Oregon astronomer J. Hugh Pruett thought the explanation was "persistent vision," meaning that Arnold had stared into the sun and its image persisted in his vision even after he was no longer looking at it. Pruett was certain that the discs were not meteors, because "meteors do not dip and sway."

The same day, Associated Press science writer Howard W. Blakeslee had seen jet planes and been mistaken about the details—such as shape and speed—that suggested otherwise. At the proving grounds in White Sands, New Mexico, Lt. Col. Harold R. Turner voiced the same view, only to change his mind the next day and identify Arnold's objects as "meteorites," apparently meaning meteors (meteorites are meteors that have crashed to earth).

None of these theories were especially persuasive, but they were only the first of many to come. Ohio State University astronomer J. Allen Hynek, whom the Air Force hired in 1948 as its scientific consultant on UFO matters, argued that Arnold had been wrong about the objects' distance and that he probably had seen large but ordinary aircraft only six miles away.[5]

In three books published between 1953 and 1976, Harvard University astronomer Donald H. Menzel, an energetic debunker, advanced six separate explanations for Arnold's objects. In the first of these books he argued, rather incredibly, that 500 mph winds—not known to exist anywhere on earth—had blown snow down the Cascade hogback, notwithstanding Arnold's clear statement that conditions were calm or the likelihood that his plane would have been severely damaged, even torn to pieces, if caught in winds of that magnitude. Apparently not entirely convinced himself, Menzel offered an alternative theory, that rapidly circulating air had pushed mountain fog around; the sun reflecting on this moving mist created mirror-like reflections.

By 1963, when his next UFO-debunking book appeared, Menzel (along with co-author Lyle G. Boyd) was putting forth three new explanations—mirages, "orographic clouds," and "wave clouds in motion." In his last book, written with Ernest H. Taves, Menzel pronounced this explanation: Arnold had seen "merely raindrops on the window of his plane," never mind Arnold's assertion (undisputed in any meteorological record) that atmospheric conditions were clear and that he had rolled down his window to make sure he wasn't seeing simple reflections. Even Menzel, not ordinarily known to qualify his opinions about anything, reluctantly but candidly admitted that he did not know "definitely" that his latest theory (the others, unmentioned, long since having been dropped into the memory hole) was valid.

In recent years other would-be debunkers have revived the meteor hypothesis, in the face of a number of problems, such as the objects' speed (far too slow), their trajectory (horizontal), and duration (too long). Scottish debunker James Easton has argued that Arnold's objects were merely pelicans—leading one wag to coin the term "pelicanist" to characterize one who proposes hard-to-believe solutions to puzzling UFO sightings. Along with many other problems, the pelican idea has one elemental flaw: even to see pelicans, Arnold would have had to be so close to them that he could have immediately identified them.

The official Project Blue Book explanation is that the objects were mirages, while, contrarily, Fred Johnson's sighting of what are almost surely the identical phenomena is listed as unexplained. More than half a century later, it is safe to say that Arnold's sighting is also unexplained—notwithstanding nearly six decades' worth of confusing, mutually exclusive efforts to persuade the unwitting otherwise.

Believing It

On the evening of the following July 4, United Air Lines Flight 105 was about to fly out of Gown Field, in Boise, on its way to Seattle. Shortly before he boarded the airliner, a DC-3, a man asked the pilot, Capt. E. J. Smith, if he or his crew had seen any of those flying saucers everybody was talking about. Smith laughingly responded, "I'll believe them when I see them."

Eight minutes later, at 9:04, Smith, his co-pilot First Officer Ralph Stevens, crew, and passengers were passing over Emmett, Idaho, at 7000 feet when something appeared in the sky ahead of them and at their elevation. Stevens blinked the landing lights to alert the other aircraft to their presence. As he did so, he drew Smith's attention to the object. As the two watched, four other objects joined the first. Together they moved in a "loose formation."

Smith and Stevens's immediate impression was that these were small private airplanes returning from a Fourth of July celebration somewhere. Their second impression was more confusing. The more they looked, the less the things looked like aircraft. They looked flat and circular. The two pilots decided to call for another set of eyes and summoned stewardess Marty Morrow to the cockpit. Taking care not to influence her perception, they simply pointed in the general direction. Morrow gaped in disbelief, then exclaimed, "Why, there's a formation of those flying discs!"

Relieved that their eyes and brains were in working order, Smith radioed the Ontario, Oregon, control tower. Would personnel there step outside and report whatever they saw? As it turned out, they saw nothing. Later Smith wondered if they had looked toward the plane rather than away from it, to the west. In any event, the objects were still in view from the airliner's perspective, and Smith was led to think that the objects were more distant (perhaps as much as 30 miles) and even larger than he had originally thought. The witnesses could make out enough detail to notice that the objects' bottoms were smooth and their tops rough. They were a dark gray in color.

At that point the objects seemed to merge[6], then they disappeared toward the northwest. Moments later, another group came from the left front, three of them in a line, a fourth on its own. This time the objects were at a higher altitude than the airliner, which was now cruising at 8,000 feet over eastern Oregon's Blue Mountains. After a short period of time, they sailed away at a remarkable rate of speed. From the appearance of the first group to the disappearance of the second, the sighting lasted 12 to 15 minutes.

In an International News Service account that went out on the wires the next day, Smith said, "In all the time Ralph and I were flying during the war, and in my 14 years with United Air Lines, I've never seen anything like it. . . . Frankly, I'm baffled."

Mystery and Madness

In the days following Arnold's sighting, the Northwest was in-undated with reports of shiny, fast-moving discs. The age of UFOs had begun, and Arnold unhappily found himself at the center of it. Reporters and curiosity-seekers called his home at all hours, making normal family life—he and his wife Doris had two small daughters—effectively impossible. Then on the afternoon of July 3, an old friend, Col. Paul Wieland, back from Germany where he had served as a judge at the Nuremberg trials of Nazi war criminals, called and suggested the two go fishing in remote Sekiu, Washington, out on the Olympian Peninsula, where nobody could find them.

The two flew out soon afterwards and stayed overnight in a Sekiu inn. They were disappointed to learn that fishing had stopped. A red tide had engulfed the inlet, killing the Chinook salmon by the thousands. Arnold thought the tide was "mysterious" and even sinister ("I admitted red tides into my collection of phenomena along with flying saucers," he would write), but in fact it is a known natural phenomenon caused by algae infestation. Specialists call it Harmful Algal Blooms, or HABs. By now Arnold was getting jumpy, and things would only get worse in the days and weeks to come.

Arnold and Wieland abandoned their expedition and headed toward home. They landed at Boeing Field in Seattle to fuel up. There, Arnold learned about Smith and Stevens's sighting of the previous evening. He was elated. One could not ask for better, more qualified witnesses than an airline crew, Arnold thought. Smith had a particularly stellar reputation as a pilot. Arnold wandered the terminal buying every newspaper he could find, seeking as much information as possible. One of them carried a picture Coast Guard Yeoman Frank Ryman had taken the night before in Lake City, Washington. It depicted a disc-shaped light source—perhaps not the most exciting or conclusive image, but among the very first taken of a flying saucer. Arnold was thrilled. He wanted to see a glossy blowup and thought he might find one at the Seattle office of International News Service.

So focused on what he wanted to do that he completely forgot his friend, who was patiently awaiting his return, Arnold set out on foot to find the INS building. After a number of missteps, he arrived there and met with a reporter. On learning who he was, the reporter ushered him out of his office and led him to the ante-room, where Arnold was introduced to two visitors: Capt. Smith and First Officer Stevens. When he walked into the room, they were studying the Ryman photograph.

Arnold and Smith hit it off, eventually repairing to a coffee shop to continue the conversation. In due course Arnold remembered Wieland and had to excuse himself. As he did so, he joked that maybe he and Smith would meet again "on Mars." They would meet again soon, but much closer to home.

Back in Boise, at the Air Force's request, Arnold prepared a report of his experience and sent it to Wright-Patterson Field, in Dayton, Ohio. Around the middle of the month, Lt. Frank M. Brown and Capt. William Davidson, military intelligence officers stationed at Hamilton Field, in California, interviewed Arnold in person. Arnold found the officers friendly and open. They went out to dinner, and afterwards Arnold took them to the Boise air-port, where Capt. Smith—"Big Smithy," Arnold called him—was scheduled to land around 9:30 for a short time between flights. After that meeting, Arnold and the officers returned to Arnold's home to look over the mail he had received in the wake of his sighting. Before Brown and Davidson left, they encouraged Arnold to contact them if anything interesting came his way. Then they flew back to Hamilton in an A-26 bomber.

While all of this was happening, Arnold was intermittently mulling over one letter in particular. It had come from Evanston, Illinois—a suburb immediately north of Chicago, on Lake Mich-igan—and carried the letterhead of the obscure Venture Press (later, Clark Publishing Company). The writer was a man named Ray Palmer, of whom Arnold, by his own admission indifferent to anything but utilitarian printed matter, had never heard.

Palmer, however, was known to many around the world as a controversial, even notorious, character. Born in Milwaukee in 1910, he had become an active presence in early science-fiction fandom. In 1938, through his writing and self-promotional skills, he was appointed editor of Ziff-Davis's *Amazing Stories* (the first SF magazine, founded by genre pioneer Hugo Gernsback a dozen years earlier) and the companion pulp, *Fantastic Adventures.* Palmer favored loud, lurid yarns which, because they amounted to Westerns ("horse operas") in futuristic interplanetary garb, were dubbed "space operas"—not meant flatteringly.

Even worse, Palmer was now championing something he marketed as the "Shaver mystery," based on the bizarre tales of a Barto, Pennsylvania, welder with the unlikely name Richard Sharpe Shaver. Shaver alleged that in the early 1930s he began hearing voices inside his head. He learned that in vast caverns underneath the earth's surface dwell evil beings named deros, the degenerate remnants of an advanced race that had lived on the surface until 12,000 years ago, when the sun started to beam negative energies. Those who did not escape the earth in spaceships were forced underground. They brought much of their technology with them and used it for evil ends, such as battling the tiny minority of their fellows, called teros, who had not devolved into sadistic idiots. Mostly, though, the deros beamed negative energies surfaceward, causing madness, violence, and plane crashes, and they kidnapped surface humans to rape, torture, and even eat.

By his own admission, Shaver had spent time in a mental hospital. He had, it need hardly be said, no real evidence to back up his outlandish assertions. Still, no small number of his readers responded with enthusiasm, citing their own or others' strange experiences or theories which they were sure validated Shaver's. Many SF fans and readers of *Amazing* and *Fantastic*, on the other hand, were furious to the point of obsession. They complained to editor and publisher about the magazines' growing focus on "true" Shaver-related material (including articles, often written around reports culled from Charles Fort, about possible alien visitation) and SF stories inspired by it. By the late 1940s Ziff-Davis, weary of the uproar, directed Palmer to publish no more Shaver material.

Meanwhile, Ziff-Davis was laying plans to move its operation from Chicago to New York City. Palmer was disinclined to move with it. So was Curtis Fuller, editor of another Ziff-Davis publication, the more sedate and mainstream *Flying*, whose readership consisted of pilots and aviation buffs. Palmer's experience promoting Shaver had convinced him that there was a large, untapped audience eager for said-to-be-true accounts of psychic phenomena, ghosts, lost civilizations, strange creatures, falls of substances from the sky, spontaneous human combustion, and a broad range of mysteries real and imagined. When flying saucers came along, Palmer already was familiar with comparable aerial anomalies, such as the turn-of-the-century unidentified "airships" and the "foo fighters" of World War II. These had already figured in *Amazing* and *Fantastic* pieces on otherworldly visitors.

Like Palmer, Fuller had little interest in pulling up roots. For one thing, Fuller's wife Mary was in precarious health and under constant care for tuberculosis. If they were to stay in Chicago, they would have to start their own publishing business. Together the two men came up with the name Venture Press (later abandoned because they learned that the name had already been taken) and decided to publish a digest-sized, true-mystery magazine which they would call *Fate*.

This was the background to the letter Arnold picked out of his mail in mid-July. As Arnold would write subsequently, "At the time, had I known who he was, I probably wouldn't have answered his letter. . . . Later I found he was connected with the type of publications that I not only never read but had always thought a gross waste of time for anyone to read." Not knowing this, however, he was intrigued enough to inquire of journalists of his acquaintance if they had ever heard of Venture Press or Ray Palmer. None had.

Nonetheless, on impulse Arnold wrote back. Palmer responded immediately with an offer to pay him for a written account of his sighting. Arnold wasn't interested; he had received other, similar offers, and they didn't tempt him, either. Out of courtesy, he sent Palmer a carbon copy of the letter he had written for the Air Force. Palmer persisted, however. In a quick letter back, he mentioned a sensational incident he had learned about in a letter from one of the alleged witnesses, two "harbor patrolmen" from Tacoma, Washington. The harbor patrolmen had seen several flying saucers and collected pieces of some strange "stuff" that one had ejected. If he sent him the expense money, would Arnold investigate and write an article about what he found?

Never one to let his reservations get in the way of the pursuit of a story, preferably a scary story, Palmer neglected to mention a salient fact, namely that his correspondent, one Fred L. Crisman, was already known to him. Crisman, an *Amazing* reader, was among those who responded to the Shaver tales with a fantastic yarn of his own: during the war he had fought his way out of a dero-infested Burmese cave with a submachine gun. It is highly unlikely that Palmer believed this to be true.

It is just as improbable that Arnold would have believed it. If Palmer had told him about it, chances are that the farce and tragedy that would become known as the "Maury Island incident" would never have taken place. As it was, Arnold was—understandably—eager for any evidence that would both validate and shed light on his sighting, for which he had received no small amount of ridicule. If there was actual physical evidence of the flying discs, who could doubt them any longer?

Farce and Tragedy

The day after Brown and Davidson departed, Arnold talked with Dave Johnson, aviation editor of Boise's *Idaho Statesman*. Johnson had had his own sighting from the air, and he told Arnold that Wright-Patterson had asked for his complete written report, too. In the course of the conversation, Arnold raised the subject of Palmer's offer to investigate the incident on Maury Island, in Washington's Puget Sound. Johnson urged him to accept the money—$200, an impressive sum by 1947 standards. That afternoon Arnold wired Palmer, and the money arrived the next morning.

On July 29 he began his adventure, taking off at 5:30 A.M. from a pasture near his home and heading out through a clear, calm sky in the direction of Tacoma, with a planned refueling stop at La Grande, Oregon. Over North Powder, Oregon, he began a gentle descent in preparation for landing, while above him and 10 miles to his right an Empire Airlines plane did the same.

At 6:55, as he was at 5,000 feet over the La Grande Valley, 20 to 25 "brass-colored objects that looked like ducks" approached him head-on. He thought they were in fact ducks, but he wasn't positive, and if they weren't, he wanted them on film. He grabbed a camera and proceeded to film the procession, which turned sharply at about 400 yards from him. "I was a little bit shocked and excited," he would recall, "when I realized they had the same flight characteristics of the large objects that I had observed on June 24. These appeared to be round, rather rough on top, and to have a dark or a light spot on top of each one. I couldn't be absolutely positive of this because it all happened so suddenly." Arnold attempted to follow them, but the objects, whatever they were, outdistanced him.

After he landed at La Grande, he asked members of the airline crew if they had seen the objects. They said they had observed nothing out of the ordinary. The exact nature of the objects remains uncertain. Whatever they were, they were quite small, at maximum 30 inches in diameter. When developed, the film shed no light on the matter. Only one or two of the objects had been captured, and the images were so tiny as to be meaningless.

Late in the afternoon, following a brief stop at Chehalis, where he considered staying for the night, Arnold summoned up enough energy to resume the flight to Tacoma. There, he brought his plane down on the runway of a small private airport. The couple who ran it warned him that lodging was hard to come by in Tacoma. As he phoned one hotel or rooming house after another without success, he despaired of finding a place to sleep. Finally, he called the Winthrop, the city's major hotel, and was startled and bewildered when the clerk told him that there was a reservation for Kenneth Arnold. Arnold had not made one for himself, nor could he figure out who could have done it for him; when he left Boise he wasn't even sure he would fly all the way to Tacoma.

In retrospect, these two events—the sighting of unidentified objects, the unexplained hotel reservation—would influence Arnold's perception of all that followed during his stay in Tacoma. He would become convinced that dark forces were shadowing him, and common sense would desert this ordinarily common-sensical man. To other eyes things would appear more mundane, more human-scale, but Arnold would go to his grave convinced that he had stumbled upon something eerie beyond comprehension.

In fact, he was the victim of a cruel hoax. The hoax was the creation of Fred Crisman, lifelong con man. Crisman persuaded his friend Harold Dahl to go along with the joke. It entailed their pretending to be harbor patrolmen who had encountered six doughnut-shaped objects while at work near Maury Island, three miles off the coast of Tacoma. The incident was reported as occurring on June 21 (three days before Arnold's encounter), when Dahl, his 15-year-old son Charles, and two other employees were on patrol in a small boat. They saw five strange craft circling the sixth, which was having difficulty maintaining altitude. Apparently in trouble, it descended to about 500 feet directly above the boat, and then it began spewing two kinds of substances, one like lava rock, the other a white metal. As the stuff rained down on the boat, Charles's arm was broken and his dog was killed. Dahl caught much of the incident on film.

Dahl told this story to Arnold the evening of the latter's arrival in town. He went on to relate another unusual incident. The following day, June 22, a threatening stranger in a dark suit had called on him. The mysterious man knew everything, down to the smallest detail, about the encounter on the island. He warned Dahl not to talk about it to anyone. Nonetheless, Dahl averred (rather oddly, given the just-stated, seemingly inexplicable weirdness of the [alleged] circumstances), he took the man to be a crackpot. He then relayed his flying-doughnut-and-residue experience, Dahl informed Arnold, to his "superior," Crisman. Dahl's boss then went to a Maury Island beach and collected samples of the materials the doughnut ships had dropped.

Naturally, Arnold wanted to see the stuff as soon as he could. So they left the hotel and went to Dahl's secretary's house, where it was stored. When Dahl produced a piece of it, his guest immediately thought he recognized it for what it was: common, ordinary lava rock. (It turned out, however, to be molten metal slag from a smelter.) The realization did not encourage Arnold to embrace the story, but it was not enough to discourage him—tragically, as events would show—from a willingness to continue the conversation the next day.

In the morning Dahl was there, in the company of Crisman. Crisman, who dominated the conversation while Dahl sat silent, had found additional samples of the saucer material on the beach when he went there to investigate, he said. While he was collecting it, one of the doughnuts "circled the bay as if it was looking for something."

At this point Arnold's breakfast arrived, and his attention turned

to both the plate in front of him—he had not eaten since the previous noon—and the pile of clippings next to it. As it happened,
one clipping described a saucer sighting over Mountain Home,
Idaho, on July 12. The witness reported that as the object passed,
a cinder-like substance like lava ash had fallen from it.[7] Arnold
decided that maybe Crisman and Dahl were telling the truth,
after all. He decided to bring in his new friend E. J. "Big Smithy"
Smith.

Smith arrived the next day and took over the interviewing of
the two men.[8] The following morning, Crisman and Dahl showed
up at the hotel room with samples of the two substances. Arnold
and Smith immediately identified the white metal as the "ordinary aluminum which certain sections of all large military aircraft are made of," in Arnold's words. "If this was truly the light
metal that Harold Dahl said was spewed from these strange aircraft, we knew, or thought we knew, that it was a fake." Yet Arnold persisted in believing that Crisman and Dahl's story was in
some sense authentic. He did not even raise his eyebrows when,
after he asked to see the film, Dahl swore he had given it to
Crisman, who swore he had misplaced it.

Instead, Arnold decided to take up Brown and Davidson on
their expressed wish to be informed of any new developments that
Arnold heard about on the flying-saucer front. As Arnold recalled
it, Crisman was "very enthusiastic" at the idea of a military intelligence investigation. Dahl, on the other hand, turned white. He
wanted nothing to do with it. Soon after the call was made, he left
the room. By 4:30 that afternoon, Brown and Davidson were in
Tacoma.

That evening Crisman regaled them with his and Dahl's story,
as the two officers looked over the 25 to 30 fragments. As it grew
late, Crisman began winding down—he had been, Arnold would
write vaguely, "reviewing some of his own experiences" (his close
shave in the Burma cave?)—but offered to hurry home to get a
box of yet more samples the officers could take back with them

to Hamilton Field. At that point, Brown and Davidson visibly lost interest, excused themselves, and were gone.

"My mind was going around in circles," Arnold would write. "I recall how badly [sic] I felt that I had asked Brown and Davidson to come to Tacoma. Even though they were as polite and nice as you could ask, they gave me the impression they thought Smith and I were the victims of some silly hoax."

Smith and Arnold never saw Brown and Davidson again. The two officers went to nearby McChord Field and told its intelligence officer that the Maury Island story was an obvious hoax. At 1:30 A.M., as it flew back to Hamilton Field, the B-25 on which the officers were traveling developed a fire in its left wing. The wing broke off and sheared off the tail. Near Kelso, Washington, the bomber plowed into the ground, killing two of its occupants—Brown and Davidson. If Arnold had not summoned them to Tacoma, if Fred Crisman and Harold Dahl had not conjured up a bald-faced falsehood, if Ray Palmer had not taken it seriously (or at least pretended to), they would not have been aboard.

Arnold and Smith learned of the crash from Crisman, who called their room around 9:20 that morning. He had just heard the news on the radio. Crisman came over, and not long afterwards, Arnold called Palmer and spoke with him for the first time. At one point Crisman asked to be put on the line. After he got off, Palmer told Arnold he recognized the voice. It belonged to someone who had phoned him a number of times from various parts of the country. Then Arnold recalled that on the previous day, he had asked Crisman how he and Dahl learned of Palmer. Crisman replied that he was a regular reader of *Venture Magazine*. No such magazine existed. Venture was only the name of a publishing company that at the time was publishing nothing.

Later that day, Smith and Arnold drove to the pier to meet Crisman, who was to take them to the island in his "harbor patrol" boat. It turned out to be nothing more than a small, beat-up fishing boat, and it wasn't working. They noticed that the engine looked as if it hadn't worked in a long time. Moreover, the extensive recent damage allegedly caused by the falling metal and rock was nowhere apparent. As if to sink his credibility to new depths, Crisman said that the film Dahl had taken of the flying doughnuts had disappeared from Crisman's office.

Knowing they were not going to get to the island in Crisman's nonfunctioning vessel and exhausted by Crisman's company, Arnold and Smith left. They never saw him again.[9]

They returned to the hotel room, where they took a call from United Press reporter Ted Morello. An anonymous phone informant, Morello told them, was predicting that Smith would be called to Wright-Patterson Field to meet with military-intelligence people there (he wasn't). The caller claimed that a shell from a 20mm cannon had downed the B-25 and that both Arnold's plane and Smith's airliner had been shot at on a number of occasions—an allegation the two rejected as preposterous.

On August 8, following an investigation, Fourth Air Force spokesman Lt. Col. Donald L. Springer issued a statement declaring the Crisman/Dahl story a hoax. It had all started when—as Air Force interrogators learned from Dahl and Crisman's confession to them—the two hoaxers sent fragments to Palmer as a joke. In the accompanying letter they suggested that they "might" have come from a flying saucer. The joke had blossomed from there.

Years later, in an interview with journalism historian Herbert Strentz, Associated Press reporter Elmer Vogel remembered visiting Dahl's house while working on the story. As they stood on the back porch, Dahl's wife flew out of the door waving a butcher knife. For a frightened moment, Vogel thought he was a goner. He breathed easier when he saw that the object of her wrath was her husband, beneath whose nose the blade was pointed dangerously close. "I'm tired of being embarrassed by your lies!" she shouted. "Tell this man the truth." Truthfully, Dahl admitted that he had lied.

Visitors

Arnold and flying saucers were not quite through with each other. This ordinarily incurious man was in the grip of an obsession. He wanted to know what the discs were. Mail poured into his house, most of it detailing people's experiences with the saucers and even weirder phenomena. By his estimate he would eventually receive as many as 10,000 letters.[10] Arnold maintained a relationship with *Fate* and Ray Palmer, writing an article (no doubt with a lot of uncredited assistance from Palmer) for the first issue of the magazine (Spring 1948) and two follow-ups in the Summer and Fall issues. The latter two covered UFO activity, already bewildering and awe-inspiring in its diversity and complexity. The Summer article, titled "Are Space Visitors Here?", concluded:

> Well, there you have it. Many people have seen them; photos have been taken of them, both visible and "half" visible, in the air and in the water; they've come down, gone sideways, gone up; they're blue and green and fiery; they are spheres, cones, torpedoes; they go incredibly fast or impossibly slow (for aircraft); radar can see the ones you can't; they whine and they roar and they explode; they flame and they flash; scientists explain 'em and can't explain 'em.
> But *don't say they aren't here!*

With his tape recorder in tow, Arnold flew around the Northwest whenever he wanted to talk with someone who had had a sighting or other unexplained encounter. In due course he spent, he would guess, some $30,000 pursuing such inquiries. He interviewed persons who had seen saucers, but he also met with the individuals who swore they had seen humanoid entities who could have been space people.

For example, there were the flying men. On the afternoon of

January 6, 1948, an elderly woman named Bernice Zaikowski, who lived on a farm outside Chehalis, Washington, and eight children told of seeing a man equipped with long silver wings. He was hovering over Mrs. Zaikowski's barn, manipulating instruments attached to his chest. There was no propeller or other obvious means of propulsion, but the figure, who flew in an upright position, easily maneuvered about. He ascended until he could no longer be seen.

Arnold spoke with her and also, months later, with a man from Grassy Butte, Oregon. At dawn on September 16, he allegedly saw two "flying persons" passing through the southern sky at about 200 feet altitude. Their movement was slow enough that the witness got a good look at them. The wings were narrow and rounded at the tips. The fliers' legs seemed unusually short.

Another encounter claim came from a woman named Ellen Jonerson of Canby, Oregon. She was, according to Arnold, a "University of Oregon graduate and a very intelligent person." Though the thought did not occur to Arnold, Jonerson's story has more an elfin quality than anything. In any event, she did not mention seeing a flying saucer in association with the tiny man she noticed in her neighbor's yard.

She was working in her own yard when her eyes fell on the back of a 12-inch figure. As she tried to reconcile ordinary perception with what those eyes were telling her, the figure turned around, revealing a stocky build and a face that was either naturally dark or heavily tanned. He was clad not in a spacesuit but in rather more ordinary, if undersized, garb: a plaid shirt and overalls. A skullcap covered the top of his head.

Recovering her wits, Jonerson dashed inside her house to phone a friend, presumably in the interest of securing an independent witness. When she stepped outside shortly thereafter, he was "waddling" away in the direction of a 1937 Dodge parked on the street. Rather than go around it, he walked under its running board and vanished.

Outlandish as the story undoubtedly was, Arnold would re-member it all his life and often speak of it, recalling how im-pressed he had been with Jonerson's straightforward testimony. He wished, however, that she had done what she could have done: "run over and grabbed the little fellow," as she put it.

But the most bizarre of all was the tale of Samuel Eaton Thomp-son. As Thompson, a retired and marginally educated railroad man in his 70s, told it, he was passing in his car through a wooded area between Morton and Mineral, Washington, on March 28, 1950, when he stopped to take a break. Stretching his legs, he wan-dered along an old logging trail until he came to a clearing, where he encountered a craft "shaped like two saucers fused together" (almost a cliché of later UFO description), perhaps 80 feet wide and 30 feet high. It was hovering just above the ground, with steps leading from the open door. On those steps children were playing.

They were not, of course, ordinary children. They were "beau-tiful," darkly tanned, with dark blond hair flowing to their waists. They were also nude. Shortly afterwards, their adult equivalents—similarly unclad—showed up at the door, watching Thompson as if fearful of his intentions. After he managed to persuade them that he meant no harm, they invited him into their ship.

They spoke—interestingly, like Thompson himself—in an "un-educated" English, and while friendly and good-natured, they seemed curiously naïve, unable even to explain how their ship flew. They operated more by instinct than by intellect, and they ate what we would now call organic foods (not a phrase with which Thompson was familiar). They were, they told him, from Venus; Thompson himself had been a Venusian in a former life. (In another peculiar detail, when he related this to Arnold and his wife a day or two after the alleged incident, Thompson did not appear to have the word "reincarnation" in his decidedly limited vocabulary.) Thompson spent a total of 40 hours in their com-pany. At one point he went home to pick up a camera so that he could photograph the Venusians and their ship. Sadly, the pictures did not turn out. "It was just like trying to take a picture of the sun," he lamented. "That film was just blank."

To every appearance, Thompson was sincere, and probably fully as naïve as the Venusians he described. Arnold decided that he was no hoaxer—a conclusion with which anybody who has heard the tape of the interview is likely to agree. On the other hand, not being devoid of all good sense, he was unprepared to believe that Thompson had been aboard a Venusian spaceship in any objective sense. Arnold decided that Thompson had undergone a visionary or "psychic" experience, whatever that actually means.

Arnold would have other sightings of his own. One took place as he was flying near Susanville, California, one day in 1952. He saw two objects with a craftlike configuration, except that one was transparent. They looked as if they were "alive," he thought, reflecting a once-popular speculation that UFOs themselves are living entities or "space animals." On occasion Arnold would wonder in statements to newspaper reporters if these creature-UFOs had "the power to change their density and appearance." But he did not rule out the possibility of craft and crews from other worlds, and sometimes his ruminations took on a distinctly occultish cast. These sorts of ideas came Arnold's way via his mail—not from his reading of mystical literature, which always challenged his attention span—or from conversations with the esoterically inclined and abundantly imaginative Palmer.

On the afternoon of July 9, 1966, Arnold filmed a balloon-like object over Idaho Falls, Idaho. Though its appearance by Arnold's own admission was not especially anomalous, he was convinced it was moving against the wind and thus at least a candidate for UFO status.

In 1952 he and Ray Palmer released a book titled *The Coming of the Saucers*. It consisted of material taken and revised from earlier *Fate* articles the two had done. The book rehashes Arnold's sighting and the Maury Island affair and covers a range of other material. Arnold would complain for the rest of his life about the money he had lost from taking Palmer's advice, though for some reason he never seemed to hold it against Palmer personally. Doubleday had approached him, he said, with a $50,000 offer to write a flying-saucer book. Knowing nothing about writing books, he decided to seek guidance from Palmer. Palmer urged him to turn down the offer; the two would publish the book themselves and keep the sure-to-be-big take for themselves. Thus *The Coming of the Saucers*, from which Arnold never took a cent.

Back from the Twilight Zone

By the time the book appeared, Arnold was ready to return to the normal life of a taciturn, conservative-Republican Westerner. He dropped out of involvement with UFOs, reemerging only in the occasional newspaper interview. In 1962 he ran unsuccessfully for the GOP nomination for lieutenant governor of Idaho. In June 1977 he participated in the First (and only) International UFO Congress, sponsored by *Fate* and held at Chicago's Pick-Congress Hotel. There he met Palmer—who had long since sold his share of the magazine and started up his own modest publishing venture in small-town Wisconsin—for the first time in many years. His first words to Palmer were, "There's my old buddy." (I know this because I heard them. I was at Arnold's side.) While at the Congress, Arnold got to hear author, scientist, and ufologist Jacques Vallee remark that the UFO phenomenon could as well be called the "Arnold phenomenon."

In 1987 he consented to an interview with ufologist Greg Long. Even four decades later, he was bitter about the way he had been treated. He remembered "the nameless, faceless people ridiculing me. I was considered an Orson Welles,[11] a fraud. . . . I loved my country. I was very naïve about the whole thing. I was the unfortunate goat who first reported [the phenomenon]." In those early days he believed—probably with reason, given the Hoover-era FBI's interest in anyone who could be watched in the name of "national security"—that the government was monitoring him and causing trouble for him, including a 1950 tax audit. "Governments are more afraid than anything else of Joan of Arcs, religious saints, or 'phenomena' that cause their self-destruction," he said, adding, "When it happens to you, you're completely helpless."

Palmer died in August 1977 while on vacation in Florida. Arnold survived a few more years. He passed away in a Bellevue, Washington, hospital on January 6, 1984. Flying saucers live on.

3

Killed by a Flying Saucer

REPORTS OF CURIOUS aerial phenomena have been fixed in the popular consciousness for more than half a century. The worldwide sense of wonder associated with the widely publicized sightings of the late 1940s and the early 1950s has mostly dissipated, however. UFO reports continue to spark a range of emotions, of course: astonishment or, on occasion, fright from direct witnesses; puzzlement or jeers from others, that is, those without personal experience of the phenomenon. What is also missing is also forgotten: the sense of expectation.

In the dawning years of the UFO era, few imagined that answers would not be forthcoming in fairly short order. Either a flying disc would crash, thereby establishing both its reality and, at least by inference, its maker; or the persons—if persons they were—flying the discs would reveal themselves. In so doing, they would also let us know what they were up to.

It was the latter issue that brought military agencies into the forefront of UFO investigation. If there were unidentified, apparently unauthorized aircraft sailing through the nation's airspace, it was incumbent upon any official body involved in national defense generally and air defense specifically to investigate the reports, determine their significance, and act accordingly.

As early as September 23, 1947, Lt. Gen. Nathan F. Twining, in charge of the Air Materiel Command, headquartered at Wright Field (soon to be renamed Wright-Patterson Air Force Base), Dayton, Ohio, wrote his superiors to remark that "the phenomenon reported is something real and not visionary or fictitious." He urged that "Headquarters, Army Air Forces, issue a directive assigning a priority, security classification and Code Name for a detailed study of the matter." Maj. Gen. Charles P. Cabell, later to be chief of Air Force Intelligence, echoed the sentiment: "The conclusion appears inescapable that some type of flying object has been observed." Wright Field's own Intelligence Chief, Col. Howard McCoy, agreed, remarking that "it is obvious some types of flying objects have been sighted."

The very first investigations were conducted out of the A-2 section of the Fourth Air Force, based in Hamilton Field, California. Army Air Force Chief of Staff Gen. Carl Spaatz, concerned about the outbreak of sightings in the Northwest (of which Kenneth Arnold's was only the first to attract national press coverage), ordered the section to "open a file." The officer in charge of Hamilton's A-2 section, Lt. Col. Donald L. Springer, gave the job of running down reports and witnesses to two of his brightest young men, who would die for their efforts: Capt. William L. Davidson and 1st Lt. Frank M. Brown, killed in a plane crash on their way home from Tacoma, Washington, after determining that a claim of UFOs and physical evidence from Maury Island was a fabrication.

Still, it was clear virtually at the outset that only a relative handful of reports were hoaxes. Overwhelmingly, the witnesses were sincere and sane. No serious observer of what was going on thought—at least after the days and weeks following Arnold's sighting—that the flying discs were the confabulations of the gullible and the mentally disordered. Overwhelmingly, the people who reported seeing them were credible, solid citizens, and some—such as military personnel, scientists, and pilots—were particularly credible witnesses.

What is probably the first post-Arnold sighting of a UFO by an Army Air Force pilot occurred four days later, on June 28. First Lt. Eric B. Armstrong left Brooks Field in San Antonio, Texas, that morning with an intended destination of Portland, Oregon. By 1:15 P.M. he was 30 miles north of and 10,000 feet above Lake Meade, Nevada. Noticing some movement below him, he turned his gaze to five or six white disc-shaped objects flying smoothly toward the southeast. They were small—only three feet in diameter—but they were moving fast enough that they were soon out of sight.[1]

The Air Force—no longer the Army Air Force, as of the summer of 1947—needed to know what was going on. On December 30 the Air Force Chief of Staff gave the go-ahead to an official project, under a classified name (Sign; in subsequent public discussion, it was called "Project Saucer") and at A2 restricted classification (A1 being the highest level of classification). It was under the direction of Air Materiel Command (AMC) and worked out of Wright-Patterson. Its first day on the job was January 22, 1948, and its first big case was one that had happened earlier that month—one that had the potential both to solve the flying-saucer mystery and to expose the possible danger the strange objects posed to America's national security.

The Mantell Incident

In its evening edition of January 7, 1948, the *Louisville Courier* ran a chilling headline, as if to confirm everyone's most nightmarish fears about the mass of flying saucers being reported in the skies of Earth: F-51 and Capt. Mantell Destroyed Chasing Flying Saucer.

Beyond those stark words were mystery and controversy sufficient to go on for decades to come. The already complex real story would be further complicated by wild rumors and speculation. Project Blue Book head Edward J. Ruppelt called it one of "the classics," and it was certainly that to the first generation of UFO enthusiasts. To the first Air Force investigators, it looked very much as if an interplanetary spacecraft had downed an interceptor aircraft and killed its pilot.

The pilot was Kentucky Air National Guard Capt. Thomas F. Mantell, Jr., 25 years old, an experienced flyer, a veteran of the Normandy invasion. The episode is even today known as the Mantell Incident.

Early on the afternoon of January 7, the Kentucky State Highway Patrol took calls from anxious citizens of Maysville. They were reporting that a strange object was passing over town. The patrol notified Godman Field's military police and asked if they knew of an airplane in the area. (Godman, located in Louisville, 80 miles to the west, served Fort Knox.) The message was relayed to the Godman tower and to T/Sgt. Quinton Blackwell, who in turn called Wright Field in Dayton, Ohio, to see if it knew anything about air traffic over Maysville. The reply was negative. Shortly afterwards, the highway patrol reported it was now hearing about sightings from Owensboro and Irvington. The object, said to be circular and 250 to 300 feet in diameter, was on a westward flight path.

Hearing that, Blackwell started scanning the sky. At 1:45 he spotted something and pointed it out to a private and a lieutenant in the tower with him. The base commanding officer, Col. Guy Hix, was alerted, and he and a growing number of observers watched what they would variously describe to inquirers from the Air Force's Project Sign as looking like a "parachute with the bright sun shining on top of the silk," "round and whiter than the clouds that passed in front of it," "an ice cream cone topped with red." Col. Hix stated, "It was very white and looked like an umbrella. I thought it was a celestial body. I can't account for the fact it didn't move. I just don't know what it was. It appeared about one-fourth the size of the full moon and white in color. Through the binoculars it appeared to have a red border at the bottom at times, a red border at the top at times. It remained stationary, seemingly for one and a half hours."

At that moment four F-51s were heading in Godman's direction on a ferry mission. The interceptors were being flown from Marietta Army Air Base in Georgia, where they had been grounded for routine maintenance before being returned to Standiford Air Field in northern Kentucky. Capt. Mantell, who led the formation, took a radio call from Blackwell, who urged the pilot and his fellow pilots to approach the subject and see exactly what it was. Mantell was able to spot it himself in short order, reporting that it was "in sight above and ahead of me, and it appears to be moving at about half my speed or approximately 180 miles an hour." It was, he went on, "a metallic object or possibly reflection of sun from a metallic object, and it is of tremendous size." At that juncture, without notifying his companions of his intentions, he took a sharp right turn and a steep ascent.

One of the pilots had already begged off the UFO pursuit, noting that his plane was running low on fuel. He went on to Standiford while the other two pilots struggled to catch up with Mantell. They were already getting uneasy about the intercept attempt. At 16,000 feet the air was getting perilously thin, and only the right wingman, 1st Lt. Albert Clements, had an oxygen mask. As he hastily donned it, the left wingman, 2d Lt. B. A. Hammond, measured his breathing carefully. By the time they had followed Mantell to 20,000 feet, however, they were ready to abandon the chase. They were now over Bowling Green, Kentucky, and they still had seen nothing out of the ordinary. When they said as much to Mantell, he shouted, "Look, there it is out there at 12 o'clock!"

Clements looked, and there it was: "a bright-appearing object," he told the Air Force, "very small, and so far away [that I was] unable to identify it as to size, shape, color. . . . Its position was slightly lower and to the left of the sun." Clements suggested that they level off and try to get under the object, but Mantell expressed a desire to continue the ascension up to 25,000 feet. If after 10 minutes they were no closer to it, they would give up. The time was 3:15. Mantell informed Godman that the thing was "directly ahead of me and slightly above and is now moving at about my speed or better. I am trying to close in for a better look."

Clements and Hammond made it up to 22,500 feet before deciding that this was getting too risky. They descended to a more comfortable altitude and pointed themselves again in the direction of Standiford. When Clements radioed Mantell to let him know what they were doing, they got no response. Clements saw Mantell's plane "still climbing almost directly into the sun," and that would be the last time he saw it. Mantell was about to become a fatality of the age of flying saucers.

No more than a minute or two later, William C. Mayes, who lived in the country outside Franklin, witnessed Mantell's last moments. As he would tell investigators, he heard a "funny noise as if [the pilot] were driving down and pulling up, but [the plane] wasn't, it was just circling. After about three circles the airplane started into a power dive slowly rotating. The plane was so high I could hardly see it when it started down. It started to make a terrific noise, ever increasing, as it descended. It exploded halfway between where it started to dive and the ground. No fire was seen."

Not far way, a farm woman named Carrie Phillips, sitting in her living room, heard a loud, explosive sound. She leaped to her feet and to the front window just as a plane crashed on her property 750 feet from the house. Later, when fire fighters from Franklin pulled Mantell's almost decapitated body from the wreckage, they recovered a shattered wristwatch which had stopped at 3:18.

At 3:50 the object was no longer visible from Godman tower. Having refueled at Standiford, Clements was on his way back to see if he could find Mantell. He couldn't. It would not be long, however, before word of his death spread far and wide. No one then could have imagined that an obscure aviation tragedy would be noted, debated, and remembered throughout the world for decades to come.

Reports of unidentified objects in the sky were continuing. At 7:35 a "dancing" object with alternating green and red lights was observed over Clinton County Air Base, outside Wilmington, in southwestern Ohio. In Columbus, southwest of Wilmington, Lockbourne Tower personnel watched a bright light with an amber-colored exhaust trailing it. It made a sharp, rapid descent until it hovered close to the ground for perhaps 10 seconds before shooting back to its original position. The sky was cloudy at the time, ruling out an identification based on radical misperception of an astronomical object; there were, in any case, no stars visible in the overcast.

In 1977 William E. Jones, a corporate attorney and private UFO investigator, located a witness to the Lockbourne sighting. Albert R. Pickering, a civilian air controller, was working a mile from the tower at a direction-finding station off the north-south runway. Around seven, as he looked through the window, he spotted a "great big round red object" coming down through the mist. His immediate conclusion was that a plane was about to crash in flames. His second conclusion was that this was unlike anything he had ever seen before. The phone rang just as he was reaching for it. The tower asked if he was seeing something over his shack.

Pickering judged it to be the size of a one-car garage. It circled three times, each circuit taking 30 seconds and encompassing perhaps 100 square feet. It then circled the entire base, streaked at fantastic speed to a place slightly southwest of where it had first appeared, and stopped so suddenly that it might as well have run "into a wall," Pickering thought. Moments later it sailed casually to the base's perimeter, then went straight down, either touching the ground or coming very close to it. It then ascended until it got just beneath the clouds, where it hovered before heading off to the northwest.[2]

Then as now, attempts to reconstruct what happened to Capt. Mantell get confused when the nearby Ohio sightings are incorporated into the Kentucky part of the story. It is virtually certain that the two episodes are unrelated, connected only by their misleading proximity in time and space.

The Solution

For much of 1948, a significant faction within Project Sign believed that the flying discs were unearthly machines. Though they did not take every report at face value and were able to explain a number of sightings in prosaic terms, they were convinced that eventually they could firmly document the reality of otherworldly visitation. They embarked on the Mantell investigation with that in mind, according to Ruppelt's history of the early Air Force UFO project.

It soon became clear, though, that this was not going to be the big case everyone was hoping for. A flying saucer had not zapped Mantell's plane. To all appearances, he had simply flown too high and blacked out from lack of oxygen. Disillusioned, Sign wanted any explanation it could find. It found one from a Pentagon major who was willing to assure newspaper reporters clambering for an answer that the object was indeed from outer space. It was the planet Venus.

In 1952 the newly appointed head of Blue Book, Ed Ruppelt, was asked to take a fresh look at the case. He thought the Venus explanation did not make a whole lot of sense, and he wondered where the Pentagon major, who had no experience in UFO investigation, had gotten the idea. Ruppelt talked with Blue Book's scientific advisor, Ohio State University astronomer J. Allen Hynek, who sheepishly admitted that he had suggested it to the officer. He agreed with Ruppelt that this was a less than compelling identification. Yes, the object seen from Godman had been in roughly the same position in the sky as Venus, but in daylight the planet would have been invisible for all practical purposes.

In January 1948 the U.S. Navy was conducting a project called Skyhook, involving balloon launches designed to test the level of cosmic or other radiation in the atmosphere. Sign—not to mention the witnesses themselves—hadn't known about it, but Ruppelt at Blue Book did four years later. In fact, as Ruppelt learned as he reviewed the records, two witnesses—each of whom thought at first it was a UFO until he looked at it through a telescope—had actually reported that the object was a huge balloon. Ruppelt would write:

> When first seen by the people in Godman Tower, the UFO was south of the air base. It was relatively close and looked "like a parachute," which a balloon does. During the two hours that it was in sight, the observers reported that it seemed to hover, yet each observer estimated the time he looked at the object through the binoculars and sizewise the descriptions ran "huge," "small," "one fourth the size of the full moon," "one tenth the size of a full moon." Whatever the UFO was, it was slowly moving away. As the balloon continued to drift in a southerly direction it would have picked up stronger winds, and could have easily been seen by astronomers in Madisonville, Kentucky, and north of Nashville an hour after it disappeared from view at Godman.

Moreover, the wind patterns were consistent with the movement of a balloon. All that remained, Ruppelt deduced, was to find the place where the Skyhook was launched. Unfortunately, flight records were unavailable to him. Informally, sources at Wright-Patterson suggested—incorrectly, as it turned out—that the launch was from Clinton County Air Base, where un-balloon-like sightings had been made on the evening in question. In later years, Ruppelt's successors would declare as simple fact that the Skyhook was from Clinton.

It wasn't. No less than Charles B. Moore, a weather scientist who had been deeply involved in the Skyhook project in the late 1940s, testified that no Skyhooks were flown from Clinton before July 9, 1951. With Moore advising them, ufologists Barry Greenwood and Robert G. Todd in the early 1990s traced the launch to one from Camp Ripley, Minnesota, at 8 A.M. on January 6, 1948.

This virtually certain solution notwithstanding, the Mantell Incident took on a life of its own and became a saucer legend which survived well into the 1970s and even today yields the occasional advocate. The cosmic-ray balloon identification ("Skyhook" was still a classified name), interestingly, was proposed in 1949 by Sidney Shallett in a *Saturday Evening Post* article, but in the January 1950 issue of *True,* in a widely read article arguing for an extraterrestrial origin of flying saucers, aviation journalist Donald Keyhoe declared that the "lightninglike maneuvers" of Mantell's object alone ruled out a non-UFO explanation, though nothing in the witness testimony—unless Keyhoe is conflating it with the reports of the witnesses at Lockbourne—speaks of such maneuvers. Keyhoe would not even concede that lack of oxygen was responsible for the crash. He cites the opinion of an anonymous pilot: "It looks like a cover-up to me. I think Mantell did just what he said he would—closed in on the thing. I think he either collided with it, or more likely they [the UFO's occupants] knocked him out of the air."

In a book that grew out of the *True* article, Keyhoe declared that his government and military sources were certain that the object had been a "huge space ship—perhaps the largest ever to come into our atmosphere." The Air Force "must have known the truth from the start—that Mantell had pursued a tremendous space ship. That fact alone, if it had exploded in the headlines at that time, might have caused dangerous panic." No wonder the Air Force had issued patently phony explanations. The Mantell Incident, Keyhoe wrote, "might even be the key to the whole flying-saucer riddle."

In the luridly titled *Flying Saucers on the Attack* (1954), Harold T. Wilkins, a British writer of eccentric disposition, windily argued that "some lethal ray of immense power and unknown type had been directed at Mantell and his plane by the entities in the weird and vast machine, who may have deemed that they were going to be attacked, or wished to demonstrate to terrestrial military power, with its anti-aircraft batteries, the folly of any closer approach." More than three decades later, in a 1977 book, ufologist Len Stringfield wrote of speaking with someone who claimed to have been "Mantell's wing man." The anonymous man said he had seen "what appeared to be tracer" fired at Mantell's aircraft. In reality, the two real wingmen, Clements and Hammond, testified to nothing more dramatic than the sight of Mantell's F-51 ascending.

Even more fantastic stories circulated among contactees—individuals who claimed to be in personal contact with friendly, benevolent space people. George Hunt Williamson wrote that Mantell's final words were, "There are windows, and I can see people in it!" George Adamski, on the other hand, had it on the authority of no less than his friend Ramu of Mars that this was an "accident which we regretted deeply. . . . Members of the crew had noticed Captain Mantell coming toward them and knew that his interest was sincere, not belligerent." Unfortunately, he got too close, and the "power radiating from their ship" sheared off one of his plane's wings, "allowing a suction to take place which pulled the entire plane into it, causing an immediate disintegration of both the plane and his body."

On the other hand, another contactee, Orfeo Angelucci, had a different story from his own space contacts. According to them, the craft was "one of the remotely controlled disks." Mantell was trying to capture it just before the crash.

On April 24, 1965, according to an Englishman named Ernest Arthur Bryant, a spaceship landed near a rural Devonshire village. One of the space people promised, "One month from today we will bring you proof of Mantell." On June 7, a little late, a blue light beam delivered aircraft parts which, unfortunately for Bryant, proved not to be from an F-51, as aviation authorities easily determined.

Mantell Redux

The Mantell tragedy has a sequel of sorts, another interceptor crash involving an aircraft from the Kentucky National Guard. It also occurred in January, albeit eight years later.

In the early evening of January 31, 1956, some residents of southern Indiana reported seeing what they thought might be UFOs. When word got to the National Guard Airfield in Louisville, jet fighters were scrambled. The unit's commander, Col. Lee Merkel, went along, but for some reason (probably having to do with what was available at the moment) flew in a propeller-driven F-51, the same type of airplane Mantell had piloted.

The jets, which raced far ahead of Merkel's relatively slow-moving plane, saw nothing. Merkel stayed on course and eventually reported something moving along a cloud bank above him. It was, he said, luminous and blinking. He ascended until he got to 30,000 feet, which put him above the light. He radioed Louisville that he was now in the process of closing in on it. It would be his last message.

According to one account, a few minutes later his F-51 exploded several hundred feet in the air above a farmhouse south of Bloomington. The wreckage damaged the house, and portions of it were scattered for a quarter of a mile around. Not surprisingly, Merkel did not survive the disaster.

As it happens, Merkel was a friend of radio broadcaster and UFO buff Frank Edwards. Edwards, not always the most reliable source, claimed that unlike Mantell, Merkel was well supplied with oxygen.

In contrast to the Mantell incident, the Merkel case is sketchily documented, so it is hard to know what to make of it. The vague description we have of the light Merkel saw is amenable to a variety of interpretations.

Dogfight over Fargo

Another once-classic pilot sighting played out on the evening of October 1, 1948, over the skies of Fargo, North Dakota.

At 8:30, North Dakota Air National Guard 2d Lt. George F. Gorman, manager of a construction company in his civilian hours, was returning to Fargo from a cross-country flight. It was still relatively early, and he took the opportunity to put in some extra night-flying time. He pointed his F-51 west, toward Valley City, and when he got there, circled around and went back to Fargo. Still not ready to land, he amused himself by watching from the air a football game in progress in a field at the north end of the city.

He was circling at 1,500 feet when he saw a Piper Cub 500 feet beneath him. Moments later, he spotted something more interesting, a light moving from east to west between the tower at Hector Airport and the football field. A quick radio check with Hector elicited the puzzled reply that, as far as the tower knew, only the F-51 and the Cub were in the air. Like Mantell before him but fortunately without the sad consequences, Gorman announced he was going to close in on the unidentified object. He later provided this statement to Sign:

After the initial peel off, I realized the speed of the object was too great to catch in a straight chase, so I proceed to cut it off in turns. At this time my fighter was under full power, my speed varying between 300 and 400. The object circled to the left, I cut back to the right for a head-on pass. The pass was made at apparently 5,000 feet, the object approaching head-on until a collision seemed inevitable. The object veered and passed apparently 500 feet or less over the top above me. I channeled around still without the object in sight. The object made a 180 degree turn and initiated a pass at me. This time I watched it approach all the way and as it started to pull up, I pulled up abruptly trying to ram the object until [it went] straight up with me following at apparently 14,000 feet. I stalled out at 14,000 feet with the object apparently 2,000 feet above me circling to the left. We made two circles to the left. The object then pulled out away from me and made another head-on pass. At this time the pass started and the object broke off a large distance from me heading over Hectic Airport to the northwest at apparently 11,000 feet. I gave a chase circling to the left trying to cut it off until I was 25 miles southeast of Fargo. I was at 14,000, the object at 11,000 when I again gave the aircraft full power [trying] to catch it in a diving turn. The object turned around and made another head-on pass. This time when pulling up, I pulled up also and observed it traveling straight up until I lost it. I then returned to the field and landed.

As Gorman would tell Sign representatives, the object was white and ball-shaped, six to eight inches in diameter. It blinked at slow speed and did not blink when it accelerated. Sometimes, he thought, its speed was close to 600 mph.

While this was going on, air traffic controller L. D. Jensen radioed L. N. Cannon, pilot of the Piper Cub, and asked him what
he thought. He and his passenger, Einar Nelson, of nearby Moor-
head, Minnesota, were preparing to land at the north edge of
Hector at the time. Cannon said the object was in the north and
heading speedily toward the west on a steady course.

After landing, Cannon and Nelson rushed over to the tower
and listened to Gorman's ongoing radio contacts. The object
seemed to be "moving very swiftly, much faster than the 51,"
Cannon would recall. He "tried to get a better view with a pair of
binoculars but couldn't follow it well enough." In the meantime,
Jensen was watching the object from the tower's south window. It
appeared to be a thousand feet in the northwestern sky, sailing
over a field on a straight course. He was in continuing communication with Gorman but at the moment couldn't see his plane.

Sign had investigators in Fargo within hours. Besides interviewing all the witnesses, they used a Geiger counter to check the F-51
for radiation. They were excited when they got a positive response,
but they soon learned that a recently flown aircraft registers the effects of cosmic rays. In other words, the reading meant nothing.

Gorman almost certainly encountered a balloon, the Air Force
decided. The object's evasive maneuvers were a product of the
pilot's imagination, neither the first nor the last time that a pilot,
including some more experienced than Gorman, had been so
fooled in interacting with a balloon. The Air Weather Service was
even able to identify the balloon responsible for the confusion. It
is worth noting, too, that the other witnesses did not see the maneuvers Gorman claimed to have observed.

Even so, as the UFO age picked up steam, Gorman's sighting
became famous, with writers and enthusiasts suspicious of the
Air Force suggesting that the explanation was absurd or duplici-
tous. Over the years, the Air Force would have a well-deserved
reputation for concocting often dubious solutions, but this is not
one of them. On the other hand. . . .

A Dogfight in Cuba

In his book Ruppelt reports an encounter which occurred over Cuba on September 24, 1952, as an example of the kind of error that Gorman made. An independent examination of the pilot's account—quoted below—does not compellingly lead to that conclusion, however. In his official report, Navy pilot William N. Straugh relates that at 7:25 P.M. he was flying near the base at Guantanamo Bay. As he was ascending to 4,000 feet, he noticed another object—an orange light approaching from the east. He knew there was another Navy jet in the area, but as the light effected a left turn, he realized that it was something else. Straugh attempted an intercept but managed to get no closer than 8 to 10 miles from it. According to his report:

> It had a greenish tail that looked to be five to six times as long as the light's diameter. This tail was seen several times in the next 10 minutes in periods of five to 30 seconds each. As I reached 10,000', it appeared to be at 15,000' still in a port turn. It took approximately 40 degrees of bank to keep the nose of my relatively slow . . . plane on the light. At this time I estimated the light to be in a 10 to 15 degree orbit.
>
> At 12,000 feet I stopped climbing, but the light was still climbing at a faster rate than I was. I then reversed my turn from port to starboard and the light appeared to reverse also. I was not gaining distance. . . . It appeared to be moving north over Guantanamo City. As I turned north, the light appeared to move west over Leeward[,] and then due south of the base I tried the same thing to the east. As I turned back to intercept it, the light appeared to climb rapidly, at approximately a 60-degree angle from approximately 25,000' to approximately 35,000', and then start a rapid descent.

The light was then at its greatest distance of about 20 miles away. . . .

While the light was still at approximately 1,500', I deliberately placed it between the moon and myself three times to try [to] identify a solid body. [Two crew-members] were in the plane with me and observed all maneuvers of the light and had a good view of the light passing the moon[;] however, neither of us saw a solid body. Considering the light was possibly from an aer-ologist's wind balloon, we did not see a shadow of the balloon against the moon.

During the descent, the light appeared to slow down at approximately 10,000' at which time I made three runs on the light. Two of them were 90 degree collision course runs and this light appeared to travel at a tremen-dous speed across my bow, accelerating rapidly at the 2 o'clock position and slowing at the 9 o'clock position.

One run was so close that the light blanked out all view of the lights on McCalla Field. At this time the light started another rapid rate of descent and seemed to cross over Caimanes in a left turn and head straight toward the base, then turn left again and pass over the dredge located northeast of McCalla. It then leveled out over the mangroves, hovered over the water for approximately three seconds in a cove east of Hospital Cay, and then faded quickly out. In the last descent, I was in a dive and as the light faded out I was at ap-proximately 1,500' and continued on down to 100' or-biting over the spot where the light disappeared. No disturbances could be seen by [Straugh and the other two witnesses], with the moonlight on the water. The light disappeared at approximately 2010Q and a po-lice boat was dispatched at 2015Q to search the area. In the meantime, a harbor patrol boat had gone through the area being orbited by the plane and upon being questioned later, had seen nothing unusual. At 2115 the search was discontinued.

Straugh was shaken. "Of these facts stated," he wrote, "some could possibly be explained as an optical illusion. Others seem too strange for an explanation." To his credit he did not let matters rest there. He sought to investigate his experience by trying to duplicate it with a light-bearing weather balloon which he arranged to have released the following evening. Without quoting the account, Ruppelt simply declares, "He duplicated his dogfight—illusions and all." Well, maybe. In a separate report of this second incident, Straugh wrote:

> The balloon was released prior to my takeoff but I intercepted it at 2,000' and made various . . . runs on it from all angles and at different speeds. Many of the illusions seen on the previous night could be duplicated by maneuvering the plane appropriately. I tracked the balloon through 12,000' and made my runs on it from as far away as 10 miles. I could always intercept and pass it at any predetermined position as against the fact that I could not get close to the other light, which at the time appeared to be moving away from me at each attempted approach.

Uneasily acknowledging that this last fact was hardly a replication of the previous night's experience, Straugh tried to rationalize the discordant detail by suggesting that maybe the light—or balloon, as he held it to be—was at an higher altitude than he thought it was and his rate of climb was insufficient to reach it. Still:

> The rate of ascent of the light on the 24th was the most weird and also the hardest to explain. When the light

of the 24th was at 25,000', it was seen by two passengers and myself at the same instant to start a climb at an angle of approximately 60% and at a terrific rate of ascent. At this time the light which had been a large bright glow was now a very red point which could have blended with the stars, if it had not appeared to be moving.

Straugh was reduced to iffy speculation about leaks in the presumed balloon (causing descent) and vertical air currents (ascent). The light's violent maneuvers were probably an illusion triggered by "tight turns at high speed with resultant vertigo to myself"—unmentioned in his first report. He attributed the light/balloon's "last fast descent" to the possibility that "I may have cut the balloon with my prop on the third run."

My last three-quarter turn was diving port in a position northeast of the light which could have produced the illusion of the light arcing over Caimanera and the bay, and setting [sic] in the water. The lights crossing from starboard to port could have been the result of my plane being in a vertical turn and the light descending straight down instead of going horizontally. At the time of intercept I thought my wings to be almost level and the light traveling in a flat circle, but due to the aforementioned vertigo, a pilot cannot rely on his sense to establish altitude.

This labored effort to dispose of an experience Straugh clearly found disturbing tells us, I suspect, that he very much did not want to be accused of seeing a UFO. The balloon explanation for the Gorman sighting is straightforward and convincing. Straugh's theory, on the other hand, seems almost like a parody of an explanation.

4

Estimation Extraterrestrial

SOMETHING—A BIG rocket-shaped something with flame shooting out of its tail, if you took the witnesses' testimony literally—zoomed past an airliner in an early-morning moment in the summer of 1948. The duration of the sighting can be counted in seconds. Its effect would be numbered in decades. In a sense, after the Chiles-Whitted encounter, nothing would be the same. After that, it was curtains for UFOs.

Not, obviously, that the sightings would cease. The sightings were and are unstoppable. But after the Chiles-Whitted affair had played out, unidentified flying objects were no longer an urgent Air Force issue but an Air Force problem. Thereafter, UFO investigation became a low-priority item, no longer focused so much on national security as on public relations. From the summer of 1947, some influential people in the armed services judged flying-disc reports a waste of time, at least after it became reasonably clear that superior but highly secret Soviet aircraft were not penetrating American airspace at will.

Understandably, given what was known or suspected of advances in Soviet weapons and aviation technology after World War II, as tensions between Stalin's closed, secretive state and the West chilled into the Cold War, the Air Force first suspected that the Russians were improving on rocket and other technology they got from captured German scientists and engineers. These suspicions carried over from the ghost-rocket scare of the previous year. Ghost rockets are mentioned prominently in early American military discussions.

Lt. Col. George D. Garrett, who well remembered the intense concern ghost rockets had caused at the Pentagon, was still serving with the Intelligence Collections Branch in 1947 as flying saucers were breaking out all over. His superiors, including Collection head and Garrett's immediate boss, Col. Robert Taylor, directed him to find out what was going on. Other service branches and government agencies helped provide him with information as he commenced preliminary inquiries focused on worries about a link between the saucers and the Soviets.[1]

At his direction the Intelligence Division (T-2) at Wright Field searched its classified collections. There it uncovered a paper titled *German Flying Wings Designed by Horten Brothers,* dated July 5, 1946. The Horten brothers were two brilliant German aeronautical engineers. Maybe the Russians had developed flying discs out of the Hortens' ideas and designs.

As July ended, Garrett noticed something odd: pressure to solve the mystery of the discs had eased. Garrett and his FBI liaison, Special Agent S. W. Reynolds, were perplexed. They had thought they were at the forefront of the official investigation, and they knew they had solved nothing. They still had no idea what the discs were. The silence from above, however, led them to suspect strongly that somebody did. And that in turn led them to suspect that the discs were secret American devices.

Garrett prepared a document in which he listed 16 cases of high credibility. From these cases he concluded that someone had developed high-performance disc-shaped aircraft. Now all he had to do was find out who in the American defense establishment had accomplished as much. With Reynolds[2] he circulated the document among research and intelligence agencies, every one of which—to the two investigators' astonishment—said it knew nothing of any such aircraft. When Wright-Patterson's commander, Gen. Nathan Twining, saw the document and the responses, he called on Col. Howard McCoy to convene experts there and begin a new secret investigation under a new project.

Estimate of the Situation: Extraterrestrial

It was a sighting that, more than any other, came close to convincing an influential faction within the U.S. Air Force's UFO-investigative agency, Project Sign, that intelligent beings from another world were visiting the earth. Others were certain that the witnesses *must be* mistaken, that what they claimed to have seen could not possibly exist; therefore, they saw something else, something much less extraordinary. Even today, more than five decades later, the case remains controversial because its implications are . . . well . . . cosmic.

It is, however, undisputed that at 2:45 A.M. on July 24, 1948, an Eastern Airlines DC-3 was passing 20 miles to the southwest of Montgomery, Alabama, at 5,000 feet. The sky was clear, and a full moon shone brightly. To the pilot, Capt. Clarence S. Chiles, and copilot, John B. Whitted, it seemed an ordinary night and an ordinary flight. And then Chiles spotted something. He pointed it out to Whitted, directing him to look at the "new Army jet job."

The words were barely out of his mouth when the object was upon them, moving in their direction perhaps 500 feet to their right and the same distance above the airliner's altitude. It was no "jet job." To them it looked like an immense structure, perhaps 100 feet long, torpedo-shaped, with two rows of large, square windows through which an intense, almost blinding white light could be discerned. "The fuselage appeared to be about three times the circumference of a B-29 fuselage," Whitted would report. Underneath the craft was a blue glow. A stream of fire shot some 50 feet out of its rear, in the fashion of a huge missile. Whitted remembered thinking that it resembled nothing so much as "one of those fantastic Flash Gordon rocket ships in the funny papers."

No sound accompanied the object's passing, nor did it leave any turbulence in its wake. Within 5 to 10 seconds it had ascended sharply, dipped into light, broken clouds at 6,000 feet, and disappeared from sight.

Besides Chiles and Whitted, only one other person on the plane witnessed it. Clarence L. McKelvie, of Columbus, Ohio, was staring drowsily out the window when he saw something shoot by. He would call it a "strange, eerie streak . . . It was very intense, not like lightning or anything I had ever seen. I could discern nothing in the way of a definite shape or form, but I was so startled that I could not get my eyes adjusted to it before it was gone." Later, when interviewed by Project Sign's Lt. Robert Schneider, McKelvie confirmed the pilots' assertion that the object had been moving along a generally straight course at a slightly higher elevation than the DC-3's.

Shortly after the object's departure, Chiles radioed Eastern in Columbus, Georgia, and asked the radio operator to call nearby Fort Benning to see if it could shed light on the sighting. Chiles and Whitted thought it possible that they had seen some kind of experimental aircraft, but Benning replied that it knew nothing of any such flight.

By the time they landed their DC-3 at 3:49 in Atlanta, the story was already spreading, and so were theories about it. The first—and, as history would document, the most persistent—was that the witnesses had observed a meteor and imagined the rest. In their first newspaper interview, with reporter William Key, Chiles and Whitted were asked directly what they thought of that particular explanation. Not much, they said; they had seen plenty of meteors, and this was not one of them. It was a "man-made thing," they insisted. When interviewed in the mid-1960s by atmospheric physicist and UFO investigator James E. McDonald, they were still maintaining as much.

Always quick with an explanation, well-considered or otherwise, for UFO reports, the Pentagon suggested that a weather balloon was probably responsible. The speculation was withdrawn almost as quickly, when an anonymous Air Force spokesman conceded the absence of any balloon or plane resembling a "double-decked, jet-propelled, wingless transport shooting a 40-foot flame out of its back end."

In any event, as the Air Force commenced its inquiries, the story got more and more interesting. On August 10 the officer in charge of the Sixth District Office of Special Investigations (AFOSI, roughly the Air Force equivalent to the FBI) interviewed Walter Massey, a ground-maintenance crewman stationed at Robins Air Force Base in Georgia. Massey related that two hours prior to the Chiles-Whitted sighting, he was "standing fire guard on a C-47"—the military version of the DC-3—and facing north when he spotted something coming from that direction. At first it looked like a "stream of fire," but when it passed directly overhead on a straight, level course, he could make out the details. It "appeared to be a cylindrical-shaped object with a long stream of fire coming out of the tail end. I am sure it [was] not a jet since I have observed P-84s in flight at night on two occasions." He thought it was the size of a B-29 or "a little larger in circumference. It was too large for a jet. It seemed to be a dark color and constructed of an unknown metallic type material."

He estimated that it was at 3,000 feet but acknowledged that was a guess. Asked if he saw windows, he pointed out, "It would be hard to tell if there were windows and a divided deck could not be recognized from the ground." The object reminded him of a German V-2 rocket that he and a fellow soldier had observed in Europe during the Battle of the Bulge, except that the one over Georgia was bigger and faster.

In addition to Massey's sighting, which investigators thought might well be of the same object the Eastern pilots had seen, Sign personnel learned of a July 20 report from The Hague, Holland. "It was a poor report, very sketchy and incomplete," Edward J. Ruppelt, chief of a subsequent Air Force UFO project, would write, "and it probably would have been forgotten" if not for the Chiles-Whitted encounter four days later. The Dutch witnesses allegedly observed through high, broken clouds a rocket-shaped structure with two rows of windows.

In *The Report on Unidentified Flying Objects* (1956) Ruppelt would reveal for the first time the effect of these developments on a Sign faction which had suspected for some time that flying-saucer sightings could be best explained as evidence of extra-terrestrial visitation. The pro-ET group, which included Sign's director Lt. Schneider and Air Force-employed civilian aeronautical engineer Alfred Loedding, had been looking for a case which would clinch the argument it had been conducting with two smaller factions, one holding that the discs were secret Soviet air-craft, the other that the discs had no reality outside the minds of misguided or overly imaginative witnesses.

The extraterrestrialists seized upon the Chiles-Whitted sighting and linked it with other pilot reports, including Kenneth Arnold's and several by military aviators, to conclude that only their explanation seemed adequate to account for the data. They prepared a classified document, titled "Estimate of the Situation," to make their point. Authorship has been variously ascribed to Schneider or to Loedding (the best available current evidence, based on testimony of the Loedding family, indicates the latter). In any event, in later years, as the Air Force's relationship with UFO sightings grew ever more antagonistic, the Estimate would prove to be such an institutional embarrassment that for years afterwards the Air Force would essentially accuse Ruppelt of lying about its existence.

Just prior to the writing of the Estimate, Schneider appended a page to Sign's Chiles-Whitted file, in which he considered the sighting from an aerodynamics perspective. A wingless, rocket-shaped structure was technically feasible, he said. He added gingerly, "That this development is possibly of foreign origin would seem to be a logical premise." The Estimate would make clear what he meant by "foreign origin."

The Estimate went through channels, starting with Wright-Patterson's Technical Intelligence Division, where Sign was housed, and wending its way up to the Air Force Chief of Staff, Gen. Hoyt S. Vandenberg. Along the way, apparently, it generated fierce controversy and concerns about public panic such as had manifested in October 1938, when the Mercury Theater's notorious radio drama based on H. G. Wells's *War of the Worlds* had frightened at least some Americans into believing that a Martian invasion had begun. Vandenberg rejected the Estimate on the not unreasonable grounds that without physical evidence, this extraordinary hypothesis remained unproved. A few months later, the Estimate was declassified. All copies were ordered burned.

Most were so disposed of, but a few were quietly claimed by those who had access to them. Ruppelt himself saw one, apparently in the possession of a fellow Air Force officer, in 1951. He remembered it as a "rather thick document with a black cover . . . printed on legal-sized paper. Stamped across the front were the words TOP SECRET." If any copies survive, they are probably gathering dust in attics. Over the decades UFO historians have conducted energetic but fruitless searches for a document that has become, to some, the ufological equivalent of the Holy Grail.

In the aftermath of the Estimate's rejection, the pro-ET faction at Sign was given its walking papers[3] and control of the project turned over to the UFOphobes. The project was renamed, appropriately enough, Grudge. It was formalized on February 11, 1949, on the unspoken but, at least among insiders, universally understood premise that—in the caustic words of Ruppelt, himself no believer but at least relatively open-minded in his skepticism—reports were to be "evaluated on the premise that UFOs couldn't exist. No matter what you see or hear, don't believe it."

Since UFOs couldn't exist, the object Chiles and Whitted saw could not be one. Grudge personnel went back to something the project's scientific consultant, Ohio State University astronomer J. Allen Hynek, had written when Sign asked for his assessment. Hynek had conceded that "no astronomical explanation" could account for what the airline pilots had described—that is, "if we accept the report at face value." Employing a practice all subsequent generations of UFO debunkers would emulate, Hynek (who eventually would take a more sympathetic view of UFOs and witness testimony) airily swept aside what Chiles and Whitted had actually said. After all, he declared, the "sheer improbability of the facts as stated . . . makes it necessary to see whether any other explanation, even though far-fetched, can be considered." Therefore, it followed that Massey, his statement to the contrary notwithstanding, must have seen not a V-2-like craft but an "extraordinary meteor," and moreover, he had seen it not two hours before Chiles and Whitted but *at the same time*. As for the Eastern pilots, they had mistaken the train behind the extraordinary meteor for a "ship with lighted windows."

Solved. Ever since, "meteor" has been the official explanation.

In the 1960s James E. McDonald, a University of Arizona atmospheric physicist who energetically investigated UFO reports before his untimely death in 1971, conducted separate interviews with the pilots. According to McDonald, "Both pilots reiterated to me . . . that each saw *square* ports or windows along the side of the fuselage-shaped object from the rear of which a cherry-red wake emerged, extending back 50–100 aft of the object. To term this a 'meteor' is not even *qualitatively* reasonable. One can reject the testimony; but reason forbids calling the object a meteor."

Of course it is impossible to prove that Chiles and Whitted did *not* see a meteor. Astronomer and skeptic William K. Hartmann, an investigator for the University of Colorado UFO Project,[4] was certain that they had. He pointed to a February 9, 1913, sighting of a meteor display seen from Saskatchewan to the New Jersey coast. One witness said the meteor "resembled a large aeroplane or dirigible, with two tiers of lights strung along the sides." More recently, British ufologist Jenny Randles has averred that the Chiles-Whitted object is "easy to identify" as an "incandescent bolide."

Flaming Cigars

The Chiles-Whitted sighting, however, does not exist in a vacuum. Explanations that insist on misidentification require the object to be seen against a dark, nocturnal background in which dim and bright areas of flaming fireballs create the impression of windows.[5] "Meteor" does not come immediately to mind when one encounters a report like the one that follows. It took place on April 5, 1946, more than a year before anyone had heard of the concept of "flying saucers," and the principal witness, Army Air Corps Capt. Jack E. Puckett, served as Assistant Chief of Flying Safety on the staff of Gen. Elwood Quesada. On the day in question, he was piloting a C-47 transport plane on a scheduled flight from Langley Field, Virginia, to McDill Field, Tampa, Florida.

"At approximately 6 P.M., while flying . . . at 4000 feet northeast of Tampa," he would recall, "I observed what I thought to be a shooting star to the southeast over the Atlantic Ocean. My co-pilot, Lt. Henry F. Glass, and my engineer both observed this object at the same time. This object continued toward us on a collision course at our exact altitude. At about 1,000 yards it veered to cross our path. We observed it to be a long, cylindrical shape approximately twice the size of a B-29, with luminous portholes."

The sighting occurred over a three-minute period—long enough to rule out any possibility of its being a meteor. A stream of fire, half the length of the object, shot out from behind it. The witnesses estimated its speed to be around 2,000 mph. The object eventually disappeared over the horizon.

The similarities between this and the Chiles-Whitted case—even to the scale of the flame to the object preceding it—are remarkable.

A few months later, another suggestive incident—though this was not a pilot sighting—occurred on a farm eight miles north of O'Neill, Nebraska. It was a fall evening, and Gladys McCage, who was holding a lantern and two milk buckets, was returning from the barn, her four-year-old son in tow. Mrs. McCage noticed a yellowish orange light heading in their direction at a "terrific speed" from the northwest. It turned red, then stopped and hovered almost directly above them. The terrified little boy threw himself to the ground. Mrs. McCage dropped what she was holding, grabbed him, and fled toward the house. As she was doing so, the object ascended and shot off toward the northeast.

She had gotten a good look at it before she made her escape. It was cigar-shaped and "huge . . . It would have filled a football field. . . . There were windows in this 'thing' and it [made] a terrific amount of noise. . . . I had a sensation like there was a 'vacuum' and I could have been pulled skyward but I didn't stand still to find that out. There was yellowish blue flame or fire shooting out near the back. . . . There were no wings; it traveled too fast for a plane in '46."

On July 11, 1947, over the Bay of Biscay (off the coast of France and Spain), at around 10 A.M., the British pilot of a Viking transport on its way to Argentina spotted an elongated oval- or cigar-shaped object at 16,000 feet, or 8,000 feet above the airplane. The pilot, Capt. Norman E. Waugh, pointed it out to First Officer Peter Roberts and Radio Officer Stuart Chinneck. The UFO, a metallic gray in color, descended about 1,000 feet and passed by the right side of the aircraft, moving at an extraordinary speed and leaving a long vapor trail. At its closest it was five to six miles away. The report says nothing about windows or portholes, but if the UFO had them, it may have been too far away for the witnesses to observe them.

In 1950 another classic airline-pilot sighting echoed the Chiles-Whitted report in some significant details. It took place around 9:30 P.M. on May 29 as a Nashville-bound American Airlines DC-6, with Capt. Willis T. Sperry at the controls, passed over Mount Vernon, Virginia, at 8,000 feet after having left Washington Airport not long before. Sperry's attention was focused on a map which he was pulling out of a briefcase when suddenly he heard copilot William Gates shout, "Watch it! Watch it!" Gates had caught sight of a fast-moving, brilliant blue glow, estimated to be 25 times that of the brightest star, on what looked like a collision course. Sperry, who quickly spotted the light himself, quickly steered into a sharp, 45-degree right turn. When the airliner leveled off, the object stopped and sat motionless for approximately half a minute. By this time eight passengers were watching it along with Sperry, Gates, Flight Engineer Robert Arnholt, and the stewardess.

Sperry turned to the left to keep it in view. Then the object flew past the plane, circled it, and reappeared on the right side, then hovered for 10 or 15 seconds. Sperry banked right toward it, but the object abruptly resumed its flight. It passed in front of the moon, and in silhouette the crew and passengers could see a cigar- or submarine-shaped structure. It had no wings or other protrusions. The blue light remained visible at the front of the UFO,[6] which took up almost the entire diameter of the moon. It then headed eastward, moving upward on a 30-degree ascending course. It disappeared after about 60 seconds at a speed Sperry characterized as "fantastic . . . without a doubt beyond the limits of any known aircraft speeds."

Later, after the sighting attracted newspaper publicity, Sperry heard from another pilot, Capt. Henry H. Myers. Myers had been flying another American DC-6 at the same time, heading east toward Washington. The airliner was at 19,000 feet about halfway between Nashville and Knoxville, 450 nautical miles from where Sperry's craft was, when Myers and his crew saw what they first took to be a shooting star plummeting from the sky. They were startled when, as it reached the horizon, it stopped. Moments later, it began to move horizontally. It was obvious that this was no shooting star.

During World War II Myers had been President Franklin D. Roosevelt's personal pilot. Perhaps for that reason, he asked Sperry not to reveal what he had seen. Sperry honored his request and said nothing about Myers's sighting until the latter's death. "We correlated the time of my sighting and his," he told ufologist Robert Barrow in the mid-1970s, "and it was exactly the same time."

Another report differs from Chiles-Whitted's in some important respects but also bears some interesting similarities. It is relatively little known but in its way most impressive.

At 9:26 P.M. on March 20, 1950, the pilot of a Chicago and Southern DC-3 airliner flying from Memphis on its way to Little Rock beneath a clear, cloudless sky spotted something unusual off to the left. It was a light, clearly not a star, and apparently not an airplane, and it was approaching them. It had, Capt. Jack Adams would report, "an unusual bluish and brilliant glow, flashing on and off far more rapidly than the normal blinking of civilian aircraft lights." The flashing was occurring every three seconds.

Adams drew copilot G. W. Anderson's attention to the object. By now it was growing larger and approaching at great speed. It passed in front of them but about 1,000 feet above. It was tilted at an angle so that only the bottom was now visible. Nine to 10 "portholes" circled the bottom, at about three-fourths of the distance from the center. A soft purple or bluish white light emanated from them. "The pattern was clear and consistent," Adams would recall. The object "did not change shape as it darted past." It was in sight for some 45 seconds, moving at an estimated 500 mph. It was apparently 100 feet in diameter. Adams and Anderson deduced that the object was a flat disc, with the white light probably in the center of the top side.

The UFO disappeared to the north. As soon as it vanished from view, Adams notified the tower at Little Rock. The plane was still in the air when Mutual Broadcasting Network newscaster—and hard-core UFO buff—Frank Edwards learned of the sighting and conducted an interview with Adams. Soon afterwards, he played the recording on his radio show.

The two witnesses told reporters that they were "flabbergasted." Not long before their own sighting, they had openly ridiculed those benighted souls who believed they had seen flying saucers. "But when you see something with your own eyes," Anderson said, "you have to believe it."

On his return to Memphis, Adams was interviewed by two local Air Force Intelligence officers, Maj. Dewey H. Orr and Maj. Richard K. Easley. When the officers tried to convince Adams that he had seen no more than a meteor, he angrily rejected the idea. Eventually, the Air Force's UFO project would classify the sighting as unexplained.

At least Adams was able to discuss his sighting with others. That was not the case, according to his widow, with another Air Force officer, Maj. Robert J. Waste. The incident came to the attention of the late California ufologist Paul Cerny when he was a guest on a call-in radio show in the early 1970s. Mrs. Waste phoned to recount a sighting her late husband and others had experienced on September 3, 1954. Cerny, a respected and conscientious investigator, conducted follow-up interviews and tried, without success, to get the other witnesses to discuss what they had seen.

In Mrs. Waste's account, her husband, a bombardier-navigator on a B-47, and other members of the crew were 25,000 feet in the air between east Texas and western Louisiana on a relatively clear, sunny afternoon with good visibility. At 4:30 Carswell Air Force

Base, Fort Worth, notified them to look out for a suspected UFO. It didn't take them long to find it. To their astonishment, they learned that it was just about as close as it could be to their aircraft without colliding into it. It was 100 feet above them, hovering.

The object was slightly larger and longer than the B-47's fuselage. It looked like an enormous, streamlined, silver missile, except that it had two rows of oval-shaped "windows" on each side. A long orange "tail" streamed out from behind it.

For the next hour the UFO alternately paced and circled the B-47, performing maneuvers that the witnesses deemed nearly unbelievable. Eventually it effected a sharp, fast ascent and disappeared. Meantime, Waste and another crewmember, using their personal cameras, snapped a number of photographs of it.

When the B-47 landed at Barksdale Air Force Base, the B-47 crew, along with the crews of two other bombers that had participated in the exercise, was held incommunicado. The pictures were confiscated and never returned. After three days the crews were released, instructed not to discuss the matter even with wives. But eventually, Waste confided the story. Mrs. Waste kept silent about it for 20 years before finally passing it on to Cerny.

Though not particularly compelling, another case with Chiles-Whitted overtones is mentioned here for whatever it is worth. It came from over the Gulf of Mexico, at 8:30 P.M. on January 22, 1956. The witness was Flight Engineer Robert Mueller, aboard a Pan American airliner heading from Houston on its way to Miami. The pilot himself was not at the controls but inside. Copilot Tom Tompkins was in the left—pilot's—seat in the cockpit, with Mueller occupying the copilot's seat to the right.

At the moment the UFO appeared, Tompkins was bent over adjusting the radio direction finder. Mueller, who was looking forward, was at first too stunned to speak. By the time he found his voice, the object was gone. Fellow airline pilot and UFO witness

William B. Nash interviewed Mueller and sent an account to ufologist Leonard Stringfield:

> In his opinion, [the object] was something very solid. There was partial moonlight and only small wisps of high cirrus. There was a front visible over the southern U.S. to the left. The object must have been very large, he said, and it crossed from the southern horizon to beyond the front in about six seconds. It was only about 30 degrees up from level sight traveling from [south-southwest] to [north-northeast]. Prior to this sighting Mr. Mueller was a complete skeptic regarding UFOs.

Mueller's sketch showed a cylindrical object, its body emanating a pale blue luminescence. A yellow, flaming exhaust shot out from the back. Mueller did not think this was a meteor, despite some obvious similarities.

5

Grounding the Saucers

THE SUMMER OF 1952 ushered in a dramatic upsurge in UFO reports, overwhelming the well-meaning but under-budgeted Blue Book, then under the direction of Capt. Ed Ruppelt, and alarming the highest reaches of the U.S. government. Until then, officialdom thought it had the UFO question well in hand. Air Force investigations were generally low-key affairs, and the previous year, 1951, had been a relatively quiet one. The year 1952, however, would set in motion a series of events that would push UFOs to the far fringes of respectability. The UFOs did not do that themselves. They received considerable help from a secret CIA scientific panel convened in response to the events of a tumultuous summer.

A Month of Mystery

When they first saw the glowing amber light ahead of them, the pilot and copilot of a Capital airliner at 1,500-feet altitude thought it was from an approaching civilian airplane, or maybe from a flair. They were 10 miles south of the Potomac River, near

Washington, D. C. It was 8:18 P.M. on July 10, 1952. As they watched it, they saw that the light was not in fact moving, thus rendering their identification moot.

They watched the light for the next 10 minutes. It was motionless all the time, until suddenly, as the pilots told Air Force investigators, "it climbed rapidly in a turning attitude and turned into the northwest."

At 3:30 on the afternoon of July 12, the sky clear, two swimmers lay on the beach at Round Bay, Maryland, six miles northwest of Annapolis. One was the president of an insurance company, a frequent flyer quite familiar with air traffic. He happened to glance upwards, squinting in the bright light. His eyes fell on a passing transport plane 9,000 feet above, moving in the direction of Norfolk, Virginia. Then, when the plane was directly overhead, the man observed four white oval objects, each approximately one-third the size of the transport. Clustered together, they were approaching the plane at a high rate of speed. Half a mile behind it, the witness informed the Air Force, "All four objects stopped abruptly in mid-air behind the transport, maintained their formation, hesitated for a full second, did a right-angle turn, and then immediately resumed their original high speed and headed approximately south. They were in sight for about three seconds more, then disappeared in mid-air."

The other witness, a woman, confirmed the report in all its details.

Not quite 12 hours later, at 3 A.M. on July 13, 60 miles southwest of Washington, D.C., a National Airlines DC-4 on its way to the city from Jacksonville, Florida, encountered a bluish white luminous sphere. First seen hovering in the western sky, it soon ascended to 11,000 feet, the airliner's altitude, and stopped two miles off its left wing. The UFO then paced the aircraft. To get a better look at it against the dark background, the pilot turned off all the external and internal lights. Almost immediately, the object shot off at an estimated 1,000 mph.

In its official summation the Air Force noted, "No other air traffic was reported in the general area at the time of the sighting. No activity or condition which could account for the sighting, no physical evidence, and no attempt to intercept or identify the object has been reported. . . . Due to the occupation and probable experience of the reporting observers, the reliability of information is considered to be excellent."[1]

At 9:30 A.M. on July 14, three objects in triangular formation passed over the outskirts of Washington. Eight witnesses watched them cut a 75-degree arc through the sky before disappearing from sight in the hazy southeast horizon. The observers, employees of a Naval weapons factory, described them as shiny, metallic discs. Five minutes later, two similar objects—these, however, positioned vertically—appeared out of the southwest, moving along at a brisk clip, one behind the other in a straight line. After 35 seconds the UFOs were obscured in factory smoke.

Just before 8:12 P.M. on the same day, 8,000 feet over Chesapeake Bay, the sky was clear, almost completely dark an hour after sunset. The Pan American Airways DC-4 on its way from New York City to Miami was approaching Norfolk on automatic pilot, ferrying ten passengers and three crew members. The latter were Capt. Fred V. Koepke, First Officer William B. Nash, and Second Officer William H. Fortenberry. Nash was in the pilot's seat, Fortenberry in the copilot's. It was Fortenberry's first run on this particular course, and Nash was acquainting him with the landscape.

Then, as if out of nowhere, six crimson dots appeared in the sky at 30 degrees to the east and just beyond Newport News. The two men said almost simultaneously, "What the hell is that?" Whatever they were, they were approaching the airliner at a terrific rate of speed. They looked almost like tracer bullets, but of course that is not what they were; they were "clearly outlined and evidently circular," Nash would write; "the edges were well defined, not phosphorescent or fuzzy in the least." They had a glow even more intense than that of hot coals, and they were "20 times more brilliant than any of the scattered ground lights over which they passed or the city limits to the right." Their altitude was, the observers would estimate, 2,000 feet.

They were passing well below the airliner. It took them only seconds to cross half the distance between their original position and the plane's location. In Nash's account, "We could observe that they were holding a narrow echelon formation, a stepped-up line tilted slightly to our right with the leader at the lowest point, and each following craft slightly higher."

At this juncture the lead object abruptly slowed, causing the second and third to "waver" as if taken by surprise. They came close to passing the leader, "so that for a brief moment during the remainder of their approach the positions of these three varied." Like a stream of tracers, the UFOs then shot over Chesapeake Bay. Now they were about half a mile from the witnesses, heading rapidly toward and below the right-hand side.

Nash released his safety belt and jumped to the window on the right—Fortenberry's—side. In the process he lost sight of the objects for a short time, but Fortenberry was watching them all the while as they passed below. Together the two saw them flip on edge, "the sides to the left going up and the glowing surface facing right." The bottom surfaces seemed dark, but the exposed edges, also unlighted, looked approximately 15 feet thick, with a flat top surface. From this perspective, they resembled giant coins.

"While all were in the edgewise position," Nash would recall, "the last five slid over and past the leader so that the echelon was now tail-foremost, so to speak, the top or last craft being nearest to our position. Then, without any arc or swerve at all, they all flipped back together to the flat attitude and darted off in a direction that formed a sharp angle with their first course, holding their new formation." The change in direction was so abrupt and radical that Nash could only compare it to "a ball ricocheting off a wall."

As this formation peeled off toward the west, Nash and Fortenberry saw two comparable objects, only brighter, shooting from beneath their right wing and heading toward the others at the same altitude. The two observers had the impression—unprovable, of course—that the brighter glow was connected with the greater acceleration of the two new UFOs which seemed to be trying to catch up with the others. When they did, they joined the rear of the echelon.

Moments later, all the objects went dark, now invisible against the black sky. Then in an instant they blinked on again. They continued their passage over the bay until they were 10 miles beyond Newport News, at which point they started to rise until they were well above the DC-4's altitude.

"As they climbed," Nash wrote a couple of years later, "they oscillated up and down behind one another in an irregular fashion, as though they were extremely sensitive to control. In doing this, they went vertically past one another, bobbing up and down (just as the front three went horizontally past one another, as the initial six approached us. This appeared to be an intelligent error, 'lousing up the formation')—they disappeared by blinking out in a mixed-up fashion, in no particular order."

All of this took place in about 15 seconds. Nash and Fortenberry could only gape uncomprehendingly. They agreed that if either had seen it alone, neither would have said a word. Together, however, they couldn't be mistaken. As they overcame their initial shock, Nash went back into the plane to ask—choosing his words carefully—if anybody else had seen anything out of the ordinary. Capt. Koepke, who was engaged in paperwork, hadn't. Neither had any of the passengers.

Nash radioed Norfolk to report his sighting, which was quickly forwarded to the Air Force. Koepke took control of the airplane as the two witnesses reconstructed their experience with the use of a Dalton Mark 7 computer. The computer simulation established the plane's precise location in relation to various geographical markers. This also enabled them to judge where the objects were, how far they had traveled while under observation, and how fast they were going. They reenacted the sighting no fewer than seven times, trying to get as accurate a reading as possible; in each case, the duration came to at least 12 seconds, arguably two or three more. The objects had traveled about 50 miles in that time. In the end, they determined to their satisfaction, not to mention their astonishment, that the objects had traveled at 12,000 mph. By their estimation the UFOs were 100 feet in diameter and 15 feet thick.

In the course of this conversation, they happened to notice an airliner approaching theirs from the south (theirs was, of course, heading south). Even with the two large aircraft moving toward each other at 500 mph, the other plane appeared almost to be standing still compared to the discs. The effect was to underscore the extreme strangeness of what they had encountered just minutes before.

They arrived in Miami after midnight. Just before 8 a.m., Air Force representatives called them to arrange an interview. Later that morning the two were interviewed separately at first for nearly two hours, then together for half an hour. The officers, led by Air Force Wing Intelligence Officer Maj. John H. Sharpe, had already done their homework. By consulting weather records, they had already established that a temperature inversion could not have been responsible. They had collected seven other reports of unusual aerial phenomena in the area the previous evening, one from a Navy lieutenant commander who with his wife had observed a formation of reddish discs traveling at great speed and effecting an abrupt, radical turn.[2]

Nash and Fortenberry were unusually skilled observers, thus able to take in a great deal of detail even given the relative brevity of their sighting. Both were Navy veterans trained, as military pilots, to identify and describe objects in the air and on the ground even under the briefest or most adverse conditions. (Nash had

10,000 hours as a transport pilot, and Fortenberry, who had flown Navy fighters, had been a Pan American pilot since 1945.) "We memorized the contours of every ship in the German and Japanese Navies," Nash noted in a 1962 letter to Harvard University astronomer and UFO debunker Donald H. Menzel. "We did this also with all enemy aircraft. Needless to say, we had to learn all of our own air and sea craft, too. We had to draw outline sketches of any of them in tests. These, once learned, were flashed upon a screen, first at a 10th of a second and later at 1/100th of a second. . . . We had to tell the instructor the type, nation, and number of craft we had seen. . . . We had all the time in the world to make our [UFO] observations."

The lieutenant commander the Air Force men had mentioned wrote a letter to the *Norfolk Virginian-Pilot* to recount his own sighting. The witness, an officer on the cruiser *Roanoke*, reported seeing eight red lights moving in a straight line, then vanishing. His sighting took place about 15 minutes before Nash and Fortenberry's.

Another possible witness, whose testimony emerged years later, wrote a UFO-research organization in 1970 to recall a sighting he had experienced one evening in July 1952 in New Jersey. He could not recall the exact date, and he did not mention Nash and Fortenberry's encounter, of which he appeared unaware. It happened, he thought, "about 9 P.M." He had seen seven glowing orange discs moving at a remarkable pace in staggered formation toward the southwest, in the general direction of Chesapeake Bay. Scientist/ufologist Michael D. Swords, who found this obscure report, writes:

> One wonders whether a formation of discs flew over Camden, New Jersey, at 8:00 P.M. or so (rather than 9:00) heading southwest toward Newport News, and at 8:12 P.M. reversed their direction and encountered Nash and Fortenberry. Thereupon two more of their number were about to join, or rejoin, them and they

pivoted, reassembled, and flew off toward the west. We
could never prove this scenario, but the correlation of
attributes is extremely intriguing. Perhaps one of the
UFO classics just got better.

A possibly confirmatory sighting occurred two nights later. The
Pan Am report got headline treatment all across the country and
aroused the curiosity of Paul R. Hill. Hill was an aeronautical engineer employed at Langley Air Force Base, in Hampton, the sister city to Newport News. When he read about the encounter, he
wondered if the UFOs might engage in a repeat performance and
decided to be in the right place in case they did. As he looked out
over the waters of Chesapeake Bay at 8 o'clock on the evening of
July 16, he spotted two amber-colored lights coming in from the
south at about 500 mph.

"These slowed down as they made a 'U' turn at the southern
edge of the Peninsula," Hill related. "They moved side by side
until they revolved around each other at a high rate of speed in a
tight circle two or three hundred feet as a third UFO came racing
up from the direction of Virginia Beach [to the southwest] and
'fell in' several hundred feet below the first two, forming a sort of
'V' formation. A fourth UFO came in from up to the James River
and joined the group which headed on south at about 500 mph."

Hill's observation came, of course, in the middle of a huge,
already-noted national UFO wave. The most sensational part of
it, however, was just three evenings away, and it would all happen
in the same area where Nash and Fortenberry, Hill, and others
had sighted anomalous aerial phenomena.

Three nights later, on July 19, a Saturday, at 11:40, seven "pips"
or "blips" appeared on the radarscope at Washington National
Airport. They indicated that objects in the sky were moving at
100 mph and 15 miles south-southwest of the capital, in an area
where no aircraft were known to be. Moreover, they were not
traveling on registered flight paths. Air traffic controller Edward

Nugent, who first noticed the pips, joked about a "fleet of flying saucers" when he spoke with his superior, Harry G. Barnes, senior air traffic controller for the Civil Aeronautics Administration (CAA). Soon afterwards, in a nationally syndicated story, Barnes recorded his impressions:

> We knew immediately that a very strange situation existed. . . . Their movements were completely radical compared to those of ordinary aircraft. They followed no set course [and] were not in any formation, and we only seemed to be able to track them for about three miles at a time. The individual pip would seem to disappear from the scope at intervals. Later I realized that if these objects had made any sudden burst of extremely high speed, that would account for [their] disappearing from the scope temporarily.

An independent check of the radar determined that technical glitches were not causing phony returns. Barnes phoned Howard Cocklin at National's other radar station, at Tower Central a quarter-mile away. Cocklin reported that his radar was tracking the objects, too. Not only that, he could see one—"a bright orange light"—through the window. Ten miles to the east, a civilian controller at Andrews Air Force Base radar was telling Barnes that the only aircraft in the sky was a C-47 transport an hour in the distance. Then an airman on the ground phoned the tower with news of unidentified objects nearby. Following directions, Airman William Brady, who had taken the call, looked to the south, where he observed, as he would tell Blue Book investigators, "an object which appeared to be like an orange ball of fire, trailing a tail[;] it appeared to be about two miles south and one-half mile from the Andrews range. It was very bright and definite, and unlike anything I had ever seen before. . . . It made kind of a circular movement."

As he was opening his mouth to alert others in the tower, the object suddenly stopped, hovered, then "took off at an unbelievable speed." It was gone in a "split second." Moments later, another fireball, looking like the first, showed up. "It made an arc-like pattern and then disappeared," he said. "I only saw each object for about a second."

Now Barnes's scope was tracking unknowns east and west of Andrews. Andrews's interceptors could not be launched, however, because the runway was undergoing repairs. Frenzied arrangements were made to send a squadron from the Delaware-based Newcastle AFB.

At 1 A.M. Capt. S. C. Pierman, a Capital Airlines DC-4 pilot, had just lifted off from National when he learned that radar was monitoring unknowns nine miles away. In short order they were four miles away, then closer and at his 10 o'clock position. Pierman looked out and at first could see only another DC-4 in the distance. Then other things came into view: six bright, fast-moving lights, white in color, with no visible tails. He watched them for the next 14 minutes. Radar confirmed their presence. As Barnes would state, "Each sighting coincided with a pip we could see near his plane. When he reported that the light streaked off at high speed, it disappeared on our scope." The objects were tracked performing maneuvers—extraordinarily rapid climbs and descents—which were well beyond the performance characteristics of even the most advanced earthly aircraft.

Meantime, in the growing excitement, some witnesses were mistaking stars and other prosaic stimuli for UFOs. Nonetheless, unknowns were still being observed and sometimes—though not always—showing up on radar screens. On one occasion the three radars—the two at National, the other at Andrews—followed the same object at the same time. It was there for half a minute before vanishing.

Around 3 A.M. another airliner, this one piloted by Capt. Howard Dermott, was approaching National from Herndon, Virginia, when a UFO appeared behind it and shadowed it in its flight. Unnerved, Dermott asked National if it had anything on its radar. It did, and it was where Dermott thought it was: at an eight o'clock position. Four miles from landing, both pilot and ground radar saw the object turn away and disappear.

This was the last sighting for a while, a fact that had its own at least ostensible significance. Shortly afterwards, the squadron from Newscastle showed up. The jets patrolled the skies until their fuel ran low and they were forced to return to Delaware. With them out of the way, the UFOs came back, which led Barnes to suspect that the objects were monitoring radio traffic. Earlier, when he had directed Pierman toward a specific object, it would inevitably shoot off. Barnes was certain that whoever was inside the UFOs was always a step ahead of the human beings on the ground, in the air, and at the radarscopes. According to him:

> The only recognizable behavior pattern which occurred to me from watching the objects was that they acted like a bunch of small kids out playing. It was helter skelter, as if directed by some innate curiosity. At times they moved as a group or cluster, at other times as individuals over widely scattered areas. I could safely declare that they could make right-angle turns and completely reverse their flight. . . .
>
> I'm positive they were guided by some intelligence. If no planes were in the air, the things would fly over the most likely points of interest—Andrews Field, the aircraft plant at Riverdale, the [Washington] Monument, or the Capitol. One or two circled our radio beacons. But as soon as an airliner took off, several would dart across and start to follow, as if to look it over.

The targets continued to appear until about 5:30, when Barnes's scope contained as many as seven or eight.

Sightings and blips were registered the following evening, the twentieth. There were sporadic sightings during the week. One, an aerial encounter, happened over Maryland at noon on the twenty-second.

Two Air Force pilots, identified in official records only as Col. Bailey and Maj. Kemper, flying over Stafford, Maryland, in a C-45 spotted a brilliant, oblong-shaped object dancing in the sky 70 degrees to their right at 6000 feet. It was approaching the plane in what looked like "spurts," an irregular movement in which no acceleration or deceleration was apparent. Finally, it turned away on the same path as the C-45. "The spurting motion continued but in a vertical plane coming up 'step fashion.' " Both Bailey and Kemper changed their angle of vision to assure themselves that they were not seeing a reflection on the glass. What they did see, however, is unclear.

A blitz comparable to the weekend's did not start up until the next Saturday, the twenty-sixth, when at 8:15 P.M. the pilot and stewardess of a National Airlines plane encountered red, glowing objects above them, estimated to be traveling at 100 mph. Objects traveling at comparable speeds, sometimes a dozen at a time, were tracked on National and Andrews radar. A ground witness, a master sergeant who observed them visually, told Blue Book, "These lights did not have the characteristics of shooting stars. There was [sic] no trails, and they seemed to go out rather than disappear, and traveled faster than any shooting star I have ever seen."

National Radar followed blips that made abrupt direction reversals, then accelerated to a jaw-dropping 7,000 mph. At 11:30 two F-94 interceptors arrived from Newcastle. National's tower directed one of them, piloted by Lt. William Patterson, to a target 10 miles away. When Patterson looked in that direction, he sighted four white "glows," as he called them. He had barely pointed his jet in their direction before the UFOs were coming toward him. While he was still trying to process what was happening, they clustered around him. Patterson radioed the tower to ask for word on what to do next. The response was what one observer called "stunned silence." Fortunately, not long afterwards, the UFOs departed.

On the other hand, the other F-94 pilot, Capt. John McHugo, saw nothing, even when radar had targets all around him. The Washington National Weather Station reported the presence of a slight temperature inversion, enough to cause at least some bogus radar returns (by bending radar beams so that they picked up objects on the ground, not in the air). The pilots and radar operators felt, however, that these could not have explained the "good and solid" reports that coupled radar and visual observation of distinctly anomalous phenomena.

At 3 A.M., as an Eastern Airlines Constellation neared Washington, National radar noted an unknown to the rear of the aircraft. The pilot could not see the object from the cockpit, so he turned the plane around. As he did so, the target blinked off the radar screen. Then, a few minutes later, "odd lights" showed up in the vicinity of a Capital airliner which had left National and was on its way to Martinsburg, West Virginia. They were in view for 12 minutes.

Amid a growing clamor and newspaper headlines, the Air Force held a press conference on July 29 at the Pentagon. One of the participants, the Air Technical Intelligence Center's Capt. Roy James—who, according to Blue Book head Capt. Ed Ruppelt, harbored a "powerful dislike for UFOs"—speculated that temperature inversions could have caused the returns and the sightings. Though he termed this only "some possibility" and he had not participated in the investigation, having arrived from Wright-Patterson AFB, in Ohio, only that morning, the *Washington Post* announced in the next available headline, "Air Force Lays Saucer Blips Here to Heat." The national and world press followed suit.

In reality, everybody involved in the sightings rejected the explanation. The U.S. Weather Bureau expressed its skepticism in a little-noted newspaper story. Ruppelt would write that the press conference had served its purpose, which was to get journalists and politicians who were demanding answers "off our backs." (President Truman had personally expressed interest in the unfolding events.) Officially but quietly, the Air Force judged the reports to be of unknowns.[3]

All the while, July 1952 was recording remarkable encounters by pilots and others. The East Coast saw other UFO activity. One incident began at 3:20 A.M. on the twenty-third, when an Air Force F-94B pilot at 25,000 feet over Massachusetts saw a spinning round object throwing off rays of blue light as a pinwheel would. It was about a mile from him, at his altitude or just a little higher, at 270 degrees. The pilot jerked his aircraft and effected a 180-degree turn. As he was coming out of it, he switched on the afterburner to attain as much speed as possible. Meanwhile, the UFO made its own 180-degree turn and shot above the jet. The radar observer, the other witness on board the interceptor, got a good look at it, essentially confirming the initial impression that it was spinning and casting off light beams. The UFO continued on its course for a short time, then ascended at high speed and was gone.

UFO activity was just starting, however. At 3:47, between Boston and Provincetown, a trio of F-94s—with a total of five occupants, pilots and crewmen—at 15,000 feet encountered several objects, each with a "flickering white light and a swishing, circling blue light." They were 10,000 feet above the aircraft, streaking in the opposite direction like a "bat out of hell," as one pilot remarked. One of the jets got close enough to one of the UFOs to capture it on its radar for a minute. Or as the official Air Force report on the incident tells the story:

> Pilot flying on a heading of approx. 180 degrees at above location (71 degrees west, 42 degrees 10 north) when sighting object—appearing light. Possibly like green navigation light. He applied afterburner and headed toward the object. Radar observer picked up

object on his scope at approx. ten to 12,000 yards. A lock was obtained shortly thereafter and the pilot took his eyes off the object to flying his instruments and pilot (radar) scope. The object was kept in a position of 5 degrees above and 5 degrees to Port. After-burner was lighted and the F-94 closed to three thousand yards. At this time the object exceeded the limits of the scope and broke lock by what appeared on the scope as a hard break right and down. The return on the scope was approx. fifty knots [57½ mph]. The crew was not able to spot the object or on the scope after it broke lock.

A subsequent Blue Book investigation established that no other military aircraft were in the area at the time. Unfortunately, the ground radar that could have tracked the UFOs, at the Naval Air Station in Squantum, Rhode Island, was not operating at the time. Blue Book did learn, however, that weather observers stationed at Nathaniel Green Airport, in Hillgrove, Rhode Island, had seen white lights moving north at a fantastic speed at 1:28 A.M.

At 3:37, just 10 minutes before the F-94/UFO confrontation, five ground witnesses at Squantum saw two bluish green objects heading southwest. Soon they turned west, then northwest in a great arc. Suddenly they blinked out and were no longer visible. Between 3:50 and 3:54, according to a brief report in Air Force records, glowing blue-white lights were seen 14 times. An interceptor tracked one on radar for a short time.

At 7:36 a Navy radar at Jamestown, Rhode Island, picked up a target at 42,000 feet. It was traveling at high speed on a south-to-north trajectory. Jamestown alerted the radar station at Camp Hero, New York. It caught the same target, and F-94s were sent on an intercept mission. They were unable to catch up with it. F-86 Saber jets, faster than the F-94s, came to the rescue, only to fail themselves.

Other Aerial Enigmas

Elsewhere in the United States, not just on the East Coast, aerial encounters with unidentifieds were taking place. The twelfth saw two such incidents, one with a peculiar detail unmatched in any report before or since.

According to Air Force records, two F-86 fighters had just left O'Hare Field, near Chicago, and were flying over Arlington Heights, Illinois, when one of the pilots, coming out of a right turn, noticed a yellow, exhaust-spewing oblong object some 15 miles away, at about 22,000 feet, and moving along at an approximate 800 mph. The pilot accelerated toward the UFO, but within 20 seconds it had shot out of range. During the brief attempted intercept the pilot had notified ground control of what he was seeing and what he was trying to do. The second pilot did not see the UFO but overheard the radio traffic.

There had been silence, though, when a voice, speaking in an eerie tone, came over the radio, slowly stretching out the name "Casey." As it happened, Casey was the pilot's first name. Subsequent investigation allegedly failed to determine any source for the voice, though it is hard to resist the conclusion that this was a prank of some sort.

In Dayton, Ohio, that evening witnesses on the ground reported seeing two lights of blinding brilliance hovering motionlessly next to each other. A flight of F-86s had already been dispatched to chase an unidentified target and to make visual contact. Seeing the unusual lights, the lead pilot decided that they were what they were looking for, and he ordered the other jets to close in on them with him. But within moments the lights were gone "as if someone turned out a light," in the words of the official report.

On the morning of August 24, an Air Force pilot, Col. Gerald W. Johnson, had his own extraordinary encounter, which has some elements generally in common with Nash and Fortenberry's. In an F-84C interceptor he left Travis AFB, California, on his way to

Turner AFB, Georgia, and at 10:15 MST was 35,000 feet over Luna County, in southwestern New Mexico. Two miles off his left wing he noticed two ball-shaped, silvery objects flying abreast of one another, about 500 yards apart. Heading in the same direction as he was and at the same speed (290 mph), they were at the 11 o'clock position. A few minutes later, one turned to the right, passing in front of his aircraft and disappearing at high speed. Its companion was lost to sight for the same reason.

Seven minutes later, over El Paso, Texas, Johnson spotted a UFO which was either one he had already observed or one exactly like it. The UFO flew on a parallel path to his F-84C for the next five minutes. Then a second joined it and the two continued together for another three minutes. Finally, one ascended at a high rate of speed, followed a second later by the second.

In a report to Air Force Intelligence, Johnson noted laconically, "The observed characteristics of these unidentified objects were such that would lead to no conclusion." He added, however, that at times they were moving much faster than his 290 mph. That "and the fact that they could so quickly disappear on two occasions led me to believe that their flight capabilities were greater than that of any aircraft known to be flying today."

"Greatly Reduced . . . If Not Eliminated"

On August 1 the *New York Times* noted that the volume of UFO reports—prominently including those from the Washington part of the 1952 wave—had overwhelmed not only the Air Force but "regular intelligence work." All this, Air Force Chief of Staff Maj. Gen. Hoyt S. Vandenberg fretted, would lead to "mass hysteria." Something had to be done.

When things quieted down, H. Marshall Chadwell, assistant director of the CIA's Office of Scientific Intelligence (OSI), which had been monitoring the UFO situation since 1949, met with the

CIA director, Gen. Walter Bedell Smith, on December 2. Chadwell remarked that "sightings of unexplained objects at great altitudes and flying at high speeds in the vicinity of major U.S. defense installations" could not be ignored any longer. They "are not attributable to natural phenomena or known types of aerial vehicles," he stressed. In a memorandum sent from Smith's office, Chadwell urged the National Security Council to upgrade UFO investigation to a high priority.

At an Intelligence Advisory Committee meeting on the fourth, attendees listened to Chadwell speak and then signed on to an agreement to "enlist the services of selected scientists to review and appraise the available evidence in the light of pertinent scientific theories." Air Force Director of Intelligence Maj. Gen. John A. Samford promised that the Air Technical Intelligence Center would cooperate in supplying UFO data.

The fateful result was a three-day meeting convened by CIA physicist H. P. Robertson. Besides Robertson, the other participating scientists were Samuel A. Goudsmit (physicist); Luis Alvarez (physicist and 1968 Nobel Prize winner); Lloyd Berkner (physicist); and Thornton Page (astrophysicist). There were two associate panel members, missile specialist Frederick C. Durant and astronomer/Blue Book consultant J. Allen Hynek. Only Hynek, who might be characterized as a moderate skeptic, had any experience with actual UFO investigation. The rest of the group, including Durant, were as deeply unfriendly to UFOs as anyone could be. Page and Goudsmit were openly derisive.

The panel devoted a total of 12 hours to examination of six years' worth of UFO sightings and other evidence. It listened with modest interest to presentations by Ruppelt, Hynek, and Pentagon UFO spokesman Maj. Dewey J. Fournet (a private advocate of the extraterrestrial hypothesis). Robertson then drafted a report which the members approved on the morning of the seventeenth. It would be the most influential document in the history of the U.S. government's interaction with the UFO phenomenon.

In the panel's view unexplained sightings existed only because the investigations had been insufficient to uncover the true, prosaic causes. Such further investigation, however, would be a "great waste of effort . . . unless such action would benefit a training and educational program." Reports were only overloading "channels of communication with material quite irrelevant to hostile objects [presumably meaning Soviet bombers and missiles] that might some day appear." To remove that potential danger, the Air Force should play down UFOs and instead commence a "debunking" campaign to "reduce public interest in 'flying saucers'. . . . This education could be accomplished by mass media such as television, motion pictures, and popular articles," bringing in both scientists and celebrities from the entertainment world to assure people that all sightings are ultimately explainable.

A slight expansion of Blue Book for a year or two would help reassure the public and make for more effective debunking, eventually reducing "public gullibility." In perhaps its most outrageous recommendation, the panel urged monitoring of civilian UFO groups "because of their potentially great influence on mass thinking if widespread sightings should occur. The apparent irresponsibility and the possible use of such groups for subversive purposes should be kept in mind." It added that "national security agencies [should] take immediate steps to strip the Unidentified Flying Objects of the special status they have been given and the aura of mystery they have unfortunately acquired."

Blue Book immediately acted on the Robertson panel's recommendations and thereafter devoted itself more to anti-UFO public relations than to serious field investigation of UFO reports. The policy continued until Blue Book's closing in December 1969. Yet, as CIA historian Gerald K. Haines would write in 1997:

> CIA officials wanted knowledge of any Agency interest in the subject of flying saucers carefully restricted, noting not only that the Robertson panel report was classified but also that any mention of CIA sponsor-

ship of the panel was forbidden. This attitude would later cause the Agency major problems relating to its credibility.

It managed to keep the panel's existence secret for at least a few years. In 1956 a misleading, short account appeared in Ruppelt's memoirs, though he did not name the CIA and his representation of the panel's motives and views—sympathetic and thoughtful—is all but outright fiction. In 1958 and 1960 Air Force spokesmen acknowledged the existence of a CIA panel and provided short quotes from its conclusions. Only in 1966 did *Saturday Review* science columnist John Lear publish a fuller version of the panel's report.

That same year *CBS Reports*, hosted by Walter Cronkite, carried an hour on the UFO controversy, from a dismissive point of view. In a private letter to Durant, Page boasted that he had "helped organize the CBS TV show around the Robertson panel conclusions." Interviewed in 2002 by *Florida Today* reporter Billy Cox, the long-retired Durant insisted that he "wouldn't change a word" of the Robertson report.

In 1972, after he and Blue Book had parted company and he was speaking freely (and critically) of his experiences, Hynek had little good to say about the Robertson panel, whose "attention was directed largely to a defense and security problem rather than to a scientific one." Worse, "The Robertson panel . . . made the subject of UFOs scientifically unrespectable." Ever since, he remarked with not a little bitterness, "not enough attention was paid to the subject to acquire the kind of data needed even to decide the nature of the UFO phenomenon." Nothing has changed since Hynek wrote those words.

The one surviving mystery surrounding the panel concerns its recommendation that civilian organizations advocating UFO research and UFO reality be monitored. Did military and other agencies act on this recommendation? If so, how? And to what effect? These questions, never satisfactorily answered, are in any event outside this book's focus of interest.

6

Discs in Daylight

IN THE IMMEDIATE wake of Kenneth Arnold's seminal June 24, 1947, sighting and the flood of reports that filled newspapers worldwide, reporters searched for a phrase to characterize the new phenomenon. The first attempts were "flying disc" and "flying saucer." The latter stuck, and for the next few years, before "unidentified flying objects" and "UFOs"—the former first appeared in late-1940s Air Force memos, the latter acronym coming along in the early 1950s, during Lt. (later Capt.) Ed Ruppelt's tenure as head of Project Blue Book—entered the popular vocabulary, flying saucers were what those strange shapes and lights in the sky (and, more rarely, on the ground) were.

Today "flying saucer" serves less as a descriptive phrase than as a derisive one, employed by those who presume the illegitimacy or absurdity of the premise that UFOs may exist as extraterrestrial spacecraft or something comparably fantastic. Even by July 1947 it encompassed all manner of anomalous aerial phenomena, whatever their physical configuration. (Thus, cigars, triangles, boomerangs, and nebulous nocturnal lights were transformed into "flying saucers.") Still, it is worth recalling that "flying saucer" originally referred to exactly that: a disc sailing, under apparent intelligent control, through the atmosphere. The disc-shaped objects that gave flying saucers their name would play, and continue to play, a large role in UFO reporting.

As "flying saucer" went out of fashion except among cartoonists and scoffers, Northwestern University astronomer J. Allen Hynek, for two decades the Air Force's chief scientific consultant on UFO matters, coined "daylight disc" as part of a sighting-classification system outlined in his influential *The UFO Experience* (1972).[1] Daylight disc never managed to achieve household status in the way another of Hynek's categories, "close encounters" (especially "close encounters of the third kind"), did. Even so, it denotes an especially puzzling aspect of the UFO phenomenon, one that has proved particularly resistant to conventional accounting. Former UFO investigator Allan Hendry, among the more iconoclastic observers of the UFO scene, learned from considerable experience that daylight-disc reports—unlike, say, sightings of lights in the night sky—"are not as susceptible to the concern that the information is being partially or completely generated by fantasy."

The first time the word "saucer"—synonymous, of course, with disc—saw print in the context of a UFO sighting was long before flying saucers became a cultural artifact. On January 25, 1878, a Texas newspaper, the *Denison Daily News*, reported the curious experience of farmer John Martin, who three mornings earlier, while hunting, saw "a dark object high in the northern sky." According to the article, titled "A Strange Phenomenon":

> The peculiar shape and the velocity with which the object seemed to approach riveted his attention, and he strained his eyes to discover its character. When first noticed it appeared to be about the size of an orange, after which it continued to grow larger.
>
> After gazing at it for some time, Mr. Martin became blind from long looking and left off viewing to rest his

eyes. On resuming his view, the object was almost overhead and had increased considerably in size and appeared to be going through space at a wonderful speed. When directly over him it was about the size of a large saucer and was evidently at great height.

The newspaper added, "Mr. Martin is a gentleman of undoubted veracity and this strange occurrence, if it was not a balloon, deserves the attention of our scientists."

Unfortunately, however deserving, the daylight disc that John Martin saw—like the daylight discs seen by the pilots whose sightings are recounted in this chapter—has yet to attract the attention of more than a handful of scientists, most of whom have been quickly marginalized for their efforts. Science's shameful neglect of the mystery posed by reports like these, with all they imply, continues. It will take a future generation of more open-minded, courageous scientists to pick up the pieces and start to put them together.

July 6's Discs

An Army Air Force B-25, flying east from Odgen, Utah, on July 6, 1947, was 100 miles west of Kansas City and at 10,000 feet when it encountered a bright object "shaped," the crew would report, "like the top of a water tank." When first seen, at 1:45 P.M., the UFO was 10 miles away and below the left side of the bomber. By the time the pilot had flown within a mile or two of it, he and others were able to estimate that it was 30 to 35 feet in diameter.

The object ascended to the B-25's altitude and paced it at 210 mph. The pilot turned in another attempt to approach the UFO, but this time it rose still higher and vanished at 11,000 feet.

About an hour later, at 3 P.M., in Oklahoma, the pilot of a Phillips Petroleum private plane saw a disc at 10,000 feet. He shouted

Foo fighters—such as this one allegedly photographed following a military aircraft over Holland in 1943—puzzled pilots in both the European and Asian theaters during World War II. (*Faded Discs*)

A "small amber disc" trailed William D. Leet (*in cockpit*) and his B-17 crew over Austria one night in December 1944. (*Faded Discs*)

Lt. Donald Meiers, a bomber pilot, reported that "two balls of fire" followed him 20 miles down the Rhine Valley, matching his every maneuver. (*Faded Discs*)

Donald E. Keyhoe, a retired Marine Corps major, was the leading early public advocate of UFOs as extraterrestrial spacecraft. Some of the reports he championed have since been disproved. (*Faded Discs*)

In 1946 and early 1947 ghost rockets, the immediate predecessors of flying saucers, plagued Europe. Authorities suspected that they were Soviet missiles, but they were not. This photograph is said to depict a ghost rocket but could as easily show a daylight meteor. (*Faded Discs*)

Several alleged ghost rocket pieces are compared in size to a matchbox. (*Faded Discs*)

Pilot Kenneth Arnold's sighting on June 24, 1947, brought UFOs to popular attention and inspired speculation about "flying saucers." In this picture, he points to one of the discs he saw that historic Tuesday afternoon. (*Fortean Picture Library*)

The nine flying discs Arnold observed over Mount Rainier, Washington, darted through the sky at a speed that he conservatively estimated to be 1200 mph. The real speed may have been as high as 1700 mph.
(*Dezsö Sternoczky/SUFOI/Fortean Picture Library*)

Ohio State University—later Northwestern University—astrophysicist J. Allen Hynek served as chief scientific consultant to the U.S. Air Force on UFO matters. Over the years, Hynek evolved from UFO skeptic to advocate of serious investigation. He came to suspect that the best sightings were evidence of nonhuman intelligence. (*Faded Discs*)

United Air Lines pilot E. J. Smith experienced one of the most impressive early sightings, on the evening of July 4, 1947. Soon afterward, he and Kenneth Arnold became enmeshed in the notorious Maury Island affair. (*Faded Discs*)

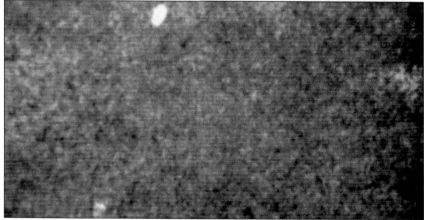

Alerted by neighbors, Yeoman Frank Ryman of the Coast Guard press information office in Seattle grabbed his camera and took this photograph in the late afternoon of July 4. He estimated the disc's altitude at 10,000 feet. "It was flashing silver in the sun," he said, "about one-tenth the apparent size of a full moon." It was in view for five minutes. (*Faded Discs*)

In September 1947, in one of the first official assessments of the UFO phenomenon, Lt. Gen. Nathan F. Twining, head of the Air Materiel Command, declared that "the phenomenon . . . is something real and not visionary or fictitious." (*Faded Discs*)

Col. Howard McCoy directed the Air Force's first UFO project. Its classified name was Sign, but the public knew it as Project Saucer. (*Faded Discs*)

Capt. Edward J. Ruppelt, who directed the Air Force UFO project in the early 1950s, later wrote a memoir which revealed Project Sign's pro-extraterrestrial conclusions. (*Faded Discs*)

Kentucky Air National Guard Capt. Thomas F. Mantell's death while chasing an ostensible flying saucer led to fears about the possibly unfriendly intentions of space visitors.
(*Fortean Picture Library*)

In this artist's reconstruction, Mantell's F-51 pursues an unidentified sky object to what would prove a fatal altitude.
(*Fortean Picture Library*)

T/Sgt. Quinton Blackwell, at Godman Field Control Tower, took a call about an approaching unidentified object, saw it himself, and directed Mantell and his fellow pilots to approach it. (*Faded Discs*)

Col. Guy Hix, Godman commander, observed the object Mantell soon would pursue, describing it as "very white . . . like an umbrella." (*Faded Discs*)

Second Lt. George F. Gorman's "dogfight" with a flying object over Fargo, North Dakota, on October 1, 1948, proved to be less than met the pilot's eye. (*Faded Discs*)

John B. Whitted and Clarence S. Chiles's near-collision with a giant rocket-shaped craft with two rows of portholes so impressed Air Force investigators that some were ready to declare that otherworldly ships had arrived. (*Fortean Picture Library and Faded Discs*)

Chiles and Whitted's dramatic sighting occurred as their Eastern Air Lines DC-3 flew over Alabama at 2:45 A.M. on July 24, 1948. (*Faded Discs*)

A powerful, articulate advocate of objective scientific UFO research, University of Arizona atmospheric physicist James E. McDonald investigated reports and debunked facile explanations for puzzling sightings. (*Faded Discs*)

Capt. Willis T. Sperry, American Air Lines DC-6 pilot, and his crew and passengers spotted an enormous cigar-shaped structure moving at "fantastic" speed. (*Faded Discs*)

A civilian aeronautical engineer employed by the Air Force, Alfred Loedding was an active figure in Project Sign and principal author of the pro-extraterrestrial "Estimate of the Situation." (*Faded Discs*)

On March 20, 1950,
between Memphis
and Little Rock,
DC-3 pilot Capt. Jack
Adams observed a
flat disc with flashing
lights. (*Faded Discs*)

Adams's copilot, Capt. G. W.
Anderson, a scoffer until his
own sighting, said, "When you
see something with your own
eyes, you have to believe it."
(*Faded Discs*)

William B. Nash, first officer of a Pan American DC-4, encountered six glowing, coin-shaped UFOs over Chesapeake Bay on the night of July 14, 1952. (*Faded Discs*)

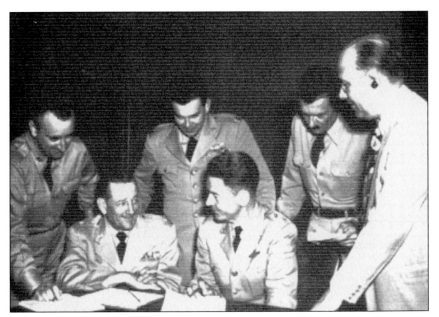

Amid mounting alarm over the Washington UFO sightings, the Pentagon held a press conference on July 29, with Air Force Intelligence head Maj. Gen. John A. Samford (*seated at right*). Blue Book's director, Capt. Ed Ruppelt (*standing in center*), also participated. (*Faded Discs*)

According to one somewhat dubious account, Eastern Air Defense chief Gen. Benjamin Chidlaw once confided, "We take [UFO reports] seriously when you consider that we have lost many men and planes trying to intercept them." (*Faded Discs*)

Though harshly dismissive of the idea that reports might suggest anything extraordinary, University of Colorado physicist Edward U. Condon headed an Air Force–sponsored but allegedly independent inquiry into UFOs. (*Faded Discs*)

Among the most impressive and extraordinary of all pilot sightings was one that took place over Alaska in November 1986. The principal witness was Japan Airlines pilot Capt. Kenju Terauchi, here pictured with a drawing of the gigantic Saturn-shaped UFO he and his crew witnessed in an episode that attracted worldwide attention. (*Fortean Picture Library*)

This diagram shows the positioning of Capt. Terauchi's Japan Airlines Boeing 707 and the "mothership" he encountered over Alaska. (*Faded Discs*)

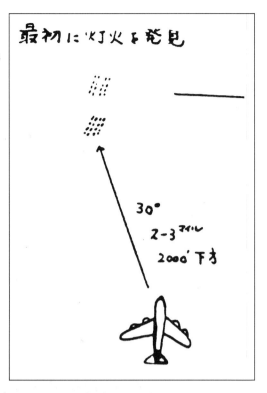

最初に灯火を発見

30°
2-3 マイル
2000′ 下方

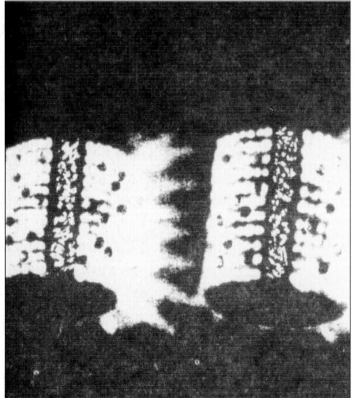

This artist's depiction of the "mothership" that Capt. Terauchi viewed over Alaska is part of the JAL case file.
(*Faded Discs*)

to his passenger, fellow pilot Henry Barbarick, but it had vanished before Barbarick could see it. A few minutes later the pilot, John Phillips, Jr., thought he saw another of the discs, but again it was gone before his companion could confirm the sighting. Just a moment later, however, a disc loomed up in front of the plane, then flew over it. Barbarick did not miss this one.

Over the next 15 minutes, as many as nine objects, moving at an almost blinding speed, showed up. Their sizes varied from that of a small aircraft to that of a transport plane. They were all saucer-shaped, with turn-up fronts and a silvery sheen. As they maneuvered, they also revolved. The effect, Barbarick told a reporter, was "like someone shooting flak at you."

Muroc Discs

Among the most impressive of early UFO sightings were those that occurred on July 8, 1947, over Muroc Air Base (now Edwards Air Force Base), in southern California. The events began at 9:30 A.M. when 1st Lt. Joseph C. McHenry, walking to his office, stopped to look at something odd in the sky: two silvery discs. Flying at 300 mph against prevailing winds, they were on a straight, northbound course at 8,000 feet.

By the time McHenry had called to three potential witnesses nearby, the discs were far in the distance. But as they were scanning the sky, they saw a third disc appear from the same area. It made a series of tight circles as it made its way north toward the Mojave Desert. McHenry told investigators:

> From my actual observation, the object circled in too tight a circle and [on] too severe a plane to be any aircraft that I know of. It could not have been any type of bird because of the reflection that was created when the object reached certain altitudes. The object could

not have been a local weather balloon for it is impossible that a weather balloon could stay at the same altitude as long and circle in such a consistent nature as did the above-mentioned object.

At 10:10, as he was warming up the engines of an XP-84 aircraft, a test pilot happened to look to the north, where he saw a weather balloon. Or so he thought at first, before he grasped that it could not be, since it was flying in the face of the wind. Moreover, the spherical, yellowish white object was moving too fast, more than 200 mph.

About two hours later, east of Muroc, at Rogers Dry Lake, Air Force personnel were watching as an aircraft prepared to conduct a seat-ejection experiment and other airplanes flew nearby to monitor it. A round object appeared under the planes, which were at 20,000 feet. As it descended, the witnesses thought the ejection had occurred sooner than planned, but as they told the Air Force:

> The object . . . was falling at three times the rate observed for the test parachute which ejected 30 seconds after we first saw the object. As the object fell it drifted north of due west against the prevailing wind. . . . As this object descended through a low enough level to permit observation of its lateral silhouette, it presented a distinct oval-shaped outline, with two projections on the upper surface which might have been thick fins or knobs. They crossed each other at intervals, suggesting either rotation or oscillation of a slow type. No smoke, flames, propeller arcs, engine noise, or other plausible or visible means of propulsion were noted. The color was silver, resembling an aluminum-printed fabric, and did not appear as dense as a parachute canopy. When the object dropped to a

level such that it came into line of vision of the mountain tops, it was lost to the vision of the observers.

Four hours later, 40 miles south of Muroc and 20,000 feet in the air, an F-51 pilot sighted a "flat object of a light-reflecting nature" at an undetermined distance above him. It was no conventional aircraft; it had no wings or fins, but it was too high for his aircraft to get any closer to it.

It was these sightings, according to an officer who would head Project Blue Book in the early 1950s, that led the Air Force to "take a deep interest in UFOs." Nonetheless, in later years, as it sought to dispose of UFO reports at almost any cost, a subsequent analyst guessed that the objects were "balloons."

Radio Interference?

In this instance, the object described was not a daylight disc in the literal sense, but certainly a variation on the theme. The sighting took place over the central Philippines at 9:55 A.M. on April 1, 1948. The witness was a P-47 pilot, 1st Lt. Robert W. Meyers, from the 67th Fighter Group.

Meyers, leading a flight of three other P-47s, was at 1,500 feet when he observed an unusual object three miles to the east and at 1,000 feet. According to Meyers's official report, it was the shape of a half moon, silvery, with a "turtle back," and it was flying in his direction at approximately 200 mph. When it passed below him, Meyers estimated that it was 30 feet by 20 feet long. His attempt to alert the other pilots, who were some distance behind them, was frustrated when his radio would not function.

Meyers turned left 230 degrees as he set out to get closer to the UFO. Meantime, the UFO executed a 90-degree left turn and leveled out. It sped off and vanished in seconds.

The Air Force report on the case remarked that Meyers was a

"reliable, non-excitable individual who appeared quite positive about his statements"—notwithstanding, presumably, the unfortunate date of the encounter.

Elongated Ovals over Oregon

At 2:25 on the afternoon of May 27, 1949, as he ferried an SNJ trainer for North American Aviation to Burns, Oregon, Joseph Shell noticed a flash of light, which led him to look in the direction of five to eight "aircraft" on a southward trek over the south-central part of the state. They were traveling at an estimated 200 to 250 mph. He thought at first that they were Air Force jets.

Suddenly, they reversed direction and were paralleling Shell's course—he was heading north—though 1,000 to 1,500 feet below it. Still not connecting what he was seeing with UFOs, Shell grew annoyed at the thought that young pilots might be hot-dogging around his flimsier plane and putting him at risk.

The "aircraft" got even closer to him. Now he could tell that they were something strange indeed. Each was metallic, with no markings, looking like elongated ovals. Each was about 20 feet long and four feet thick, and they were flying in file formation at the approximate rate of his own speed (212 mph). They eventually disappeared over the horizon.

In the Clouds

On January 30, 1950, the Air Force's Inspector General Office of Special Investigations filed this report, based on interviews with the witnesses:

> On Tuesday, 24 January 1950, while en route from
> Pope Air Force Base, North Carolina, to Bolling Air Force

Base, Washington, D.C., in C-45 aircraft No. 7122, Captain Theron C. Fehrevach was first to notice the unidentified flying object. Fehrevach stated that the C-45 was pursuing a course of approximately 26 degrees at 5,000 feet when he first noticed the object slightly to the left of the course and about 2,000 feet higher at a distance of 5 to 10 miles from the C-45.

The object was approximately 7,000 feet just above the top of the cloud level which was at this time approximately 5/10 cloud coverage. It was darker than the clouds and easy to distinguish as not being a cloud. When first noticed the object was pursuing a course between and above two rather large cloud banks, which were estimated as being two miles apart. The object moved from the left cloud to the right cloud twice and never at any time did the object show any radius of turn. It moved to a stop and proceeded back again with a fine horizontal movement, at no time varying vertical[ly] in an ascent or descent motion.

At this time Captain Fehrevach showed the unconventional aircraft to Captain Edwards who immediately altered his course some 6 degrees and climbed to 7,000 feet to be horizontally on the same level as the object. The C-45 pursued the object at approximately 160 miles per hour with a 20 mile tail wind. The C-45 at no time could overtake the object and at all times it seemed to stay between 5 and 10 miles directly in front and at the same level as the C-45. At this time Fehrevach had the passenger, Lt. Van Santen, view the object. The object then seemed to disappear in front of them by increasing its speed. The entire action thus far reported took approximately five minutes.

After a minute and a half the object was again sighted

at the same distance (5 to 10 miles) at approximately 35 to 45 degrees to the right of the course pursued by the C-45. The object then came back to a point immediately in front of the C-45. Before assuming this course the object seemed to oscillate to the right and left, a distance seeming to be about one or one and a half distance of its width. When assuming the course it appeared to disappear directly in front of the C-45 by increasing its speed until it was invisible.

The entire incident took place in approximately 15 minutes. Captain Fehrevach and Captain Edwards stated that they had been airborne some 35 to 40 minutes or approximately 1650 [4:30 P.M.] when they first sighted the object. These two pilot officers further volunteered the following information:

The object was clearer when first noticed than at any time during the following 15 minutes that they could focus on it. The unconventional aircraft appeared to be hemispherical or spheroid in shape of approximately 200 to 250 feet in diameter. The object appeared to be flat on the bottom, but this is further explained [by the likelihood] that the bottom half of the sphere could have been obscured due to a black trail which appeared to follow the object. This black trail appeared to be three or four times as long as the object was in diameter. . . . At no time during the viewing of the object was it possible to determine the actual structure. The black trail was very pronounced at the bottom. [Captain Edwards said] the object looked like an oversized parachute with a large black object hanging below it. The smoke trail would lag behind the object no matter which direction it moved.

Unsettlingly Close Encounters over Georgia

Flying an F-51 over Augusta, Georgia, on a clear, sunny day in the summer of 1951, Lt. George Kinman became aware of "something ahead, closing in on me, head on. Before I could take evasive action—before I even thought of it, in fact—this thing dipped abruptly and passed underneath, just missing my propeller.

"The thing was definitely of disc shape . . . white . . . pretty thick. . . . It looked like an oval. . . . It was about twice as big as my plane. It had no visible protrusions like motors, guns, windows, smoke, or fire."

Kinman turned his interceptor aircraft as quickly as he could, but by the time he had positioned it in the direction the UFO had gone, the UFO wasn't there—at least for the next 15 seconds. Then it reappeared, heading toward him again, dipping at the last minute again.

The routine took place several more times over the next five to ten minutes. On its last appearance the disc ascended, barely avoiding collision with the F-51's canopy.

Mini-Disc

In a cloudless sky over Misawa, Japan, on the morning of March 29, 1952, the U.S. Air Force was conducting a practice intercept. One pilot flew the intercept plane, a T-6 trainer, while two F-84s chased it.

At 11:20, as one of the F-84s overtook the T-6 at 6,000 feet, the T-6's pilot, Lt. D. C. Brigham, saw sunlight gleaming off something to the rear of the interceptor. As he focused his attention on it, he realized that it was a shiny disc which had been moving so fast that even as it decelerated it was catching up with the F-84, moving at about 160 mph. As it did so, it flipped on its edge, effecting a 90-degree bank. For two or three seconds it was positioned between the T-6 and the F-84.

Then it flipped once before passing the interceptor. It crossed in front of it, and moments later it effected an almost instantaneous upward climb.

An Associated Press account reported:

> Lieutenant Brigham estimated that the UFO at its closest point was 30 to 50 feet away from his plane. It was round, shiny as polished chromium, and seemed to be about eight inches in diameter. Throughout the observation, the disc rocked back and forth in 40-degree banks at about one-second intervals. Lieutenant Brigham saw no exhaust or protrusions, but reported a ripple in the apparently metal skin around the edge of the disc.

"No One Is That Stupid"

In 1969 a retired Air Force pilot sent a report to the civilian National Investigations Committee on Aerial Phenomena. His sighting is fairly routine, but his experience underscores the frustration and even anger that pilots both military and civilian have often felt in their interactions with official "investigators":

> In June 1952 I took off from Moody AFB, Ga., about noon, heading west. Climbing, I was about 20,000 feet when I saw an object in the right side of the windshield. I instinctively started to turn away either right or left. But my mind did not have enough information, i.e., was the object going from right to left or the reverse, or was it coming toward me or away?
>
> Upon analyzing the situation for a second or two, I

found that its position wasn't changing much. Since it appeared circular, I assumed I was flying directly behind another jet aircraft. [But] after observing it for several seconds I could see no wings, or horizontal or vertical stabilizer. Then the object started emitting thin smoke or vapor and suddenly starting climbing, relatively slow at first, then incredibly fast. The initial acceleration was in a zig-zag fashion, then straight. It was out of sight in a matter of a few seconds.

I was in a T-33 [trainer jet], climbing at about 230 mph. Nothing flying in those days could pull away from me at the rate this thing did. Although I was shaken by the incident, I did not report it at the time.

In 1959 I was assigned as a project engineer to Wright Patt[erson AFB]. I knew that an office for reporting these things [Project Blue Book] was on the field, so I went over. This was an embarrassing mistake.

[Blue Book director] Lt. Col. [Robert] Friend was the officer who interviewed me. He had to be faking. No one is that stupid. He tried to sell me on balloons. No dice. Another aircraft. Without tail or wings?

Main Brace Interloper

In September 1952 NATO forces participated in a massive exercise, called Operation Mainbrace, designed to test the alliance's ability to respond to an attack on Western Europe. A total of 150 ships and submarines took part, along with hundreds of aircraft.

At 10:53 A.M. on the nineteenth, five members of an aircrew who had landed not long before at RAF Topcliffe, a base in North Yorkshire, England, were watching a Meteor interceptor as it approached a nearby field from the east. One of them observed a white object which seemed to be following the aircraft, though at a slower speed, at a distance of several miles. The witness pointed it out to the others, and they briefly considered the possibility that they were looking at a parachute. But it was moving too fast, and it was traveling horizontally, at least for a short while before it began to descend.

In an interview soon afterwards with the *Sunday Dispatch*, Lt. John W. Kilburn said the object "was round and silvery and circular . . . We saw it reduce speed for some seconds and then begin to come down. As it lost height, it began to flutter like a leaf or, if you prefer, oscillate like a pendulum. The Meteor swerved to circle the airfield before landing. The object began to follow it but stopped dead after a few seconds. It seemed to remain suspended in the air, revolving like a top. Suddenly it took off, accelerated, and flew westwards at a terrific speed before changing course and disappearing southeast. The whole thing lasted about 20 seconds."

Kilburn recalled that as it maneuvered, the UFO changed into an elliptical shape. As it was hovering, sunlight gleamed off it. He and the others estimated it to be the size of a Vampire pursuit plane. "We are all absolutely certain that there could be no question of a balloon or an optical illusion produced by the Meteor's jets," he said. "It was a solid object. I have never seen anything like that in the sky in all my life." In his official report Kilburn characterized its acceleration speed as "unbelievable."

Three Saucers over Gloucestershire

This remarkable case remained unknown until 1997, when onetime Air Marshal Sir Peter Horsley reported it in his memoirs. In 2002 British researchers David Clarke and Andy Roberts printed a fuller account, based on newly released documents from the Ministry of Defense and from an interview with the principal witness, in their *Out of the Shadows*.

In the fall of 1952, Michael Swiney served as staff instructor at the Royal Air Force's Central Flying School, in Little Rissington, Gloucestershire. He helped train RAF and Navy pilots. On the afternoon of October 21, Swiney was aboard an RAF Meteor VII, with his student Naval Lt. David Crofts sitting behind him. They had just flown through a layer of clouds at more than 10,000 feet altitude when they were stunned to find three objects directly in front of and above them. Swiney thought they were parachutes, and he was terrified that he was going to fly right into them. He grabbed the stick from Crofts, who was flying the aircraft, to direct on a 45-degree course away.

Crofts then spotted the objects, and the two realized that these were not parachutes. Swiney was so staggered by the sight that for a few moments he suspected he was hallucinating from too little oxygen. But of course both pilots were seeing them, and that ruled out that explanation. In talking to Clarke and Roberts in 2001 he recalled that the objects were circular and hovering, two sitting level, the other slightly tilted. As the plane climbed, however, they changed position, moving toward the Meteor. "The higher we got," Swiney said, the more "they lost this circular effect [which appeared] when looking at them from underneath. As they came down to your level, they . . . took on a 'flat plane' appearance."

They were still visible when the Meteor got to 35,000 feet. They were disc-shaped, of an off-white color. A fuzzy light shone from their edges. Swiney notified air traffic control at Rissington. He was told to fly toward the UFOs. The Meteor was approaching the speed of sound and gaining on one of them—it was close enough to fill half the windshield—when the UFO turned on its side and ascended at a staggering rate of speed. This part of the incident was tracked on ground radar in Gloucestershire and Wiltshire. Radar followed the Meteor and documented the UFO's disappearance at 1,000 mph. Two Meteors were dispatched from Wiltshire, but they arrived too late to see anything. For his part,

Swiney looked for the other two UFOs, but they were "gone. Just disappeared."

Radio Intercept?

On June 25, 1954, at 5:02 P.M., John Mark was in the air and behind the controls of his Navion private plane, passing over a rural area 40 miles northeast of Dayton, Ohio. Mark, a Marine veteran and an experienced pilot with 5,000 hours inside the cockpits of both single- and multiple-engine aircraft, worked as sales manager for Atlas Tool Designers.

He was at 6,200 feet and flying at precisely 131 mph. He could see clearly; the sky was unobstructed, except for a slight haze, up to 30,000 feet. He had no trouble detecting a DC-6 high above his position. As his gaze turned from right to left, he noticed an aerial object to the southeast, 80 degrees above the horizon. It was not a balloon, he deduced quickly enough. This object, shiny and metallic, had a flat, round bottom and a cone on top of it. It had neither wings nor windows. Mark estimated it to be about 40 feet in diameter.

As it hung motionless, the pilot checked to make sure this wasn't just some reflection. First, he removed his sunglasses, moved his head so that he was getting different perspectives on the image he was seeing through the windshield. Then he rolled down his window. It was still there—until, that is, he radioed the tower at Dayton. No sooner had he done so than the UFO streaked forward, then stopped abruptly, and just as suddenly shot upward, to vanish into the overcast at 30,000 feet. Mark was convinced that the UFO had overheard his transmission and acted accordingly.

Just before the object's disappearance, however, Dayton tower was already in contact with Wright-Patterson AFB, also in Dayton (and also the home of the Air Force's Project Blue Book), to ask it to conduct an immediate radar sweep of the sky 45 miles to the northeast. The sweep picked up two blips, one evidently of the Navion and the other of the UFO. The latter, larger blip vanished from the screen within a minute.

Denmark Discs

To study a solar eclipse which otherwise would have been obscured by clouds, some 50 scientists and technicians boarded three Scandinavian airliners on June 30, 1954. The three aircraft took them to 13,500 feet over Lifjell, Denmark. They were on a steady course there at 2:17 A.M. when one man happened to look out a cabin window and do a double take. "What the hell is that?" he shouted.

On hearing these words, Ernest Graham, a British employee of the Swedish Travel Bureau, glanced out to see two silvery discs dropping out of some clouds and then taking a horizontal flight. Graham would assert, "The objects sped along the horizon keeping an exact distance from each other, both with forward edge tilted down."

Everyone on the plane saw the objects, visible for about 30 seconds. During the last 10 seconds Johnny Bjornulf focused a movie camera on the sight, but the results were disappointing, showing no more than two fast-moving, ambiguous blobs of light. Still, the sighting was featured in newspapers all over the world.

Utica Ellipse

This case had the distinction of being investigated by the University of Colorado UFO Project, otherwise known as the Condon Committee, after its director, physicist Edward U. Condon. The investigator was physicist Roy Craig, an outspoken skeptic.

Nonetheless, Craig was forced to conclude that this "is a most intriguing report, that must certainly be classed as an unknown pending further study, which it certainly deserves. . . . It does appear that this sighting defies explanation by conventional means." Craig learned of the sighting through an interview with the copilot of the Mohawk Airlines DC-3 from which the UFO had been viewed in the early afternoon of June 23, 1955.

The airliner was cruising at 3,000 feet around 12:15 when the copilot saw an object moving at "great speed" some 500 feet above them at a 70-degree angle (20 degrees from vertical). The object was, he recalled, "light gray, almost round, with a center line. . . . Beneath the line there were several (at least four) windows which emitted a bright blue-green light. It was not rotating but went straight." It looked to be 150 feet in diameter.

He and the pilot visually followed the UFO, whose speed they judged to be more than 4,000 mph, over the next several miles. As it got further from them, they saw the lights "change color from greenish to bluish or vice versa. A few minutes after it went out of sight, two aircraft (one, a Colonial DC-3, the other I did not catch the number) reported that they saw it and wondered if anyone else had seen it. The Albany control tower also reported that they had seen an object go by on Victor-2 [airway]. As we approached Albany, we overheard that Boston radar had also tracked an object along Victor-2, passing Boston and still eastbound."

Craig thought it "likely that the Boston GCA [Ground Control Approach] report was coincidental and involved a different object," but did not explain his reasoning.

Salt Lake City's Phony Sun Dog

One of the best-attested UFO sightings by a private pilot occurred over Salt Lake City, Utah, on October 2, 1961. The primary witness was Waldo J. Harris, a local real-estate broker. This is his account, as given two months later to investigator Zan Overall:

> About noon . . . I was preparing to take off in a Mooney mark 20A from the North-South runaway [sic] at Utah Central Airport when I noticed a bright spot in the sky over the Southern end of the Salt Lake Valley. I began my take-off run without paying much attention to the bright spot as I assumed that it was some aircraft reflecting the sun as it turned. After I was airborne and trimed [sic] for my climb-out I noticed that the bright spot was still about in the same position as before. I still thought it must be the sun reflecting from an airplane, so I made my turn onto my cross-wind leg of the traffic pattern, and was about to turn down-wind when I noticed that the spot was in the same spot still. I turned out of the pattern and proceeded toward the spot to get a better look.
>
> As I drew nearer I could see that the object had no wings nor tail nor any other exterior control surfaces protruding from what appeared to be the fusilage [sic]. It seemed to be hovering with a little rocking motion. As it rocked up away from me I could see that it was a disc shaped object. I would guess the diameter at about 50 to 55 feet, the thickness in the middle at about eight to 10 feet. It had the appearance of sand-blasted aluminum. I could see no windows or doors or any other openings, nor could I see any landing gear doors, etc., protruding nor showing.
>
> I believe at the closest point I was about two miles from the object at the same altitude, or a little above, the object. It rose abruptly about 1000 feet above me as I closed in giving me an excellent view of the underneath side, which was exactly like the upper side as

far as I could tell. Then it went off on a course of about 170 degrees for about 10 miles where it again hovered with that little rocking motion.

I again approached the object but not so closely this time, when it departed on a course of about 245 degrees climbing at about 18 to 20 degrees above the horizon. It went completely out of sight in about two or three seconds. . . . I can keep our fastest jets in sight for several minutes, so you can see that this object was moving rather rapidly.

All of the time I was observing the object, after getting visual confirmation from the ground, I was describing what I had seen on the radio Unicom frequency. I was answering questions from the ground both from Utah Central and [from] Provo. The voice at Provo said that they could not see the object, but at least eight or 10 people did see it from the ground at Utah Central Airport. . . .

I was returning to the field after it had departed when I was asked over radio if I could still see the object, and I reported that I could not. They said they had it in sight again. I turned back and saw it at much greater distance only for about a second or two when it completely vanished. The guys on the ground said it went straight up as it finally left, but I didn't see that departure.

The UFO was in the southern sky, off toward Provo, 23 miles away. In Salt Lake City no fewer than six ground witnesses, including airport operator Jay Galbraith, saw the object. Virgil S. Redmond had just landed his private plane when he learned of the object's appearance. He grabbed his binoculars and shared them with others as they followed the object's movement over the next 15 minutes. Galbraith said, "Whatever it was seemed to be rocking while hovering almost stationary just south of the field. At times, as it turned, it looked like a zeppelin."

Within minutes, having been alerted by the Salt Lake City Utah National Guard Control Tower, representatives of nearby Hill AFB's Security and Law Enforcement Division were at the airport interviewing the witnesses. One of them, banker Clyde Card, confirmed Galbraith's statement that when the UFO turned and evaded direct sunlight, it looked dark and cigar-shaped. When the sun was not shining on it, it was not visible to anyone without optical assistance. Another witness, Russell M. Woods, also remarked on how the object took on a cigar-shaped configuration in the absence of sunlight. This probably means only that the object looked different from a different perspective, not that it was mysteriously changing shape.

In the official report filed soon afterwards, Waldo Harris was characterized as "emotionally stable." Other pilots considered him reliable and honest. Inquiries with the U.S. Weather Bureau established that two balloons had been launched from the airport earlier in the day, but the winds "at release time would not have carried the balloons into the area of the sighting," according to the Hill report. Moreover, "Salt Lake City Air Traffic Control Center reported no air traffic in this area in a direction which could account for the sighting." The sky was absolutely clear and cloudless, with visibility extending to 40 miles.

A week after the sighting, Douglas M. Crouch, who led Hill's investigation, forwarded his findings to Project Blue Book at Wright-Patterson AFB's Foreign Technology Division (formerly Air Materiel Command). He wrote that "each of the six observers interviewed were [sic] logical, mature persons, five of whom had some connection with aviation. . . . [E]ach person was convinced that he had observed some tangible object not identifiable as a balloon or conventional-type aircraft. . . . No unusual meteorological or astronomical conditions were present which might account for the sighting." After considering and exhausting "all logical leads," Crouch stated that he could not identify the object.

This was not what the Air Force wanted to hear. Since 1953 it had shown more enthusiasm for debunking UFO reports than for encouraging serious investigations such as the one Crouch had conducted. By October 11, according to a press account, unnamed "Air Force officers in the Pentagon" were dismissing the sighting, the object of national publicity, as having been occasioned by a balloon or—more incredibly—the planet Venus.

Understandably miffed, Harris scoffed, "If the Pentagon thinks I have eyes good enough to see Venus at high noon, they are really off the beam. The object I saw was saucer shaped, had a gray color, and moved under intelligent control. I got within three miles of it, and that is a lot closer than Venus is. I have seen a lot of balloons too, and this was no balloon. It just doesn't make sense for the Pentagon to make such statements. Balloons move with the winds and air currents. This thing flew directly against a 10 mph wind and at terrific speed."

Harris did not add, though he could have, that if this was Venus, it was a particularly remarkable manifestation of Earth's sister planet. For a time during his sighting, he had observed the object in front of a distant mountain, which would have meant that Venus had moved into the lower atmosphere. In any event, if any further refutation of this unlikely hypothesis were needed, Venus—even if it had been visible, a big *if*, of course—was off to the southwest, while the mountains were to the south-southeast.

A month later, on November 9, Blue Book's head, Maj. William T. Coleman, Jr., stated in a letter to Zan Overall that the Air Force still had no opinion on what the Salt Lake City object may have been, "pending receipt of information from several firms carrying on upper air research in that area of the United States." The implication was that the balloon theory was still in play. Evidently, however, the inquiries went nowhere, and Blue Book eventually ended up with an explanation that was no less unsatisfactory. Its final summary of the case reads:

> Sun at time and date of this sighting was in a direction coincident with that reported for UFO. UFO was reported to be at elevation of approx 22 degrees above horizon while absolute elev[ation] of sun f[ro]m Salt Lak[e] area was 46 degrees 59' 42" at time of sighting. This would put obj[ec]t approx 24 degrees below sun. It is noted that weather conditions at time of sighting indicate high cirrus clouds. Cirrus clouds are associated with ice crystals. Sun dogs, which are associated with ice crystals[,] form at 22½ degrees and sometimes 45 degrees f[ro]m sun. All indications in this case are directed toward obj[ec]t being a sun dog. It is significant that witnesses on ground observed obj[ec]t to be stationary while airborne witnesses [sic] indicate motion—probably his own. There is no available evidence which would indicate the obj[ec]t of sighting was not a sun dog.

In reality, precisely zero evidence supports the sun dog identification. To start with, ground witnesses quite specifically mentioned movement. So does Crouch's Hill AFB report. Of Galbraith's testimony, that report notes its reference to an object "climbing and changing altitude. It seemed to go east for some time and hover in one position, then the last he remembered it was going west, climbing. . . . Some of the maneuvers were at rapid speed, and some were slow. At one time it climbed quite fast, with abrupt changes of direction." Another witness, according to Crouch's report, was Robert Butler, who watched the object rise straight up at a high rate of speed, then turn west at a slower pace. Duane Sinclar said, "I saw it in one position low on the horizon, and the second time it was to the right and higher, maybe eight to 10 thousand feet variation. It was approximately five minutes between the two sightings."

An additional element of fiction in the Blue Book report places "high cirrus clouds" in a sky that weather reports, which the Air Force had in its possession from Crouch's inquiries, said did not exist. As already noted, the sky was clear. Beyond that, the object Harris saw bore no resemblance to a sun dog (otherwise known as a mock sun). One scientist intimately familiar with the phenomenon, atmospheric physicist James E. McDonald, interviewed Harris in October 1966 (until that conversation, Harris had not known of the Blue Book identification). Harris observed that while sun dogs are big, the object he and others had seen was small. The habitually blunt-speaking McDonald rejected the Air Force claims as "nonsensical" and "balderdash." He pointed out, "The altitude of the noon sun at Salt Lake City that day was about 40 degrees, and sundogs, if there had been any, would have occurred to right and left at essentially the same angular altitude, far above the position in the sky where Harris and others saw the object hovering."

Willow Grove's "Credible Observer"

At 3:15 on the afternoon of May 21, 1966, a Luscombe aircraft piloted by William C. Powell, with Muriel McClave in the passenger seat, passed over Willow Grove, north of Philadelphia, at 4,500 feet through a mostly clear sky. Powell was an experienced pilot, starting in World War II, later flying airliners, then working as a test pilot before his current job as a pilot for a major national corporation.

Below him, Powell observed a flight of jets from Willow Grove Naval Air Station as they climbed northward. After they were out of sight, he noticed what he thought was another aircraft. First it was heading in the direction of the departed jets. Then, all of a sudden, it abruptly turned 160 degrees and shot toward Powell's plane. The object, he and his companion could now see, had no vertical tail fin. It was disc-shaped, with a white rounded dome that glistened in the sun. A red cone jutted out below.

The UFO flew by to the right of the aircraft and slightly below the Luscombe's altitude, as close as—in Powell's estimate—100 yards. Its flight was smooth and it emitted no exhaust. Then it was gone. There were no windows or markings on the structure, which was as visible, Powell would say, as a passing Cadillac. He thought it was 20 feet in diameter, while McClave guessed something like 40 feet.

Two days later, Powell reported the sighting to the Willow Grove NAS. The officer to whom he related the sightings said that he had had his own sighting some years earlier, but that was as far as official interest extended. Later, through a civilian UFO group which learned about the report accidentally, James McDonald heard of the incident. He interviewed the two witnesses both by phone and in person several times. He was sufficiently impressed to use the case as an example of "credible observers reporting an incredible object."

Vertical Egg

On November 4, 1970, as the Spanish Air Force participated in interception exercises with U.S. Air Force aircraft, two Spanish F-86 pilots encountered a strange object which they first mistook for an American jet. The incident happened over the northeastern part of Spain, in the La Rioja region, over a two-hour period beginning at 11:15 A.M.

They were alerted to its presence by a ground radar station, which said it had something on its screen moving at high speed and maneuvering oddly. Assuming it to be a USAF F-4 Phantom, the Spanish pilots—Capt. Saez Benito and Lt. Luis Carbayo Olivares—tried to find it. A short time later, they decided to return to their home base in Zaragoza. On their way they happened to see a glowing object. On the assumption that it was the F-4, they ascended to match its altitude and pursue it. They quickly learned, however, that it was closing on them. As it drew nearer, it took on the appearance of a vertical, metallic egg-shaped structure, about 20 feet in diameter. It had a "crest," as the pilots called it, on its top. One-third of the way up from its base were two square windows. This was no F-4.

The pilots decided to fly behind the object so that they could see what it looked like from the rear. Instead, the UFO began to make rings around the two jets at a dazzling speed; then it got behind them, and whatever they did from then on, they could not shake it. It stayed on their tails and frustrated their every effort to outmaneuver it.

Growing ever more anxious about their situation, which left them feeling vulnerable to an intelligence with uncertain intentions, they contacted the radar stations at Zarazoga and Toledo. Both radars had the UFO on their screens. With their fuel running perilously low, the pilots knew they had to get back to base. They commenced a descent, which their pursuer easily matched. It kept on them for the next 50 to 60 miles before it abruptly shot upward at an extraordinary rate of speed. It then disappeared from both sight and radar screen.

Illinois Approach, Swirling Compass

Hugo W. Feugen of Mendota, Illinois, flew an Aeronca Champ aircraft. On November 28, 1974, at 11:43 a.m., flying it from DeKalb to Mendota, in a sky with a light haze keeping visibility to six or seven miles, he passed over the small town of Shabbona. As he did so, he was checking his map to be sure he was still on course.

When he looked up briefly, he was shocked to see that the plane's compass was rotating counterclockwise at the rate of four or five rpm. Alarmed, he looked around to see what might be causing the problem. Turning to his left, he spotted a round, disc-shaped object of dull-silver color pacing his aircraft, which was moving at about 80 mph. It appeared to be a quarter of a mile away. If that estimate was correct, it would be, he judged, 120 feet long and 30 feet thick.

In the next eight to 10 seconds, the compass continued its odd counterclockwise rotation. Then the UFO tipped slightly, revealing what—in the very short time he had to look—Feugen thought might be a depression on top. It streaked away so fast that Feugen characterized its disappearance as happening in the time of a "flick of a finger."

Disc in a Thunderstorm

Ufologist Raymond E. Fowler learned of a sighting an airline pilot had confided to a friend, Allegheny Airlines Flight Capt. Robert L. Hobson. Fowler subsequently collected statements from the witness, who preferred to remain anonymous, and quizzed him at length concerning an encounter which occurred on July 6, 1975, 30 nautical miles north-northwest of Wilkes-Barre, Pennsylvania. The witness provided this statement:

> I was . . . in the captain's seat of a BAC 111 turbojet, at an altitude of 17,000 feet, eyeballing a line of thunderstorms that lay across our normal route of flight. The storms lay in a NE-SW line, the SW end of the line ending in the Wilkes-Barre area, and the line running NE as far as I could see, and the radar painted it all the way across the tube on the 60-mile scale.
>
> The closest storm lay at about our 10 to 11 o'clock

position and the radar showed a significant rain gradient, and lightning was visible to the eye. We were operating in clear air [with] good visibility and cloudless skies above and behind us. Our heading was about SSE.

At the time we saw the disc, the closest storm was about 20 nautical miles from us on the radar and the disc was somewhere between us and the storm. My First Officer and I saw the disc at about the same time. We both watched it intently.

The airplane was on auto-pilot and we were closing on the object. Our airspeed was about 300 kts [nautical miles per hour]. It quickly took [on] a disc-like shape. At this point, it was lower than we were and moving from our left to right, or roughly E to W.

My initial impression was that we were looking at a balloon. . . . The prevailing winds in these latitudes are W to E, and this westward flight of the balloon puzzled me. However, I know that thunderstorms will often create a strong counter-clockwise flow of air and a balloon on the north side of a storm might well drift westward.

I quickly realized that the speed of the object was far higher than you might expect even in the strongest wind. . . . I asked the Air Traffic Control Center (New York) if he had a radar target at 11 o'clock [relative to the airliner's nose] and about 10 miles [away]. He said, "Negative, no target in that area."

Very shortly after that, it made a sharp—more than 100 degrees—turn to the left and flew right into the thunderstorm. . . . We never saw it again after it entered the storm.

The pilot told Fowler in a follow-up interview that the object was about one-third the apparent size of the moon as viewed through the aircraft's windshield. That suggested, according to Fowler's calculations based on the proximity of the cloud line it was positioned in front of, more than 100 feet in diameter. Though Fowler, like the pilot, deemed the balloon identification unlikely, he sought a second opinion and spoke with persons from the National Oceanic and Atmospheric Administration in Washington, D.C. "When I described the UFO event to this office," Fowler would write, "they were of the opinion that it was not any kind of balloon."

Santa Monica Phenomenon

Floyd P. Hallstrom of Oxnard, California, was a pilot with long experience and distinguished career. On January 1, 1978, he had been flying 37 years, more than half of them as a Navy combat crewman. He had also served as crew chief to admirals, one of them the commander-in-chief of the Atlantic Fleet.

On the day in question, he was following a friend, Jim Victor, to Browns Field in San Diego. Hallstrom was behind the controls of a Cessna 170A, and Victor was delivering a plane to a waiting customer. Once the delivery was made, Hallstrom was to fly Victor back home. Nothing about the day or the operation was out of the ordinary—that is, until Hallstrom found himself over Santa Monica. He was at 7,500 feet, and he had lost sight of Victor's aircraft. As he looked straight ahead trying to spot it, something caught his eye just to the east of the haze over Los Angeles International Airport. Hallstrom assumed that he had found his friend.

He watched the object for a minute, becoming ever more puzzled as it seemed to grow larger. Then he realized that it was heading toward him and thus couldn't be Victor's plane, or maybe any plane at all. "I could see no wings on this aircraft," he recalled soon afterwards, "although at this time I could see windows

which appeared to be passenger windows. . . . As it drew closer . . .
I was able to determine that there were no wings or horizontal
empennage assembly to the aircraft as a conventional aircraft."
He briefly considered the possibility that it was a helicopter before rejecting the idea because it was moving too fast.

The dome-shaped object passed beneath him to his left at
6,000 feet. Viewing it from angles of 30 to 45 degrees, he said, "I
was able to make out the complete form of a saucer shape or
round object. . . . I could see the dome, also very vividly clear, including all the windows." It consisted of a bright, sun-reflecting
metal like "highly polished chrome or stainless steel." He estimated that 16 to 20 evenly spaced windows circled the dome,
some 20 feet in diameter, just above the base, 30 feet in diameter.

The UFO flew smoothly past Hallstrom's Cessna at an estimated 650 mph. The witness drew a quick sketch of it while it
was still in view. After about one minute it was gone.

Lake Michigan's Rolling Disc

A jumbo-jet pilot who requested anonymity encountered a silvery disc over Lake Michigan at 4:45 P.M. on July 4, 1981. Moving
in an arc at a high rate of speed, the UFO came into view in front
of and just above the pilot's line of vision. At one point it rolled, in
the process allowing the witness to see it from the side. Along the
edge he saw six evenly spaced "portholes." He estimated that the
disc was 10 times as long as it was high.

The UFO disappeared to the north.

7

The New War of the Worlds

HAVE UFOS ABDUCTED aircraft?

The question has been asked since the early days of the UFO controversy. As we have seen, some writers claim that UFOs have shot down aircraft. The famous January 7, 1948, case of F-51 pilot Thomas F. Mantell played a big role in the imaginations of early ufologists who suspected visiting aliens of harboring sinister intentions. Hostility theories competed with more benign readings of extraterrestrial motivation in the UFO literature of the 1950s and beyond.

British ufologist Harold T. Wilkins, author of *Flying Saucers on the Attack* (1954), referred to the "apparent hostility of some types of flying saucers," linking them to plane crashes among other unhappy occurrences. In the July 1, 1955, issue of his *C.R.I.F.O. Orbit,* the American Leonard H. Stringfield fretted that UFOs "pose a serious problem for military aviation," noting "the sudden rise in jet crashes—the causes of which are not satisfactorily explained." He went on:

> [W]e cannot prove that any one of the recent air crashes was caused by UFO action. . . . Reflectively, it is al-

ways plausible for two pilots, at the same moment, to misjudge their course, but the *spontaneous or simultaneous* crash or explosion of four, five or eight separate aircraft demands a more rationalized explanation than pilot misjudgment or routine failure. We may even suppose, on mathematical chance, that some extraordinary failure could simultaneously befall four or six aircraft but, again, hardly with the shocking *frequency* as noted in recent dispatches.

None of the cases Stringfield went on to cite amounted to much—at least as evidence for UFO-jet interaction, hostile or otherwise—and were quickly forgotten.

In a like vein M. K. Jessup wrote in his *The Case for the UFO* (1955), "The unexplained, and unannounced[,] crashes of planes over land are numbered in dozens. . . . [T]here is a strong element of mystery in many of them. It is the rule, and not the exception[,] that the major catastrophes come without warning." The same year, in *The Flying Saucer Conspiracy,* Donald E. Keyhoe linked UFOs to a variety of air disasters and mysteries, highlighting several incidents that would become—even if undeservedly—staples of the folklore of UFO hostility.

Death at Walesville

One tragic incident took place in Walesville, New York, on July 2, 1954. As Keyhoe told the story, radar at "Griffith"—actually, Griffiss—Air Force Base picked up an unidentified target over Utica. Unable to correlate with any known aircraft activity, an F-94 was dispatched. The pilot and radar officer soon saw the object, "a strange gleaming object moving swiftly above," in Keyhoe's words. Pulling up and turning sharply, the jet approached the UFO. At that moment the cockpit suddenly filled with intense, unbearable heat. Fearing they would be burned alive, the two officers ejected. The F-94, now uncontrolled, crashed into Walesville, killing four persons.[1]

This is essentially the story that got recycled into subsequent UFO books. As late as 1975, in *The Edge of Reality*—essentially a booklength transcript of conversations between scientists and ufologists J. Allen Hynek and Jacques Vallee—Vallee was insisting, over Hynek's expressed skepticism, that the "mechanical malfunction . . . was caused by a UFO."

In later years, however, Kevin D. Randle was able to reconstruct the incident from records, some of them unavailable to earlier writers. He learned that somehow Keyhoe had conflated two separate incidents, one occurring on the evening of July 1, the second late in the morning of the next day. In the first, hundreds of residents of Utica and surrounding towns called in to report the presence of a "silvery balloon-like object" over the city. Visible for about four hours, it was seen from a passing airliner and judged to be at 20,000 feet. According to an Associated Press account, "Col. Milton F. Summerfelt, commander of the Air Force Depot at Rome, said the object appeared to be a plastic balloon about 40 feet long and partially deflated."

If this was a UFO, it was a singularly unimpressive one. There seems no reason to quarrel with the balloon identification.

Project Blue Book's investigation of the crash incident the next day determined the following:

> The F-94C took off at 11:05 A.M. EST for an operational training mission out of Griffiss Air Force Base, New York, on 2 July 1954. The aircraft was only a few miles out when the Griffiss control tower operator called the pilot to advise that he was being diverted to an active air defense mission. A vector of 50 degrees and 10,000 feet altitude was given to intercept an unidentified aircraft. The pilot experienced some difficulty

finding this aircraft and the controller then informed him of a second unidentified aircraft in the area. This aircraft was [later] identified as an Air Force C-47, tail number 6099. At this time there were no indications of F-94 malfunctions as stated by the pilot and the C-47 pilot. . . .

The ground controller [then] gave the F-94C pilot a heading of 240 degrees back to the first unidentified aircraft. The F-94C was at 8,000 feet, flying above the tops of the broken clouds. It was evident that the unidentified aircraft was not found above the clouds, so the pilot started to descend below the clouds. It was evident that the unidentified aircraft was going to Griffiss Air Force Base. During the descent there was intense heat in the cockpit and the engine plenum chamber fire warning light came on. The pilot shut down the engine and the light remained on. Due to the critical low altitude and the fire warning, the pilot and the radar observer ejected and were recovered without injury.

In other words, the second unidentified aircraft turned out to be another military plane, this one on its way to Griffiss. The abandoned F-94C flew on for another four miles before slamming into a house in Walesville. It killed a mother and injured her daughter, then hit an automobile at a nearby intersection, killing three persons inside.

The Air Force's investigative report, dated August 17, 1954, was classified for many years. Declassification finally occurred more than four decades later, after ufologist Jan L. Aldrich requested that it be made available. According to the Air Force, "a malfunction of the aircraft fire detector circuit" was responsible for the accident. "Inasmuch as the pilot acknowledged changing engine power settings and flight altitude during the attempted second interception," the Air Force wrote, "it appears that the pilot interpreted a normal, non-automatically controlled temperature rise as an overheated cockpit condition. Since there was no evidence of in-flight fire, the fire warning indication received by the pilot was probably due to" the above-stated malfunction.

Still, however distorted the telling of the circumstances, an F-94C *did crash* in upstate New York on the day in question. Another story told around the same time, on the other hand, appears to be the product of somebody's imagination.

In *C.R.I.F.O. Orbit*[2] for November 4, 1955, Len Stringfield recounted a conversation with "lecturer and private UFO researcher" Robert Coe Gardner. Gardner claimed that in February 1953 no less than Gen. Benjamin Chidlaw, head of Eastern Air Defense, had confided to him, "We take these [UFO reports] seriously when you consider that we have lost many men and planes trying to intercept them." Without explaining just exactly *why* this high-ranking officer with many grave responsibilities had chosen to confide this explosive information to a lowly saucer buff, Gardner went on to recount a strange story for which he provided no source. At least Stringfield does not mention one.

On a late summer day in 1939, Gardner related, a military transport left the Marine Naval Air Station in San Diego for a routine flight to Honolulu. About three hours afterwards, several urgent distress signals sounded from the plane, followed by eerie silence. Later, the plane came limping back to execute an emergency landing. When Air Station personnel entered the plane, they found every man in the crew, including the copilot, who had lived long enough to fly the craft back to its base, dead of unknown causes.

Each of the bodies bore large, gaping wounds. The outside of the plane was similarly marked. Those who touched parts of the craft came down with a mysterious skin infection. The .45 automatics carried by the pilot and copilot as service pieces had been emptied and the shells lay on the floor. A smell of "rotten eggs" pervaded the interior.

The incident was immediately covered up. Air Station personnel were sent away from the site, leaving identification of the bodies to three medical officers.

There is no evidence that anything like this ever happened, at least in real life. (It is possible that it appeared originally as a story in a pulp magazine, but if so, no one has been able to produce it.) Gardner, a minor figure on the early UFO scene, had a reputation as a spinner of yarns and a shader—at best—of truth. In a recent memoir longtime UFO personality James W. Moseley recalls a 1954 conversation with former Blue Book head Ed Ruppelt and Pentagon UFO spokesman Albert M. Chop. Ruppelt mentioned Gardner's habit of telling lecture audiences that high-level government sources had slipped him previously unreleased UFO photographs. It turned out that he had simply clipped these pictures from newspapers.

A Saucerful of Asparagus People

Fred Reagan was flying his single-engine Piper Cub one day in July 1951 when he and it plowed into a passing flying saucer. Or so reported a story under Reagan's by-line in the May 1953 issue of the men's adventure magazine *Action*.

Instead of shattering and falling to earth when it hit the pulsating, lozenge-shaped craft, however, the plane remained in the air, mysteriously frozen to the spot even as Reagan was thrown out and hurled toward the ground. Suddenly a "sticky, clinging force" pulled him in the opposite direction, up toward the UFO. The next thing he knew, he was inside a dimly lit room.

Standing around him were glistening figures, about three feet high and resembling "huge stalks of metallic asparagus." He abruptly fainted. When he revived soon afterwards, he heard a metallic voice speaking in a kind of stilted English out of a loudspeaker. The voice apologized for the collision, which had not been intentional. The beings meant no harm, the voice said; theirs was a peaceful mission whose purpose was to observe our primitive civilization. To make up for the accident, the saucer crew had taken the liberty to examine Reagan's body, in which they detected something known to human beings as "cancer." They "adjusted" the tumor "as a slight reparation for the loss that we have caused you." The voice added that he should say nothing of this, because no one would believe him.

His next memory was of awaking in a hospital bed. He learned that he had been found unconscious in a farmer's meadow, near the wreckage. Though the plane had clearly fallen thousands of feet and hit the ground with considerable force—the engine was buried six feet into the ground—Reagan himself had not a bruise on him.

The *Action* story ended with this postscript:

Saucer Passenger Dies

Atlanta—May 16. Fred Reagan, who made headlines last year when he claimed to have been a visitor
aboard a flying saucer, died today in the State Asylum
for the Insane.

Cause of death was determined to be degeneration
of brain tissue due to extreme atomic radiation.
Authorities are unable to offer an explanation.

The story has been mentioned occasionally, though not often, in UFO literature. It also served as inspiration for an episode of the television show *One Step Beyond,* which aired between 1959 and 1961 and featured dramatizations of supposedly true experiences of the paranormal. As late as 1969, Gordon Creighton of England's influential *Flying Saucer Review* wrote that the case's relative obscurity probably had to do with its fantastic nature; back in the early 1950s, he suggested, "it seemed altogether too preposterous. . . . To be quite honest . . . despite years of trying, I have failed to find anyone who can or will throw any light upon the story for me, or authenticate it. *It may be untrue. But I do not think that it is* [Creighton's italics]. It contains far too many elements which, in this summer of 1969, seem to me to possess the ring of truth but which very understandably may not have seemed to possess it in 1951."

Creighton failed to grasp a simple fact of popular culture: that the pulp men's adventure magazines, long gone from the publishing scene but once available at every newsstand, routinely carried stories identified as true but in reality concocted by imaginative staff writers. The authentic-sounding alleged clipping that closes the story never existed, as proved by Canadian researcher Kurt Glemser in 1972 after his inquiries sparked a search for the relevant records by Georgia's Vital Records Unit. Fred Reagan—at least a Fred Reagan who had a head-on collision with an extraterrestrial spacecraft—did not exist, either. If any doubts remained on that score, ufologist T. Scott Crain laid them to rest in the late 1970s, when extensive research only confirmed the obvious. The yarn, he wrote, "appears to be the ramblings of a ghost writer's vivid imagination."

A Vanishing in the Upper Peninsula

On the opening page of *The Flying Saucer Conspiracy*, the book in which he introduced the Walesville incident to the lore of fatal aircraft/UFO encounters, Donald Keyhoe wrote, "It was the evening of November 23, [1953] and wintry darkness had settled over Michigan. At an isolated radar station Air Defense operators were watching their scope. . . . Suddenly the 'blip' of an unknown machine appeared on the glass screen." A UFO was passing over the Soo Locks.

In very short order, an F-89 from "Kimross [sic]"—actually, Kinross—Field[3] was dispatched to investigate. Lt. Felix Moncla, Jr., piloted the interceptor, with Lt. R. R. Wilson sitting behind him as radar observer. As Ground Control Intercept (GCI) radar watched, the F-89 passed over Sault Ste. Marie, Ontario, just north of Kinross on the far eastern tip of Michigan's Upper Peninsula veering west/northwest at 500 mph toward Whitefish Bay on Lake Superior. At 100 miles from Sault Ste. Marie and 70 miles from Keweenaw Point, the jet's blip and the unknown object's merged into one, and then that blip faded from the screen. Extensive searches conducted that night and the next day by American and Canadian planes and ships found no trace of the missing aircraft.[4]

The next day one edition of the *Chicago Tribune* carried an Associated Press story under the headline "Jet, 2 Aboard, Vanishes Over Lake Superior." It reported that "the plane was followed by radar until it merged with an object" but provided no further details. The incident received no further national press attention. On November 27, however, the local paper, the *Sault Ste. Marie Evening News,* quoted a Kinross Field spokesman as saying that the "object" had been identified as a Royal Canadian Air Force C-47 transport.

Keyhoe learned of the incident the night it happened, from a retired Army Air Corps navigator. Keyhoe wrote that his informant tipped him off to a "rumor . . . that an F-89 from Kimross [sic] was hit by a flying saucer. All I know is that the plane's missing."

The following morning Keyhoe phoned the Air Force press desk and talked with Lt. Robert C. White, an Air Force Public Information Officer (PIO) at the Pentagon. White thought the interceptor had experienced engine trouble and dropped into Superior. Later, learning of the Air Force's statement to AP about the plane's merging with an "object," Keyhoe grew convinced that there was more to the incident than officials were letting on. In a second conversation, White expressed the view that the F-89 and the unidentified blip had been miles from each other; as for the apparent merging, White suggested, "They just read the scope wrong." Keyhoe rejected the idea as "incredible." And when White said the investigative report on the incident would be classified, Keyhoe became convinced that a cover-up was in place—though in fact investigative reports of all military crashes are routinely classified.

Soon afterwards, when the Air Force floated the explanation that the other blip had been of a DC-3 civilian airliner from Canada, Mutual Broadcasting System newscaster Frank Edwards, a friend of Keyhoe's, interviewed two Canadian airline pilots who, according to Edwards, "denied the whole thing . . . This Kimross [sic] thing must be something terrific, the way the Air Force has covered up."[5]

If the Air Force explanation—C-47 or DC-3 (the same aircraft, but one military, the other civilian)—was already confused, it muddied waters further with conflicting accounts given to Moncla's widow. An Air Force representative first informed her that his F-89 had flown too low[6] and crashed into the lake. A second officer who called on the family, however, told a different story. Mrs. Moncla wanted to know if it would be possible to recover her husband's body. It would not, the officer replied, because the aircraft had exploded at a high altitude.

Then on June 28, 1956—or so Ohio ufologist Tom Comella would assert in *Fate* magazine six years later—Master Sgt. O. D. Hill, a Project Blue Book associate working out of Wright-Patterson AFB, confided to Comella's colleague Edgar Smith that the project's purpose was to "prevent another Pearl Harbor." (Smith and Comella had earlier dealings with Blue Book and so were known to the project, though neither had met Hill before this.) Asking not to be quoted, Hill related two instances of alleged UFO-related military-aircraft disappearances. Though he apparently did not mention Kinross by name, one of the cases sounded exactly like it.[7] Immediately following that meeting (in Smith's home), Smith called Comella to tell him Hill was on his way. At Comella's residence Hill repeated the stories. We have only Smith's (or Comella's) word that this conversation occurred. On the other hand, a Sgt. O. D. Hill was indeed part of Blue Book during the time period in question, and he did not disavow the story even after its airing in a national magazine.

In early 1958 Keyhoe received a letter from Robert C. Balsey, director of closed-circuit radio programs for Lackland Air Force Base in San Antonio. Balsey stated that he and his colleagues were preparing a show based on Keyhoe's *Conspiracy*. A script would soon be sent for Keyhoe's approval. On May 16 Maj. Warren Akin, Chief of Education Planning at Lackland, spoke to the San Antonio Chamber of Commerce. He gave voice to a decidedly un-Air Force pronouncement on UFOs. "Space visitors may already have been here," he declared.

In mid-June the promised script arrived at Keyhoe's office.[8] He was fascinated to see that it gave the Kinross incident major play, even quoting a radar officer—presumably 2nd Lt. Douglas A. Stuart, on duty at the time—who had observed the event. "It seems incredible," he said, "but the blip apparently just swallowed our F-89." The segment went on cite a statement from the Canadian government denying that any of its aircraft were involved in the incident. The script pointed out that whereas the DC-3 had a maximum speed of 215 mph, the "UFO" was tracked at 500 mph.

The show never aired, however, and the personnel were transferred just before the radio station was shut down. Keyhoe associate Richard Hall—Keyhoe himself died in 1988—saw the script and was impressed with its professionalism; he was also struck by its openly pro-UFO tone, extending even to a frank statement that the Air Force was hiding its knowledge of extraterrestrial visitation out of fear of public panic. Keyhoe wondered if this were not some kind of trial balloon the Air Force was launching before coming clean about its real assessment of the UFO phenomenon. But in Hall's more cautious reading, this was probably no more than the opinion of a group of UFO enthusiasts who only happened to be associated with the Air Force. Still, the affair struck him, even more than three decades later, as "extremely odd."

In due course the official Air Force account settled on a RCAF C-47 as the other aircraft. Strangely, however, the Canadian government on several occasions insisted it knew nothing of any such incident. For example, on April 14, 1961, a spokesman for the RCAF's Chief of Air Staff wrote, in response to an inquiry, "A check of Royal Canadian Air Force records has revealed no report of an incident involving an RCAF aircraft in the Lake Superior area on the above date." In a June 24, 1963, letter from the RCAF public-relations director to another inquirer, Squadron Leader W. B. Totman stated that "after extensive checking by this directorate we have been unable to come up with any information regarding an intercept of a RCAF C-47 by a USAF F-89 on November 23, 1953." Totman added that the intercept claim seemed unlikely on its face, since any such C-47 would have been flying over Canadian territory.

A unit history of the 433d Fighter Interceptor Squadron, acquired under the Freedom of Information Act by researcher Robert G. Todd, recounts the incident with some cryptic words: "The fighter and the bogey [unidentified] blips merged on the GCI radar scope and there was no further transmission from the fighter. The bogey [?] was not aware of any aircraft in the area, and GCI saw no blips break off from the target."

The last, of course, is a reference either to aircraft disintegration or to radar images of Moncla and Wilson bailing. The statement about the bogey's not seeing other aircraft is odd. Presumably, if the bogey was identified to the extent that it was communicating with Kinross, it was no longer a bogey by definition. Why not refer to it in words something like "the former bogey—now known to be an RCAF C-47"? On the other hand, this may be a laboring of the point. The confusion probably owes to nothing more than careless writing; one writer on the case argues, plausibly I think, that "bogey" is merely a misreading and the writer meant "base."[9]

Air Force records on the case are sketchy. It is not filed among its UFO data but among its accident investigations. Indeed, the Air Force had reason to think this was just another instance of an F-89C's acting up. In fact, that same day another F-89C had crashed. Worse, this F-89C was from Truax AFB, Madison, Wisconsin, of which Kinross was a satellite base.

The first F-89C crash is mentioned, though almost in passing, in Keyhoe's original account. He quotes Frank Edwards as saying, "Several witnesses said a saucer flew near the plane, just before it dived into a swamp. It may be just bunk, but I'm checking on it." After these words, the Truax crash vanishes from the narrative as Keyhoe turns his full attention to the incident, later in the day, at Kinross.

At 12:30 P.M. an F-89C flew out of Truax on a routine engine-test flight. The pilot was Lt. John W. Schmidt, the radar officer Capt. Glen E. Collins. The aircraft ascended to 40,000 feet, at which point radio communication abruptly ceased. At 12:40 a woman standing outside her Madison home saw a jet suddenly appear in the sky above her. "It was quite low, and I knew it was a jet," she told a reporter, "but there wasn't any noise like you always hear from a jet. It was just still-like. Suddenly there was something just like an explosion—oh, an awful, huge noise. The jet then plummeted to earth—just so fast your eye could hardly follow it." Another witness, this one two miles from the crash site, saw the F-89C pull up briefly, then flip over. "Then there was a puff of smoke," he reported, "and the plane seemed to dive straight down." It plowed into a marsh, killing both officers. No one, note, said anything about a UFO.

The Northrop F-89 Scorpion had been developed out of the need for a jet interceptor with long-range defensive capabilities, meaning it could travel at near-supersonic speeds and carry radar which functioned in all weather conditions. It would also be well armed with six 20mm cannon.

The first prototype took wing in August 1948. Soon it became apparent that there were serious design flaws. In 1949 and 1950 the Air Force nearly abandoned the F-89 project. Further refinements brought the F-89C, the first fully operational F-89, into being. The first of these flew in September 1951. The first F-89C squadron was the 176th Fighter Interceptor Squadron, at Truax, formed in February 1952. Between February 25 and September 22 no fewer than five F-89Cs were lost.

By this time the Air Defense Command was furious at Northrop. It grounded the interceptor and demanded that Northrop fix it at its own expense and with its own test pilots. Nine months later, in June 1953, only 36 of the 172 original F-89Cs were back in service. A number were at Truax, where the 433d Interceptor Squadron had replaced the 176th. The two F-89Cs were among the supposedly corrected models. The F-89D replaced the F-89C in active-duty units in 1954, while the latter went to reserve units.

None of this proves that the F-89C that vanished over Lake Superior was lost because of the F-89's persistent design problems, but it does make that a not unreasonable possibility, especially in the context of the fatal crash of an F-89 from a sister squadron in Wisconsin just hours before. That strikes one as more than a coincidence.

If there were not already enough ambiguity surrounding the incident, however, more was on the way. On October 30, 1968, a Canadian newspaper, the *Sault Daily Star* (published in Sault Ste. Marie), reported a discovery earlier that week of what "could be the wreckage of an F-89 Scorpion jet interceptor" 70 miles north of the city. Two Cozen Cove area prospectors found the tail section, "made of heavier metal than normally used in aircraft." Members of the provincial police speculated that it was from the interceptor missing since 1953. There was no follow-up press coverage.

Many years later Gord Heath, a researcher from Surrey, British Columbia, attempted to elicit information from the Canadian government. Inquiries addressed to Canada's National Defense Headquarters came up empty. In a July 2002 letter a spokeswoman told him that a "search for all records requested, using the Department's best efforts, has resulted in a nil reply." Heath also tried the National Transportation Safety Board, asking if the parts had ever been conclusively identified, but got no response despite repeated attempts. Understandably, he found all of this "a little strange." The incident serves to underscore the puzzling paradox of the alleged involvement (according to the U.S. Air Force) of a Canadian military airplane in the 1953 disappearance/accident, coupled with the Canadian government's repeated inability or refusal to shed any light on the matter at all.

Lost in the Bermuda Triangle

To Keyhoe, to whom the facts of the matter appeared far more straightforward than in fact they were, Kinross "might be the key to the flying-saucer riddle." (As we have seen, he had used nearly identical words to characterize another fatal aerial encounter with an ostensible flying saucer, the Mantell Incident.) In earnest conversations, he and his friend Walther Riedel (called "Paul Redell" in *Conspiracy*), a German-American aeronautical engineer and missile expert, wondered if extraterrestrials were seeking contact with earth but were frustrated because they didn't know how to communicate with us. Thus, according to this theory, the Kinross pilots had been taken alive, presumably to teach courses in English in alien universities. Keyhoe and Riedel were relieved to come to this conclusion, since, otherwise, cases like Kinross could only mean that UFOs had hostile intentions.

Seeking further evidence, Riedel showed Keyhoe a summary "based on the Navy's reports" of its investigation of the disappearances of six aircraft from the Naval Air Station at Fort Lauderdale, Florida, on December 5, 1945. Keyhoe writes that in the afternoon five TBM Avenger torpedo-bombers flew off "into a clear blue sky." When they failed to return after two hours, personnel at the station heard snatches of radio conversation from the planes indicating that they were lost, their compasses apparently having failed. Eventually a Martin Mariner flying boat with a crew of 13 was sent on a search-and-rescue mission. It, too, vanished.

"The sea was fairly calm," Keyhoe says, "and the pilots should have stalled their planes in without any serious damage. Normally, all of the crews would have gotten into their rubber life rafts. The crewman's pneumatic jackets would have kept them afloat while the rafts were inflating. . . . Even if they had crashed, which was almost inconceivable, wreckage and bodies would have been found strewed over several square miles."

Keyhoe cites a press-wire story which has an unnamed station officer claiming, "They vanished as completely as if they had been flown to Mars." Presumably, the officer was not speaking literally, but Keyhoe and Riedel were hearing him literally. Both were convinced that the saucers came from Mars, and they thought that saucers had taken the vanished planes and crews.

Keyhoe's is the first UFO-age treatment of the "mystery" of Flight 19 between book covers, and arguably the first to link the disappearance with UFOs. The case would become a staple of the "Bermuda triangle" legend, first given that name by writer Vincent H. Gaddis in the February 1964 issue of *Argosy* and the next year in a book titled *Invisible Horizons*. As early as 1952, however, a contributor to *Fate* had written of a "series of strange marine disappearances, each leaving no trace whatever, that have taken place in the past few years" in a "watery area bounded roughly by Florida, Bermuda and Puerto Rico." In the early to mid-1970s the Bermuda triangle became something of a fad, the subject of a popular (and wildly sensationalized) documentary, *The Devil's Triangle* (1970), and several best-selling books, most notably *The Bermuda Triangle* (1974), by Charles Berlitz with J. Manson Valentine. In 1975 Arizona State University librarian Larry Kusche published a devastating refutation, *The Bermuda Triangle Mystery—Solved*, which painstakingly documented the prosaic causes behind allegedly mysterious disappearances. That same year Lloyd's of London stated that "our intelligence service can find no evidence to support the claim that the 'Bermuda Triangle' has more losses than elsewhere. This finding is upheld by the United States Coastguard [sic] whose computer-based records of casualties in the Atlantic go back to 1958."

The salient fact about Flight 19 is the weather, which was not clear, Keyhoe and other chroniclers notwithstanding. In fact it was deteriorating alarmingly by late afternoon, which also affected radio communications. The flight consisted of 14 men, all students in training except for the commander, Lt. Charles Taylor. Taylor and the others were to conduct a practice bombing run at Hens and Chicken Shoals, in the direction of the Bahamas, then continue eastward another 67 miles, then go north 73 miles. Then, following a west-southwest turn, they would fly 120 miles straight home.

Unfortunately, Taylor did not know the area, and neither did the others. He thought he was over the Florida Keys, when in fact he was over the Bahamas. If he had known he was over the latter, he would have directed Flight 19 to fly westward, to the mainland. Thinking he was over the Keys, he had the planes head northward, which only put them further out over the ocean. Eventually, sometime after 7 P.M., they ran out of fuel and crashed into an ocean by now so turbulent that the planes were probably immediately chewed up and lost forever. The Martin Mariner—a kind of aircraft known, not entirely affectionately, as a "flying gas bomb"—almost certainly blew up at 7:50. The crew of the SS *Gaines Mill* witnessed the disaster and passed through the wreckage a few minutes later. The water was too turbulent to allow members to try to retrieve bodies.

The Navy conducted an extensive inquiry into the tragedy. It did not conclude that the missing aircraft and the men inside them had been removed to another planet. It stated in its report, issued on April 3, 1946, that the "flight leader's [Taylor's] false assurance of identifying as the Florida Keys, islands he sighted, plagued his future decisions and confused his reasoning. . . . [H]e was directing his flight to fly east . . . even though he was undoubtedly east of Florida." Over the next months Taylor's mother and aunt hired a lawyer to fight the determination that the flight's commander had been responsible. In November, apparently wanting to end the matter, the Board for Correction of Naval Records put aside the original verdict. "Causes or reasons unknown" underlay the episode, it declared, unintentionally encouraging decades of mystery-mongering. Kusche, who would write a book devoted entirely to the matter, criticized the Correction Board for its exoneration of Taylor, who in his judgment did not deserve it. The exoneration, he wrote, was no more than a well-intentioned but ultimately misguided "kindness" to Taylor's mother.

Still, the association of Flight 19 and plane-napping spacecraft was so firmly ensconced in the popular imagination in the 1970s that at the climax of Steven Spielberg's hit film *Close Encounters of the Third Kind* (1977), a UFO lands, and among the first to step out of it are the flight's missing men, looking appropriately disoriented.

"Stendec"

In the already-mentioned *Flying Saucers on the Attack* Harold Wilkins addressed the mysterious disappearance, on August 2,

1947, of the British South American Airways Corporation's Lancastrian airliner *Star Dust*, over Chile. "Did 'something' intercept the plane?" Wilkins asked melodramatically, adding the purely rhetorical question, "If so, what was it?"

The *Star Dust*'s fate was a genuine aviation mystery, and over time it would be the focus of many theories, of which UFO abduction was only one.

At 1:46 P.M. the *Star Dust* flew out of Buenos Aires, Argentina, under the direction of Capt. R. J. Cook. The airliner carried five crewmembers and six passengers, and its destination was Santiago, Chile's capital, a flight that should have taken 3 hours and 45 minutes. The flight would pass over the Andes, the more-than-5,000-mile mountain range sometimes described as the backbone of South America. The range boasts many lofty peaks, but the two highest—Aconcagua and Tupungato, each more than 22,000 feet—are on the border of northern Argentina and Chile.

Three hours into the flight, the plane would cross the Andes from Mendoza, Argentina, on a route that would take it close to Aconcagua, then turn south for Santiago. All went well. Fifteen minutes before its planned arrival in Santiago, Capt. Cook contacted air traffic control to report the *Star Dust*'s approach. Then, at 5:41, four minutes before it was to land, the airliner sent a strange, single-word Morse code message: "stendec." There could be no mistake what it was—it came in loud and clear—but the operator, presumably Radio Officer D. B. Harmer, sent it fast. The man who received it, a Chilean Air Force officer, was confused. The word made no sense to him. When he asked that it be retransmitted, it was—twice. It was indeed "stendec." But what did that mean?

Whatever it meant, it was the last word ever heard from the *Star Dust*. Attempts to reestablish communication with it met with no response. Within an hour a search-and-rescue operation began. Three Chilean Air Force planes traced the route from Santiago north. The next day Chile and Argentina joined forces, conducting both air and ground searches to no avail. Searchers spotted not a trace of the missing aircraft. Pilots came from as far as Britain as the search expanded. Nothing came of any of these efforts.

In 1948 the Accident Investigations Branch of Britain's Ministry of Civil Aviation produced an investigative report which, with no wreckage to provide solid clues, could only conclude that "the actual cause of the accident remains obscure." Even so, it suggested that there was a "possibility of severe icing."

Other theories were more dramatic. One held that the airliner was carrying important documents which the Argentine government did not want to get to Santiago; thus, it had the flight sabotaged. In another story, the most popular in South America, the passengers included Nazi spies who were carrying gold bars to support them in their retirement. Others, including wishful relatives of the victims, even wondered if the *Star Dust's* crew and passengers lived on somewhere. By the early 1950s, as we have seen, flying saucers had entered the discussion.

On January 26,1998, two young mountaineers came down from the slopes of Mount Tupungato to claim they had seen a Rolls-Royce engine. Not far away they saw pieces of an airplane fuselage, and then wires and portions of wings. Finally, they came upon clothing fragments. They were not there, however, to look for a missing aircraft, and they did not come down for a few more days. On their way down they mentioned their find to a soldier from the nearby mountain station. He didn't believe them, but he mentioned the claim to the visiting Sgt. Armando Cardozo. Nine months later, Cardozo passed on the information to a local mountain climber, Jose Moiso, who had an interest in plane wrecks. In subsequent inquiries Moiso learned that the *Star Dust*—the legendary "gold plane" he had been hearing of all his life—had carried four Rolls-Royce Merlin engines.

Moiso, his son Alejandro, and a group of soldiers (including Cardozo) from the station climbed Tupungato in March 1999 in an effort to locate and recover the remains, but after a few days storms drove them from the mountain. The next climb, in January 2000, brought success, in the form of wreckage, three mummified bodies, and pieces of other bodies. Eventually, the searchers came upon the aircraft's identification plates, documents, and, most important, an intact propeller which established beyond any question that this was indeed the missing Lancastrian.

The story got front-page treatment all over the world. In January 2001 it was even the subject of an hour-long documentary on the well-regarded BBC/PBS science series *Nova*.

Work on site soon established that the plane had met a quick, violent end, with the passengers dying at the moment of the crash. It had plowed into a glacier on Tupungato's eastern face, precipitating an avalanche which quickly covered the plane, thereby rendering it effectively invisible to searchers. Over time, as it accumulated yet more ice from the often falling snow, the glacier migrated slowly down the slope, taking the buried airliner's remains—now frozen within the glacier—with it. By the time it reached the lower part of the mountain, some melting became possible and the remains reemerged.

The proximate cause of the crash was navigational error. The error was a consequence of meteorological ignorance. In 1947 little was known of the jet stream, winds which blow high in the atmosphere above normal weather systems. Few planes encountered it because few could fly as high as the Lancastrian. Thus, when it radioed that it was ascending to 24,000 feet to escape the mountains and the storms raging on them, the *Star Dust* thought it would be sailing through stable conditions. Without the sorts of sophisticated navigational aids all modern airliners possess, the pilots depended in good part on their own eyes. As the storms and clouds caused visual cues to disappear, they could judge their location by calculating the speed at which they were flying and their distance from their destination. As it turned out, they were fatally wrong.

They thought they were about to land in Santiago, when in fact they were 50 miles from it. They were flying head on into the jet stream without even knowing it, or furthermore, without knowing that their speed was not what they thought it was. The nearly 100-mph wind was slowing the aircraft, rendering all the navigational calculations not just useless but dangerous.

At 5:33, crewmembers thought the plane was now over the mountains, into Chile, and ready to land at 5:45. In reality, they were on the wrong side of the mountain, which, unseen, was looming up right in front of them. Air-crash investigator Carlos Sorini told *Nova*, "I think that in the final moments of the flight, the pilot was quite sure of what he was doing and felt quite relaxed. The passengers would never at any moment have realized what was happening. I don't think it was a bad way to die because you go from feeling relaxed to not feeling anything."

But if this is true, why the apparently frantic final message? And what was "stendec" supposed to mean? Because it was rendered clearly three times, it is unlikely to have been a familiar word garbled. It is not a phrase in any language, and it is not a code expression. Though most of the mystery covering the *Star Dust*'s fate has now been lifted, this little core of enigma remains, probably never to be penetrated.

Gone to Maser

No one disputes that Karl Hunrath, Wilbur Wilkinson, and their airplane vanished and were never found, their fate, as the old song says, as yet unlearned. What makes the story even more interesting, though, is its curious, even bizarre, background.

First, there was George Adamski. Born in 1891 in Poland, Adamski came to the United States at a very young age and spent his youth in upstate New York. Eventually he drifted westward. By 1921 he was living in California. In the 1930s he established himself as a kind of minor guru, preaching a philosophy he called "Universal Progressive Christianity" and founding the Royal Order of Tibet. He took up residence in Palomar Gardens, a restaurant on Mount Palomar's southern slope, and set up a small observatory, perhaps in imitation of the much larger and more famous one on the mountain.

In the latter 1940s, as flying saucers came into prominence, Adamski began photographing them through his telescope. In 1949 a didactic fantasy novel, *Pioneers of Space: A Trip to the Moon, Mars and Venus,* was (self-) published with Adamski's byline, though the true author was his secretary Lucy McGinnis. In 1950 and 1951 Adamski got national exposure with two articles in *Fate,* a popular digest on anomalies, the paranormal, and the occult, illustrated with his pictures of alleged spacecraft.

All of this was mere prelude to a career as "earth's cosmic ambassador," as his legion of followers would eventually dub him. Outside Desert Center, California, on November 20, 1952, accompanied by six "witnesses" watching at no small distance, he met a beautiful, angelic-looking man from Venus named Orthon. From Orthon, Adamski learned that space people had come to save us from our warmongering ways. The *Phoenix Gazette* reported the news in a tongue-in-cheek dispatch on November 24. From there, Adamski would go on to become an international occult celebrity and the ostensible author of three books (all ghostwritten) detailing his adventures with "Space Brothers" from neighboring planets and the not exactly profound philosophical and scientific insight he gained from them. Critics noted enough similarities between *Pioneers of Space* and the later "nonfiction" that many concluded Adamski was merely—out of laziness, one might add—placing himself inside his own science fiction.

But long before he was touring the world and speaking to adoring audiences, Adamski had gathered a small group of followers around him. Some were with him in the weeks before and the weeks after the fabled November contact. Among them were Jerrold Baker,

George Hunt Williamson, and Karl Hunrath. In due course Baker, a handyman at Palomar Gardens between November 12, 1952, and January 12, 1953, would grow disillusioned and become a prime source of damaging information on Adamski for UFO writer James Moseley. Williamson, far and away the most intriguing and complex figure in Adamski's orbit, soon was nearly as famous as Adamski, pursuing intersecting careers as contactee, fringe archaeologist, explorer, pre-Erich von Däniken ancient-astronaut theorist, author, and lecturer before burning out in the early 1960s. Hunrath, an electrical engineer with esoteric interests, had invented something he called, oddly, "Bosco," a device which he believed duplicated the magnetic power behind UFO propulsion. His intention was to bring down any saucer flying nearby.

Baker, Williamson, and Hunrath sought to form an Adamski Association, with the cooperation of the man himself. Soon, though, things fell apart. On January 12 a young woman named Irma, shortly to be Jerrold Baker's wife, took a tearful phone call from Lucy McGinnis, who said she was calling at Adamski's behest. Hunrath had said that his Bosco would shoot down jets as readily as it would saucers, and he didn't really care. Alarmed, Adamski kicked him, Baker, and Williamson off the property. He and McGinnis now feared that they would return with vengeance on their minds. Irma notified the FBI and the Air Force Office of Special Investigations (AFOSI). When Irma and three companions arrived at Palomar Gardens in the early evening, FBI and AFOSI officers were already there.

Adamski told the no doubt startled investigators that Hunrath had become deranged, perhaps literally possessed by a demonic entity. He charged that Williamson was a liar and a phony medium and that Baker, though harmless on his own, was so impressionable that he let the other two men lead him around. Irma thought, rightly or wrongly, that Adamski was making all this up out of anger about the three men's stated intention to leave Palomar

Gardens and his direct control and influence. For one thing, with their special knowledge of the events surrounding November 20, he may have seen them as a potential threat to the career on which Adamski had embarked.[10] Perhaps Adamski felt that he had to discredit them before they could do the same to him.

In short, we have only Adamski's word, hardly trustworthy, for the supposed jet-downing threat (or, for that matter, Williamson's supposedly fake channeling; most students of Williamson's colorful career believe him to have been deluded but at least generally sincere). On the other hand, Hunrath was known to be a mercurial character whose behavior sometimes lurched out of control. Later, Williamson himself publicly speculated that Hunrath had been under the control of evil space intelligences "from the Orion solar systems."

In any event, Williamson returned to his pregnant wife and home in Prescott, Arizona. Baker and Hunrath moved down to Los Angeles and rented an apartment together. Hunrath got work as a radio technician. In late June, Wilbur J. Wilkinson, formerly of Racine, Wisconsin, arrived in the city with his wife and three children. Hunrath and Wilkinson were old friends from Wisconsin. Hunrath had left the state several months before, to participate directly in the emerging southern California saucer scene. Meantime, he kept in touch with Wilkinson, then a foreman at an electrical plant. Wilkinson had helped Hunrath develop the Bosco. Apparently, Hunrath's promise that he would see a saucer, maybe even board one, was sufficient to move Wilkinson to pull up Midwestern roots and head for the West Coast.

What happened next is unclear. An account by James W. Moseley, based on information provided by Irma Baker, alleges that Jerrold Baker, Hunrath, and Wilkinson made regular junkets to Prescott to talk with Williamson and to sit in on channeling sessions with him. By this time all four believed that they were actually spacemen. They assumed "extraterrestrial" names, and they drove out into the desert on a number of occasions, hoping that they could attract the attention of flying saucers. Maybe their occupants would even fly them to another planet. Meantime, Wilkinson was himself going into trances and channeling messages from space people. He and Hunrath began experiencing visions, which came unbidden but often, of strange symbols. They wrote them down on paper and tacked them to whatever walls were at hand. The space people behind all this were from "Maser," known to the rest of us as the moon.

Williamson told a different, simpler story. "During his stay in [Williamson's] home" sometime in the early part of 1953, he himself had given Hunrath the symbols, which he had from his own contacts and channels. "Much of this symbolism," he wrote, "is characteristic of the ancient scroll writing of the Atlanteans and of the ancient pictographic writing of Lemuria."[11] He never met Wilkinson personally. Hunrath also visited other saucer personalities and contactees in the same period. Williamson remembered him as "a strange man who would change his mind and ideas from one moment to the next. . . . He visited Saucer researchers as a friend, then systematically began to spread rumors about them and their work which had no basis in fact."

All that is known for certain is that Hunrath and Wilkinson continued their saucer-related activities, to which Mrs. Wilkinson paid so little attention that later she could shed little light on exactly what they consisted of. The existing evidence suggests that the two men were experimenting with psychic techniques and mechanical contraptions which they thought would enable them to contact people from Maser—a name they got from Williamson. They also possessed tape recordings of channeled messages, whether their own or Williamson's is unknown.

In November, Baker went east to visit his ailing mother. On the way, he stopped in Winslow, Arizona, to call on Williamson associates Al Bailey (another "witness" to Adamski's November 20 contact[12]) and Laimon Streeter. It was there that he learned of the strange fate, several days earlier, of Hunrath and Wilkinson.

The circumstances of the two saucer seekers' last weeks are murky, but it appears that they succeeded, at least in their own estimation, in their effort to contact space people. Apparently, according to his wife, Wilkinson wrote a letter to Baker, imploring him to return to Los Angeles. He and Hunrath knew where a saucer was going to land, and they wanted Baker to join them in the long-anticipated face-to-face meeting with a spaceman. For some reason, however, Wilkinson did not mail the letter. For Baker, that would be a lucky break indeed.

Just before he disappeared, from most accounts the day before, Hunrath phoned a number of saucerian associates to denounce Adamski's photographs, which he charged had been faked. He also said words to the effect that people had left Earth for other planets; no one should be surprised if one day he went there, too, he added. At the time, it is likely that no one took him especially seriously. By that time, those who knew him knew him as a man with an oversized mouth.

On the afternoon of November 11, Hunrath and Wilkinson rented a plane at Gardina County Airport near Los Angeles. They paid for an hour's flight and flew off in a small aircraft with three hours' worth of fuel. Airport personnel assumed they would circle the flat, desert landscape around the airport for a short while. In fact, that was not their intention at all.

It can be reasonably inferred that the two did not intend to return the plane. Presumably, they paid the minimal rental fee and sailed off—leaving no flight plan—in the expectation that when the hour was up and long passed, they would be nowhere near irate airport personnel and warrant-waving law enforcement officers. They could put all such earthly complications behind as they sailed happily off to another world. In any event, they and their plane vanished. They and it have yet to be found.

In this instance, unless one thinks there really are men on the moon called Maserians, there is no reason to believe that the disappearance took place under extraterrestrial circumstances.

Hunrath, who was behind the controls, was a pilot without a great deal of experience. Almost certainly, nearly everyone agreed, the plane went down to the east, in a remote, inaccessible, mountainous location.[13] A tragedy, in other words, but not a mystery, at least not in any otherworldly sense.

As Los Angeles newspapers ran with sensational but largely inaccurate accounts about Hunrath and Wilkinson, Baker helped the latter's wife pack up and dispose of her husband's property. She had no interest in flying saucers, and she said that her husband never talked about them except when Hunrath was around. Hunrath, meantime, had disappeared with his rent unpaid. The landlord sold his property at an auction, unloading it for more money than Baker, who had hoped to acquire the material in order to answer the many questions swirling about the episode, could afford. Thus ended one of the odder incidents in the social history of flying saucers.

Mystery over Bass Strait

Early on the evening of Saturday, October 21, 1978, twenty-year-old pilot Frederick Valentich flew his Cessna 182 out of the airport at Moorabbin, Victoria, Australia, and into . . . no one knows. To this day his fate is an enigma of a particularly deep, impenetrable kind. Not a single clue that could provide an answer has emerged in the quarter-century that has passed since then. Even more interesting, in this case the link between the disappearance and the sighting of a UFO is not purely speculative. The disappearance took place, to all available appearances, *while the pilot was reporting a UFO.* Even more remarkably, the pilot's final words were caught on tape.

At the time of its occurrence, it was a front-page story in Australia and all over the world. All sorts of theories were bandied about to explain what had happened, and more than once hopeful seekers declared that the solution was imminent. Sadly, it wasn't.

As detailed in a number of books, including a privately published one devoted solely to the case, Valentich was over Bass Strait on his way to King Island when he saw another aircraft flying uncomfortably close to his. Moments later, the unidentified craft proceeded to hover over the Cessna, which suddenly developed engine trouble. At 7:06 an anxious Valentich asked Melbourne Air Flight Service if it knew of any traffic in his vicinity, just below 5,000 feet (his own altitude was 4,500 feet, he soon clarified). When Controller Steve Robey said he knew of none, the pilot complained that a "large aircraft" was just above him. He said it had "four bright, it seems to me like landing lights . . . The aircraft has just passed over me at least a thousand feet above." He couldn't tell exactly what it was because it was traveling too fast, he added.

After Robey reaffirmed the nonpresence of known aircraft, Valentich reported, "It's approaching now from due east towards me." After a few moments of silence, he resumed, "It seems to me he's playing some sort of game. He's flying over me two to three times . . . at speeds I could not identify." Then: "It's not an aircraft. It is—" Silence again. Robey prodded him, "Can you describe the, er, aircraft?" Valentich replied, "As it's flying past, it's a long shape." Silence, then, after repeating that its speed rendered identification impossible, he said it was positioned "before me right now, Melbourne."

Asked if he could now describe it better, Valentich said, "It seems like it's stationary. What I'm doing right now is orbiting, and the thing is just orbiting on top of me. Also it's got a green light and sort of metallic. It's shiny [on] the outside." A few seconds of silence. "It's just vanished." He asked, "Would you know what kind of aircraft I've got? Is it military aircraft?"

Robey didn't answer directly, instead requesting him to repeat what must have sounded like an incredible statement about a sudden vanishing. Then Valentich radioed that the aircraft was "approaching from the southwest. . . . The engine is rough idling" and "coughing."

Robey wanted to know what his intentions were. Valentich replied, "My intentions are, ah, to go to King Island. Ah, Melbourne, that strange aircraft is hovering on top of me again." Silence. "It is hovering, and it's not an aircraft." As the mike remained open, the next 17 seconds recorded a loud, metallic, scraping sound. Robey would recall "this open microphone, with just this metal pinging sound, like someone rapidly pushing the press-to-talk button . . . It started for five to six seconds, then broke briefly and started up again." And then there was silence. It has never ended.

When Valentich and the Cessna vanished, they were about 45 miles north-northwest of King Island, at which he was scheduled to land at 7:28. An air search and radio queries followed soon afterwards. More formal, better-equipped searches commenced and continued for the next four days. Nothing was uncovered except an oil slick 18 miles north of the island; analysis determined that it was from ship, not airplane, fuel.

Because the notion that a UFO could have snatched the plane and its pilot out of mid air seemed too fantastic to consider, other theories filled Australian press coverage over the next weeks. One held that Valentich had staged the incident, secretly landed, and gone into hiding. There was no evidence to support that idea then, and none has emerged to date. Others thought airborne drug dealers had brought down the plane. More plausibly, some theorized that Valentich had grown disoriented and crashed. It was not explained, however, what could have caused the hypothesized disorientation and why no trace of the plane would ever be recovered. In May 1982 Australia's Bureau of Air Safety Investigation released its official report, which acknowledged that it could not determine "the reason for the disappearance." A few months later, an independent film producer, Ron Cameron, claimed that two divers had approached him to say they had found the wreckage. A flurry of press excitement followed, until questions were raised about the divers' honesty. Unable to produce convincing evidence to back their assertion, the divers dropped out of sight, never to reappear.

According to well-regarded Australian UFO investigator Paul Norman, "Frederick Valentich was not the only person who reported a strange object over and near Bass Strait that day and night. Researchers have found over 50 reported observations in that area which occurred before, during and after his encounter. . . . The Bass Strait Flap had been building up for over six weeks prior to the pilot's disappearance."

On October 21, the date of the disappearance, several remarkable sightings took place. At 2 P.M., at Curry, King Island, an object resembling a huge golf ball sailed out of the one cloud in an otherwise cloudless sky. The object, one-fourth the apparent size of the moon and between silvery and white in color, moved west at a slow rate of speed, heading seaward. Then it stopped and with the same measured pace returned to the cloud.

Less than an hour later, two identical cigar-shaped UFOs, joined by two silver beams, were seen flying from west to east over Victoria, close to Bass Strait. Around 4:30, they took a long, sweeping curve which took them northward before shooting away. Investigators for the Victoria UFO Research Society (VUFORS) interviewed witnesses all along the UFOs' flight path, including some who had seen the objects—which were silent at all times—from almost directly underneath. They described them as three-quarters the size of a Boeing 747. The UFOs disappeared near Cape Otway (at the southernmost point of Victoria's west coast, off Bass Strait).

The most remarkable sighting was captured on film at 6:45. A Melbourne man named Roy Manifold photographed a strange object, surrounded by spray and mist, shooting out of the water near the Cape Otway lighthouse. The 35mm camera, in automatic sequencing at the time, captured the image—a cloudlike form—on two of six pictures. To theories that it *was* a cloud, Norman retorted, "The time interval between each photograph is confirmed by the setting sun's position. In the last picture the so-called cloud is already nine degrees into the shot. This means it would have been moving at 200 miles per hour. It is not possible for a cloud or puff of smoke to move at this speed on a calm day." A subsequent analysis by Ground Saucer Watch, an American group specializing in the study of alleged UFO photographs, mostly by computer-enhancement techniques, led to the conclusion that "the images represent a bona fide unknown flying object of moderate dimensions, apparently surrounded by a cloud-like vapor/exhaust residue." UFO researcher Richard F. Haines, however, suspects tampering with at least one of the photographs, suggesting that "the dark cloud-like image of frame six was somehow added after the exposure was made at Cape Otway." After examining the negative, Bill Tindale, deputy picture editor of the Melbourne newspaper *The Sun*, declared, "The alleged UFO is just a dark gray, blurred blob."

Other sightings, mostly of light sources in the sky, were logged that evening. The association of any of them with Valentich's disappearance is, of course, unproved. A story that came to light several years later, however, claimed a sighting of both a UFO *and* Valentich's plane.

Several years after the incident, four members of a family—an uncle, his son, and two nieces—came forward to relate an experience they allegedly underwent on the evening of October 21, 1978. As the story went, they were hunting rabbits at Cape Otway when one of the girls asked, "What is that light?" Looking up, the uncle spotted an airplane (apparently Valentich's, the only one that would have been in the air at the time in question) and identified it as an aircraft light. "No," the niece insisted, "the light *above* the airplane." The four watched the plane and the light until they were lost to sight behind nearby hills.

Whether this report is valid or not, the direct, undisputed evidence of the taped conversation between Valentich and Robey is sufficient to establish that the young pilot disappeared in the course of an airborne encounter with a highly unusual, fast-moving, sometimes hovering flying object. That object has never been identified, and no plausible, prosaic, non-UFO suspects have ever been brought forward. Unless evidence to the contrary should come to light, the Valentich case looks very much like the one instance in which a link between a UFO sighting and an aircraft disappearance—with all that implies—can be reasonably drawn.

Vanished Without a Trace That They Ever Were

According to a number of people, something very strange happened over the Puerto Rican towns of Lajas and Cabo Rojo on the evening of December 28, 1988. If it is what it seems to be, it is one of the most fantastic—not to mention disturbing—UFO sightings of all time. The problem, however, is that if one discards the witness testimony, which is clear and specific, there is no good independent evidence that such an event ever took place. Given the nature of the alleged event, that evidence has to exist, and it is evidence of a sort that would be extremely difficult to cover up. In the end, we are left with, at best, ambiguity, albeit ambiguity of an extraordinary kind.

Early on the night in question, witnesses in this coastal resort area began hearing and seeing jet fighters in the sky. One observer, Wilson Sosa, was a UFO investigator, and the activity attracted his attention because only a week before, he had heard of an attempted intercept of a UFO by an Air Force jet. At the time Puerto Rico was in the grip of UFO fever, occasioned by sightings of all kinds throughout the island.

At 7:45 Sosa, who lived in the Betances community in Cabo

Rojo, thought he heard aircraft "that were either from the Puerto Rico National Air Guard or from the U.S. Navy." They were too high to be seen, but Sosa had his gaze focused upward when he spotted a "humongous" triangle-shaped object "blinking with many colorful lights." He dashed inside and grabbed binoculars to get a better look.

"It made a turn back and then came over, lower, and appeared much larger," he said. "It was then that we noticed two jet fighters were flying directly behind it. When the UFO went to the west, one of the planes tried to intercept it and passed in front of it, at which time the UFO veered to the left and made a turn back, reducing its speed. The jets had tried to intercept it three times, and that's when the UFO decreased its speed, almost stopping in mid-air. It was incredible! How something that big could remain almost motionless in the air was unbelievable. . . . The second jet remained at the right side of the UFO while the first one positioned itself at the UFO's left rear side."

Sosa was not the only one watching this incredible spectacle. Others included Sosa's neighbors Carlos Manuel and Haydee Mercado. Elsewhere, Edwin and Eduviges Olmeda and their children were watching the unfolding drama, as were Edgardo and Carmen Plaza and an unspecified number of others.

Sosa: "I don't know exactly what happened, if the jet entered the UFO by its rear upper side, or what. That's when we all yelled because we were afraid there would be a collision and maybe an explosion due to it. The jet in the back just disappeared on top [of] or inside the UFO, because I was seeing everything through my binoculars and it didn't come out from the rear, the upper side or the other sides. . . . The second jet remained very close to the right side of the UFO. It looked very small alongside that huge thing. As the UFO flew a little to the west, the jet disappeared, as well as its engine sound. This was identical to what happened when the first jet seemed to disappear inside the UFO."

Carlos Mercado: "Suddenly, I saw two planes coming, each one at the side of the thing. When they got nearer to that ship . . . one of the jets came and crossed in front of that thing to the left and the other one crossed in front of it from left to right. Then, when they got next to it, we thought that they would collide with it. It stopped in mid air! The jets seemed to go inside of it, and that's the last we saw of them."

Ivan Cote (resident of the Sabana Yeguas sector of Lajas): "That was between 7 and 8 P.M. I was in the yard, and all of a sudden I saw this huge thing like a triangle with big lights and many similar blinking colored lights. Then some military jets arrived and began, I would say, to try to corral that thing, and there were other smaller red luminous objects that were around the triangle and were circling it and seemed to be protecting it from the planes. . . . Suddenly the planes seemed to enter or be sucked into [it]. . . . I thought there would be an explosion, a collision, but they just disappeared. I couldn't see them or hear them anymore."

Sosa: "That UFO was huge! I tell you that that ship was bigger than this community's baseball park. You could observe its gray metallic structure and great central yellow light that was being emitted from a huge bulging luminous circular concave appendage. At the triangle's right 'wing' tip it had brilliant yellow lights, and on the left one it had red ones."

Mercado: "It looked like a triangle. It had some lights on both sides and a great ball of light from the middle, from where the yellow light was emitted. When it veered and stopped over the Saman Pond, it divided itself, and one of the sections shot away at great speed to the east, and the other one took off to the north. These jets seemed to be trying to intercept that thing, force it to change its course, which they did on three occasions, until the thing stopped and trapped them. It grabbed them and took them both away!"

Sosa: "After trapping the jets it lowered its position and came very close to the ground over a small pond known in the area as

Saman Lake. It stood still in mid-air for a moment . . . then straight-
ened its corners and gave off a big flash of light from the central
ball of yellow light. It then divided itself in the middle into two
different and distinct triangular sections! It was just incredible!
The triangle to the right was illuminated in yellow, and the other
in red. That's when they both shot away at great speed, one to the
southeast, and the other one toward the northeast, toward Monte
del Estado. You could see red sparks falling from it when it divided itself."

Mrs. Olmeda: "It was like something out of a science-fiction
movie, incredible. From our balcony we could see everything. These
planes were circling and getting in front of that thing with the big
yellow light. . . . It was beautiful! Suddenly it stopped, and the
planes seemed to disappear inside it."

Mr. Olmeda: "That certainly was a UFO, and it was really big.
It was glowing with a big yellow light and didn't make a sound as
it flew over the area, but the jets did."

Cote: "Then another jet came, but it flew away, apparently because what they saw happened to the other two, and got lost in
some clouds while the smaller UFOs with red lights were chasing
it. That is all I saw. Those jets did disappear. My grandmother,
Josefina Polanco, saw it all, too, because I called her out to see."

Juan Acosta (one witness from a family of witnesses at Lajas):
"That thing was much bigger than the jets. Those jets seemed like
mosquitoes next to it."

Puerto Rican ufologist Jorge Martin learned of the incident the
evening of its occurrence. He wasted no time checking with official services, the first of them the Federal Aviation Administration
(FAA) office in Isla Verde. A supervisor named Ed Purcell said his
office had received no UFO reports and none of disappeared aircraft. There was, however, "some military movement down in the
southwest region in Cabo Rojo . . . apparently from the Roosevelt
Road Naval Base." The Puerto Rico National Air Guard Base in

Isla Verde said it knew nothing of the incident, but that none of its planes were in the area.

The day after the alleged incident, Martin, accompanied by Jose and Damaris Reyes, interviewed a large number of witnesses, including the ones mentioned above as well as others. Writing in the *MUFON UFO Journal*, he stated, "Up to now there are more than 60 witnesses to the incident." He also spoke with Aristides Medina, a retired U.S. Army man living in La Parguera, who claimed, "At about 8:30 P.M. a bunch of black helicopters arrived, and for hours overflew the Sierra Bermeja and the Laguna Cartagena areas without any lights. They did that until about 12 A.M. They seemed to be searching for something in that sector."

On the other hand, an interview that same day with a man in the air operations division of the Roosevelt Road U.S. Navy Base, in Ceiba, sparked no more than an expression of incredulity. Asked about the alleged UFO and associated aircraft disappearances, the man snorted, "That's absurd! It's not true, it's ridiculous. What's more, for better proof, I can tell you that we did not have any personnel in that area either day or night on Wednesday, yesterday. Whoever said that is wrong." When Martin pointed out that a number of persons claimed to have witnessed the extraordinary event, the spokesman insisted that "they couldn't have seen that because it's not true. The whole version is absurd."

Still, when Martin checked with the Federal Aviation Administration office at Isla Verde, an officer denied knowing anything about a UFO incident but did confirm that "there were air practices in that area in Cabo Rojo last night. Wednesdays are the official days for practices in that sector, and it is officially notified to the Administration as such." He was puzzled when Martin told him of the naval base's denial of air activity.

Later that day, Martin phoned the FAA office again and talked with another man, who asked that he not be quoted. According to Martin, he denied knowledge of the UFO incident but added that his office was not allowed to investigate UFO incidents. "A special investigation is done by a special division of the FAA stationed in Washington, D.C.," he asserted. If this is true, this is the first—and only—time anyone has ever heard of it.

The denials left Martin with no alternative but to speculate that the supposedly vanished interceptors were not from Roosevelt Road but from an aircraft carrier anchored 25 miles off the coast of Puerto Rico.

Martin would report that a week after the incident, "a Navy officer here on the island (whose name I can't give for obvious reasons)" informed him that radar on Naval vessels had tracked the jets as they merged with the larger UFO. "After that," the officer reportedly said, "the big target seemed to split and shot off at great speed. A lid has been placed on the whole incident." The classified radar tapes had been sent to Washington for analysis.

Or maybe not. Three airplanes do not disappear or crash or otherwise fail to return home without attracting attention and publicity. Jet interceptors are enormously expensive aircraft. Besides, families, colleagues, and friends are aware that pilots and crewmembers are missing, and they demand answers. Superior officers are held accountable. Accident investigators talk with a whole lot of people, including those who observed the disaster. Yet neither Martin nor anybody else could get official confirmation even when, allegedly, planes went missing in full view of—at least—dozens of witnesses. (Anonymous military and government informants, a rich history of such in ufology attests, are hardly ever to be trusted to do anything but expend hot air.)

The seemingly impressive witness testimony notwithstanding, the story makes no sense on its face. If anything like it did happen—and Martin is not a man known to conjure up tall tales—we are left to speculate that . . . what? The only thought that comes to mind is that, yes, witnesses saw something out of the ordinary, though it was not what they thought it was—the saucernapping of three jet interceptors—but some sort of bizarre display whose ostensible purpose was to make them think that's what they were seeing.

The Puerto Rican episode is not exactly the first in which seemingly sincere individuals talk of seeing jets vanish in the course of presumed UFO intercepts. One such case comes from Jim Cumber, who grew up to become a Utah representative of the Mutual UFO Network (MUFON). In the December 2000 issue of MUFON's monthly magazine, he recalls an experience from June 1965, when he was 16 years old and vacationing with his parents at Bottomless Lakes State Park, just west of Roswell, New Mexico.

A keen amateur astronomer, Cumber was sitting up around 10:30 that first evening gazing at the vast array of stars visible in the clear desert sky. He had left his telescope at home in Florida, so he made use of what he had, which happened to be a pair of 7x50 binoculars. Not long afterwards, he noticed the passage of what he first thought was a satellite. He focused the glasses at it until, to his surprise, it stopped abruptly between two stars, hovered there motionlessly for a few seconds, then flicked out "as if someone had turned off a light switch."

Of course Cumber knew that a satellite couldn't do that. He also realized that his "satellite" was traveling east to west, when satellites—at least in those days—orbited in the opposite direction. So he considered a balloon or an aircraft but rejected them, too; it was moving too fast for a balloon, and neither a balloon nor a plane would abruptly stop and disappear. In any event, there was no airplane sound associated with the sighting.

As he puzzled over this aerial oddity over the next few minutes, he began hearing actual airplane sounds. He looked up and even without binoculars could see four pairs of aircraft. Moving back and forth across the sky, they appeared to be searching for something. "Two pairs of the aircraft were running opposing search tracks far to the north," Cumber recalled, "and one pair was to the south. The fourth pair was moving west to east, directly above the northern edge of the campground. These two headed east and turned 180 degrees to come back west, directly over my position."

Intrigued, he put his binoculars to his eyes and kept them in view. Through the glasses he could make out the glow from their close-mounted twin jet exhausts as well as the red and green navigation lights. One pair of aircraft flew to exactly the point where the UFO had disappeared. One of them—the wingman's jet positioned to the right rear of the leader—seemed to vanish. The lights on his jet simply went out, and that was it.

A mile or two later, the afterburners of the lead aircraft glowed, indicating that the pilot was pushing the jet full throttle. The jet headed straight for Roswell's Walker Air Force Base. "All six of the other aircraft [did] exactly the same thing. They lit their burners and [dived] directly for Walker AFB. Forget the approach pattern! Within five minutes there wasn't a plane in the sky!"

From his observation of the aircraft, Cumber believes they were either McDonnell F-4 Phantoms or McDonnell F-101 Voodoos. There is, however, nothing in Walker's unit history or in the press of the period to verify that an interceptor failed to return to base and was never seen again. One can argue that the Air Force might order its pilots not to discuss a UFO intercept, but however much it might want to, the Air Force could not hide a missing interceptor and its crew. Whatever Cumber's sighting was about, it cannot have been what he thought it was about.

8

High Strangeness

CLOSE ENCOUNTERS OF the second kind (CE2s)—cases in which UFOs interact with their environment—take a variety of forms. Few of them are so dramatic as an incident that occurred in Venezuela well before the UFO era and well before anyone ever imagined a phenomenon such as a CE2. But the story, which appeared in an 1886 issue of *Scientific American*, is worth quoting in full. The writer was a U.S. government official, Warner Cowgill, associated with the American Consulate in Maracaibo:

> [A] family of nine persons, sleeping in a hut but a few leagues from Maracaibo, were awakened by a loud humming noise and a vivid, dazzling light, which brilliantly illuminated the interior of the house.
>
> The occupants, completely terror stricken, and believing, as they relate, that the end of the world had come, threw themselves on their knees and commenced to pray, but their devotions were almost immediately interrupted by violent vomitings, and extensive swellings commenced to appear on the upper part of their

bodies, this being particularly noticeable about the face and lips.

It is to be noted that the brilliant light was not accompanied by a sensation of heat, although there was a smoky appearance and a peculiar smell.

The next morning the swellings had subsided, leaving upon the face and body large black blotches. No special pain was felt until the ninth day, when the skin peeled off, and these blotches were transformed into virulent raw sores.

The hair of the head fell off upon the side which happened to be underneath when the phenomenon occurred, the same side of the body being, in all nine cases, the more seriously injured.

The remarkable part of the occurrence is that the house was uninjured, all doors and windows being closed at the time.

No trace of lightning could afterward be observed in any part of the building, and all the sufferers unite in saying that there was no detonation, but only the loud humming already mentioned.

Another curious attendant circumstance is that the trees around the house showed no signs of injury until the ninth day, when they suddenly withered, almost simultaneously with the development of the sores upon the bodies of the occupants of the house.

This is perhaps a mere coincidence, but it is remarkable that the same lapse of time should be observed in both animal and vegetable organisms.

I have visited the sufferers, who are now in one of the hospitals of this city; and although their appearance is truly horrible, yet it is to be hoped that in no case will the injuries prove fatal.

The fate of these poor people is unknown, but the kind of experience they suffered would repeat itself—fortunately, usually in milder form—in the UFO age, when from time to time witnesses in various parts of the world would suffer burns and rashes (even, albeit rarely, fatal ones) in the wake of a close encounter.

Another kind of CE2 is the physical-trace case. Here, UFOs which allegedly have landed leave marks on the ground: impressions, burns, damaged vegetation, and other effects. Incidents like these are potentially of particular value to scientific researchers, since they present materials which can theoretically be brought into a laboratory for analysis, which could presumably yield clues to the nature of the phenomenon responsible. I use the qualifying adverbs "theoretically" and "presumably" because few scientists have involved themselves in UFO studies, and then almost always in an unofficial capacity. Because of the stigma attached to UFOs, laboratories and the (usually considerable) funding necessary for proper analysis are not often available. On the rare occasions they are, as when the French government's GEPAN UFO project studied traces from a reported landing at Trans-en-Provence in January 1981, the results have been provocative.

Perhaps the most frequent CE2, though, is the vehicle-interference case. The Air-Force-sponsored University of Colorado Project (1966-1969), which sought a safely conventional resolution of the UFO mystery, admitted:

> Of all physical effects claimed to be due to the presence of UFOs, the alleged malfunction of automobile motors is perhaps the most puzzling. The claim is frequently made, sometimes in reports which are impressive because they involve multiple independent witnesses. Witnesses seem certain that the function of their cars was affected by the unidentified object, which sometimes reportedly was not seen until after

the malfunction was exposed. No satisfactory explanation for such effects, if indeed they occurred, is apparent.

Project physicist Roy Craig, who wrote these words, speculated, along with other members, about how such things could happen. Perhaps magnetic fields were responsible, they theorized—even though, in the one case in which they were able to study a car not long after an ostensibly UFO-related malfunctioning, they found no evidence of exposure to a strong magnetic field. This has led the prominent astrophysicist and project critic Peter Sturrock to remark wryly, "[The late project director Edward U.] Condon and other members of the staff apparently do not consider the possibility that an advanced civilization may know of and use physical processes with which we are now unfamiliar. Yet this possibility is perhaps the most intriguing reason a scientist would be interested in studying the UFO phenomenon!"

In an extensive study of vehicle-interference cases, sociologist and ufologist Mark Rodeghier—now scientific director of the J. Allen Hynek Center for UFO Studies (CUFOS)—found that in 35 percent of the cases, drivers estimated they were within 100 feet of the UFO. One in every three of the reported UFOs had a disc shape and a diameter of 10 to 30 feet. Most cases claimed more than one witness. Rodeghier found "35 separate statistically significant correlations." One of them, for example, correlated a light beam, physical effect on the observer, and pursuit of the vehicle.

Aircraft have reported similar effects, though these accounts have received less attention and analysis than those associated with cars and trucks. To persons in the air, the phenomenon of interference with electronic and other functions can be a harrowing experience, for the obvious reason that the witnesses are more vulnerable to fatal consequences.

A Glow on the Ocean

The U.S. Navy R5D, a four-engine transport plane, cruised on autopilot 10,000 feet over the North Atlantic through clear weather. It had left Keflavik, Iceland, earlier in the evening, on its way to Argentina, Newfoundland. It carried eight crewmembers and 31 passengers, all of them military men. All seemed routine. It was February 10, 1951, at 9:35 in the evening. The moon had set awhile before, and now only stars above and a few wispy clouds below occupied the sky.

At that moment Lt. Graham Bethune was sitting in the left—pilot—seat, putting in some of the time he needed to qualify as a commander on the R5D. He was gazing distractedly out the windshield into the scene outside when a yellow-orange glow came into view. It was, he thought, 35 to 40 miles ahead, slightly to the right and apparently on the ocean surface. He wondered if these weren't lights from a coastal village in Greenland, but if so, the plane had wandered northward, far off course.

Worried, he pointed it out to Lt. Fred Kingdon, Jr., sitting to his right in the copilot's seat. Soon the two asked Navigator Lt. Noel Koger if he was sure they were on course. He checked, and they were. Bethune and Koger pointed the glow out to Kingdon. Eight to ten minutes had passed since Bethune had first seen it, and the plane was moving in its direction at about two miles a minute. As it got closer, the glow resolved into, in Bethune's words, "a very large circle of lights. . . . As we drew closer, it gradually shifted to the right, until it appeared to be about 30 degrees to the right of our nose, and we had to look down at about a 45-degree angle. The lights had taken on a definitely large circular pattern and were now at least 12 bright white lights."

At that moment the lights blinked out. All was dark for the next minute or two, at which point a yellow, halo-shaped glow became visible on the surface. Soon it had transformed itself into orange, then a bright red, and then it shot upward in the direction of the R5D at high speed. As it did so, a bluish red color formed around the light's perimeter. As it closed in on the aircraft, crewmembers were startled, alarmed, or panicked. One fell over and hit his head on the navigating table and another hurt his arm. Bethune would recall:

> I disconnected the autopilot in contemplation of avoiding a collision by driving the airplane under [the UFO]. I never made a drastic maneuver, and probably only lost about 50 feet of altitude, because at that instant the UFO stopped its movement toward us and began keeping pace in a fixed position relative to our plane. It was now about 45 degrees off the nose of the airplane to the right, perhaps 200 feet below our altitude, and appeared to be only several hundred feet in front of us. It had a definite tilt of about 25 degrees from the horizontal. It was so large that it took up the right hand windshield, and most of the left.
>
> Throughout this sighting, none of the appearances, meaning the original lights and then the object, was ever seen above the horizon. They were always below the horizon, and when in close it was obviously below us, which also visually put it below the horizon.
>
> It stayed in this position for a minute or so. It appeared to be 300 feet in diameter, metallic like anodized aluminum, shaped like a saucer, a purple-red fiery ring around the perimeter with a frosted white glow around the entire object. The purple-red glow around the perimeter was the same type of glow produced around the commutator of an auto generator when seen in the dark.
>
> Then the object moved away from us. It made no turns, as though it was backing up about 170 degrees

from the direction that it approached us, and was still tilted. In only a few seconds it was out of sight.

During the sighting, when he realized that the UFO was not going to hit the airplane, Bethune reconnected the autopilot. He would write many years later in a privately circulated monograph on his experience:

In those "antique" airplanes, every autopilot engagement had to be coordinated with the magnetic heading of the airplane. This was done by referring to the magnetic compass, which was located on the frame separating the two cockpit windows. This is just like compasses sold for use in automobiles, consisting of a circular "needle" immersed in a transparent fluid. The fluid provides some dampening so that the needle movement is slow and steady, and relatively unaffected by turbulence. It is completely independent of all other aircraft systems. I used the reading on the vacuum-operated directional gyro to reset the autopilot.

I glanced up to note our magnetic heading, and saw that the compass was rocking back and forth. This is most unusual. I mentioned it to Lt. Kingdon, and he said, "You should have seen it when the object was close. The compass was spinning!"

We looked at our radio direction finders, which are essentially low frequency radio receivers. A ground station is tuned in, and needles point to the relative bearing of the radio transmitter. The needles were jumping all over the place. We had another compass system which used magnetic compasses located near the wing tips. That was spinning. Finally, we had a vacuum-driven compass system. Alone among our direction finding instruments, this was steady, and we used it to calibrate the autopilot. I conclude from this that the object had a very strong magnetic field, perhaps pulsing. The instruments returned to normal after the object left our vicinity.

As the regular pilot, Lt. Albert Jones, took his place at the controls, Bethune went into the cabin and spoke with the passengers, most of whom had seen the object. One was a Navy Commander—a psychiatrist—who said, apparently only half-jokingly, that yes, he had seen it but hadn't looked very hard because he didn't believe in flying saucers.[1] Bethune returned to the cockpit to urge Jones and Kingdon not to let anyone else know what they had seen, lest they be thought crazy. But Jones had already radioed air traffic control in Newfoundland to ask if radar could track the UFO. He received no response, though it eventually came to light that radar had indeed registered a blip of the mysterious object.

In 1992 Jones would remember what happened when he entered the cockpit to replace Bethune:

> The object to our right was at about 45 degrees relative to our position and slightly below. What amazed me was that when it would go from one position to another it wouldn't go like an airplane, it wouldn't lower the right wing to turn right; instead it would just move. It did this a little, and in the meantime it started moving forward of us. I took the aircraft off the autopilot and turned toward the object so that we could all get a better view.
>
> With that the object really took off, speeded up. It went over the horizon. We could see the silhouette of it going over the horizon on an angle. It wouldn't level, the "wings" weren't level, it was in a bank and went over

the horizon in three and a half or four minutes. . . . We
were on a heading of approximately 225 degrees . . .
and it was on a heading of about 270, rapidly disappearing above the horizon.[2]

When they landed at Argentina, crewmembers and several passengers were separated and interviewed by Air Force Intelligence
officers. Jones would state, "It struck me right from the start that
they knew a heck of a lot more about this than . . . they let on."
They also complained that the Navy medical officer had refused
to speak with them. They wanted Jones, the plane commander,
to order him to do so, but Jones refused.

The following May, a Naval Intelligence officer showed up at
Bethune's home while he was off duty for a few days. The officer,
oddly to Bethune's hearing, always used "encounter" rather than
"sighting" to refer to the incident.[3] He showed Bethune a number
of UFO photographs and asked if what he had seen looked like
any of them. Only one did, at least in shape, but it was too small.
Toward the end of the interview, Bethune asked where their written reports had ended up. The officer said they went to a 12-man
committee that would determine if they had any "national security impact." If not, they would go to the relevant military branch
for routine handling. "I assumed that my report was with the 12-
man committee," Bethune wrote, "and that is why the Intelligence officer was visiting."[4]

The official Air Force explanation was suitably far-fetched. On
February 14, half a week after the sighting, technical analyst Lt.
Col. Kent Parrot informed the (intensely anti-UFO) Col. Harold
E. Watson, chief of the Air Technical Intelligence Center (ATIC)
at Wright-Patterson AFB, "The inclosed [sic] cables were reviewed by this office. . . . [I]t was concluded that while there is a
possibility of the object being a meteor or a fireball, the description furnished gives reason to believe that the aircrew actually
saw an unusual 'northern lights' display." Bethune dismissed the

notion as "preposterous," since he and his fellow witnesses had seen the aurora borealis innumerable times and the UFO bore no resemblance to it.

In the 1970s debunker Philip J. Klass proposed a theory which had the witnesses seeing the moon reflected off clouds. Besides the clear discrepancies between what they reported and what the moon would look like, the moon was not even in the sky at the time. In fact, as already noted, Bethune and his companions had watched the moon sink below the horizon sometime before.[5]

Blinding Light

Ten minutes into October 19, 1953, on a flight between Philadelphia and Washington, D.C., on a night of pleasant weather and the occasional cloud, American Airlines Capt. J. L. Kidd looked down on Baltimore, just visible to the right about 30 miles away and 8,000 feet down. His copilot had his eye on something else, however: an object which was reflecting the moonlight but only intermittently visible as it passed through strands of cloud. Though he could not see its exact shape, he thought it did not resemble an airplane. Beyond that, he was certain that, contrary to legal requirement, it had no running lights.

Then it stopped moving and stood hovering in the darkness. By now, the copilot having alerted him, Kidd had his eyes on whatever it was. Even as the DC-6 got closer, it remained motionless. Uneasily, Kidd slowed the airliner down. "Give him the landing lights!" he shouted, and the copilot turned them on. Brilliant white beams shot toward the object. Within moments a blinding beam from the unknown object was flooding the cockpit even as the UFO began moving rapidly in the airliner's direction.

Kidd set the plane for a rapid descent, so radical that passengers not in their seatbelts lurched forward into the aisles. The plane fell to 5,000 feet, then resumed a straightforward flight path. Kidd radioed Washington National Airport to ask about other aircraft in the area. He was told there were none. He was also informed that ambulances would be waiting when the plane landed. Fortunately, the dislodged passengers suffered only minor scrapes and bruises.

The incident was covered in one edition of the *Washington Post* the following morning. Broadcaster and UFO enthusiast Frank Edwards spoke with a Civil Aeronautics Board representative, who confirmed that such an incident had taken place but would provide no further details.

In the Labrador Sky

On the evening of June 29, 1954, a British Overseas Airways Corporation (BOAC) Stratocruiser piloted by Capt. James R. Howard, on its way from New York City to London, was running late. It had been stalled in a holding pattern, for reasons never explained, south of Boston, and had taken a detour on its way back to its planned route over the North Atlantic. It was now cruising over eastern Canada.

"Soon after crossing overhead Seven Islands at 19,000 feet," Howard would report in a statement prepared shortly after the sighting, "both my copilot and I became aware of some [objects] moving along off our port beam [left side] at a lower altitude at a distance of maybe five miles, in and out of a broken layer of Strato Cumulus cloud. As we watched, these objects climbed above the cloud, and we could now clearly see one large and six small. As we flew on towards Goose Bay, the larger object began to change shape and the smaller to move relative to the larger."

It was around 9 P.M. local time. As he and others on the flight deck watched, the objects now were ascending, apparently to match the altitude of the BOAC plane. "Sometimes three were in front and three behind the large object," Howard said. "Then they would change position relative to the large one."

The large object, dull gray with clear edges, seemed to change shape, sometimes resembling an oval, at other times a cigar, sometimes a triangle. The witnesses disagreed over whether the UFO was *actually* changing shape, or only appearing to—in other words, an illusion created by changing light as the sun set. All could see, however, that it was taking up a good chunk of sky, comparable to a hand held at arm's length. On the other hand, some thought it looked big because it *was* close and others that it looked big because it was big. The latter were probably right. Stewardess Daphne Webster would recall seeing "one big object, cigar shaped, and six smaller ones that were going around, under and over, the big one in constant motion. Sometimes the shape of the big one stretched out."

Howard called Goose Bay to ask if it had anything on radar. (In 1954 airliners were not equipped with radar.) Goose Bay replied that it had nothing but the Stratocruiser. A Royal Canadian Air Force F-94 patrolling the area was instructed to investigate. Howard spoke directly with the pilot and vectored him toward the unknowns. Soon the jet flew over the airliner and toward the UFO, at which point—according to the navigator, who witnessed this part of the sighting without interruption or distraction—the little objects entered the larger one. Three went in from the top, the other three from the bottom. Then the large UFO vanished.

The F-94 communicated only minimally with Howard, so he and his crew never learned what the interceptor pilot had seen or if he had captured the UFOs on his radar. The entire incident had lasted 20 minutes.

When they landed the BOAC plane at Goose Bay nearly half an hour later, U.S. Air Force Intelligence officers were waiting for them. They separated Howard and First Officer Lee Boyd. Meantime, the navigator had his flight log confiscated. The stewardess sat in with passengers as they filled out report forms, probably for Project Blue Book. Years later, interviewed for a British television show, Howard recalled, "The USAF seemed rather blasé about the whole thing, frankly. The officer doing the interview gave me the impression that this sort of thing happened—if not daily, then weekly. He told me of several recent sightings over Labrador."

After his experience was the subject of international publicity, Howard received a letter from a doctor and his wife; the couple were in Massachusetts on the night of the sighting. They wrote that they had seen strange aerial objects heading toward the northeast. Their sighting occurred at the time Howard's Stratocruiser was being held near Boston, and the accompanying sketch the doctor made depicted objects very much like, or identical to, the ones Howard and his crew had seen. Ever after, Howard would suspect that the unaccounted-for holdover—in a sky devoid, as far as Howard could tell, of other aircraft—may have occurred because air traffic control was tracking UFOs on its radar screen and not knowing what to do about the fact.

In the mid-1960s the Air Force-sponsored University of Colorado UFO Project analyzed the report, one of the most publicized of airline encounters.[6] The analyst, physicist Gordon David Thayer, struggled to conjure up a prosaic solution, specifically a mirage, before essentially giving up. The case is listed as among the reports for which the project—whose leadership rejected the idea that UFOs represented anything out of the ordinary—could find no explanation. In the project's final report, formally titled *Scientific Study of Unidentified Flying Objects,* the coverage of the BOAC encounter ends with these extraordinary words, often cited by the project's critics: "This unusual sighting should . . . be assigned to the category of some almost certainly natural phenomenon, which is so rare that it apparently has never been reported before or since."

Perhaps more realistically, University of Arizona atmospheric physicist James E. McDonald, who interviewed Howard in the mid-1960s, observed, "The group of UFOs maintained relatively constant position, relative to the airline, until their departure, and lay approximately five degrees to the left of the just-setting sun. No meteorological-optical phenomenon could reasonably account for the reported phenomena."

Blinking Pattern, Compass Interference

In the mid-1960s, as he was going through the files of Project Blue Book at Maxwell AFB, Alabama, James McDonald came upon a "Record Card" which recounted a January 16, 1957, encounter as follows:

> Two a/c [aircraft] within a few miles of each other observed round objects, alternating bright and dim in light. Appeared to give off sparks. Maneuvered erratically at very high speed, and faded out in the distance after flight appearing to be along side of observing craft. Both a/c in vicinity NW of Ft. Worth during incident. B-25 dispatched to search. After 4 hour [sic] negative results.

In the "Comments" column the anonymous writer noted "insufficient data for analysis"—which, as McDonald had long since learned, usually meant that Blue Book had not bothered to seek out the data sufficient for analysis. McDonald managed to locate the primary witness, whom he identified only as "Colonel Wright— then Lieutenant Colonel Wright," and interviewed him.

From the interview he learned that Wright, a B-25 pilot, left Birmingham, Alabama, on a flight to Reese AFB in Lubbock, Texas. As he passed over Fort Worth at 8 P.M. at around 8,000 feet, he noticed a light about 45 degrees to his right and at the 2 o'clock position. His copilot suggested that the light, a soft white glow, might be from a jet's afterburner. Suddenly, however, it jumped to a 3 o'clock position, an acceleration no jet could accomplish.

Pacing the B-25 at wing level, the object—its apparent size slightly less than that of the moon—began to blink a seemingly erratic light pattern. At times the UFO abruptly accelerated and stay at its new position until it retreated just as quickly. The sighting continued for an hour as the B-25 traversed 200 miles.

At one point Wright and his copilot wondered if the UFO was signaling to them in some kind of code. They even recorded the sequence on paper, but the next day, when they showed it to Air Force experts at Lubbock, no one could make any sense of it. More remarkably, the plane's compass followed the UFO all during the sighting, even though it should have been pointed in the direction of Lubbock. It resumed normal operation after the UFO disappeared.

When they landed at Reese, the two told their story to investigating officers. They were still speaking when a second B-25 landed. The pilots of that aircraft had had the identical experience, including the compass interference. Wright's B-25 was refueled and sent up to search for the object, this time with an Air Force photographer. The search went on for four fruitless hours.

RB-47: The Perfect Case?

Considered by at least one particularly well-informed authority, aerospace engineer Brad Sparks, to clinch the case for the existence of UFOs and acknowledged even by some hard-core skeptics to be highly puzzling, the so-called RB-47 case has withstood every attempt to explain it in prosaic terms.

The incident languished in Project Blue Book files and did not see print until 1969, some 12 years after its occurrence, when it was discussed in *Scientific Investigation of Unidentified Flying Objects.* It was one of the cases the University of Colorado Project unhappily conceded that it could not explain. The project investigator who worked on the case, physicist Gordon David Thayer, dismissed Blue Book's official explanation—which was that the "UFO" was an airliner—as "literally ridiculous."

The incident occurred in the early morning hours of July 17, 1957. An RB-47 equipped with electronic intelligence (ELINT) gear, with a six-man crew, flew out of Forbes Air Force Base, Topeka, Kansas, on a mission which was to test the aircraft's guns, navigation, and electronic countermeasures (ECM).

Having completed the first two parts of its mission, the aircraft was flying over the Gulf Coast near Gulfport, Mississippi, when a signal appeared at 3,000 megahertz (MHz) frequency on the second of the three ELINT stations aboard. Frank B. McClure, who was manning it, saw that it was at five o'clock relative to the plane's position. McClure assumed it was coming from a ground-based search radar, but when the signal moved upscope and moved across the RB-47's flight path, he thought otherwise. It then went downscope. The other two stations were unable to confirm the signal, because ELINT #1 was not working at that frequency at the moment and ELINT #3 did not have the capacity to work at any time. Though he could not think of one offhand, McClure thought there must be an explanation, so he elected to say nothing.

Turning west near Meridian, the RB-47 continued its 500-mph flight at 34,500 feet. Minutes later, at 4:10, Maj. Lewis D. Chase, the pilot, and 1st Lt. James H. McCoid, the copilot, spotted an intense blue light at 11 o'clock over east-central Louisiana. It seemed to be closing on them so rapidly that collision appeared imminent. They warned the other four crewmembers that they were about to take evasive action, but suddenly the light effected an abrupt change of direction, shot in front of the plane, and disappeared at two o'clock.

McClure now found that a strong signal was registering at the two o'clock position in the 3,000 MHz range. The same signal appeared on the #1 monitor. It moved upscope, thus eliminating any possibility that it was coming from ground radar. If it had been, the signal would have gone downscope.

As plane and crew continued on their westward course into East Texas, they entered the radar-coverage area of an Air Force radar unit (codenamed "Utah") located near Duncanville. At 4:39 Chase spotted a "huge" light, apparently on top of an even larger, though unlighted, object. It was 5,000 feet below him at the 2 o'clock position. Moments later McClure's ELINT #2 was registering a UFO at 40 degrees—the one Chase was observing—and another, briefly visible to the eye, at 70 degrees.

Radioing to Utah about his intentions, Chase diverted from the flight path and headed toward the large UFO, which ELINT #2 had at 20 degrees' bearing. It was now 4:42. Chase pushed the RB-47's speed up to 550 mph, at which point it accelerated away. McClure now had two signals again at 40 and 70 degrees, but after a minute and a half only one remained, at 50 degrees. Meantime, after Utah had asked where the UFO was and Chase had told it where to look—10 miles northwest of Fort Worth— Utah tracked it on its radarscopes. At 4:50 the UFO executed a sudden stop, causing the aircraft to shoot past it. The UFO then vanished from both scopes and ELINT #2.

In 1969 James McDonald interviewed all the crewmembers. Chase told him, in McDonald's paraphrase,

> . . . there was simultaneity between the moment when he began to sense that he was getting closure at approximately the RB-47 speed and the moment when Utah indicated that their target had stopped on their scopes. He said he veered a bit to avoid colliding with the object, not then being sure what its altitude was relative to the RB-47, and then found that he was coming over the top of it as he proceeded to close. At the instant that it blinked out visually and disappeared simultaneously from the #2 monitor and from the radarscopes at site Utah, it was at a depression angle relative to his position of something like 45 degrees.

When Chase turned the aircraft over the Mineral Wells, Texas, area, as he tried to get back on his original flight path, taking him north toward Forbes, the UFO showed up again, this time to the rear. Instantly, ELINT #2 and Utah were confirming its presence. Chase turned around again and gave chase one more time. He was within five nautical miles of it when it descended to 15,000 feet and vanished both to visual perception and to electronic monitoring. It was now 4:55, and Chase was growing anxious about the aircraft's low fuel supply.

Two minutes later, on the way back to Forbes, McClure picked up a signal at 300 degrees. One minute later the UFO was observed trailing the aircraft. It and its signal continued until Oklahoma City at 5:40. For distance if not duration, the RB-47 and the UFO had set something of a record. They had stayed together for some 800 miles.

At the conclusion of an in-depth reconstruction and analysis of the case, Brad Sparks writes:

> This case certainly now ranks as the best-documented unexplained UFO incident in history. . . . All of the UFO observations by multiple visual observers, multiple ELINT receivers, and multiple radar sets, as well as the serendipitous calibrations of the UFO signals against the separately identifiable Duncanville radar signals, provide a unique tight interlocking web of intricately fitted evidence. This mass of strikingly self-consistent data demonstrates the existence of a large metallic rapidly maneuvering airborne source of powerful S-band radarlike signals and visible light—a UFO.

Violent Effects

Shortly after 7 P.M. on March 18, 1965, as a Toa Airlines Convair-240 cruised on a routine domestic flight between Osaka and Hiroshima, Japan, pilot Yoshiaka Inaba saw a UFO.

He told United Press International, "A mysterious elliptical luminous object appeared just after I had passed Himeji [near Osaka]. I was flying at the time at an altitude of about 2,000 meters. The object followed for a while, and then stopped for about three minutes, and then followed along my left wing across the Inland Sea for a distance of about 90 kilometers until we reached Matsuyama on Shikoku Island. It then disappeared." At one point Inaba, who feared a collision, turned the aircraft sharply to the right, but the UFO matched the maneuver and stayed with him.

In the course of the sighting of the UFO, which was emitting a greenish light, the airliner suffered intense interference with its radio and automatic direction finder. He tried to contact Osaka, and copilot Tetsu Umashima attempted the same with the Matsuyama tower, but neither could get through. The copilot, however, did hear panicked calls from pilot Joji Negishi, at the controls of a nearby Tokyo Airlines Piper Apache flying just north of Matsuyama. An unidentified luminous object was pursuing his plane, he reported. A third airliner also reported sighting the UFO, as did several witnesses on the ground.

Inaba, a veteran of more than 8,600 hours in the air, said later that he had never seen anything like it.

On March 22 Tokyo's *Mainichi Daily News* claimed that the sighting had attracted the attention of the American government:

> A group of aviation, astronomical, and defense experts left the United States for Japan today to investigate the reports of a flying saucer seen by Japanese pilots Thursday night, according to a message from [the] U.S., relayed by the *New York Times'* Tokyo office to the Toa Airlines Office here.
>
> The American "flying saucer" experts from the Defense Department, the Federal Aviation Agency, and the Palomar Astronomical Observatory, want to talk to [the pilot witnesses]. . . .
>
> A test conducted by the Airlines on Saturday night

under similar circumstances ruled out the possibility that the pilots saw the reflection of light from their planes.

The American mission is believed to be interested in the case because there have been several mysterious aviation accidents and flying saucers might have been involved.

The newspaper cited no source for the fantastic allegation in that last sentence, and no information on the alleged official investigation—if indeed one ever happened—has ever surfaced.

Hypnotized over Spain

Miguel Romero Fernandez de Cordoba, flying a Cessna 88 equipped for fire-fighting, was on his way to a blazing forest in the Playa de Aro area of Spain at 6:30 P.M. on July 16, 1973. The sky was clear, and the sun was just setting when a curious object came into view. It was at his altitude—600 to 650 feet—and to his right, just ahead of him. It resembled an upright egg with its bottom cut off. The top half was green, with an orange band in the middle, the rest a reddish color, all luminous. The UFO was about 12 feet high and half as wide and spinning on its axis.

The object commenced a series of unnerving sweeps around the Cessna, sometimes getting as close as six feet. All the while its speed exactly matched the aircraft's. The effect was mesmerizing. Fernandez felt at times as if he were experiencing a bizarre hypnotic attraction to the UFO, as if he could not keep his eyes off it even though flight safety demanded his full attention. His radio kept going in and out, though it remained clear long enough for him to report that he was experiencing "difficulties," though he did not explain exactly what they were.

Unlike the overwhelming majority of reported UFOs, this one

did not move silently but made a sound like sustained thunder, so loud in fact that it could easily be heard over the small airplane's engine noise.

Trying to shake his unwanted companion, Fernandez took the Cessna down to 140 feet. He began to contemplate an emergency landing on a nearby beach. But at this point the UFO effected an ascent at fantastic speed and was gone.

In the Ohio Night

Few UFO cases are so well documented as the one that occurred late on the evening of October 18, 1973, when a helicopter crew and ground observers witnessed an extraordinary mid-air encounter.

Four members of the U.S. Army Reserve had flown an Army UH-1 Huey helicopter out of Cleveland to Columbus, where they received their regularly scheduled medical examinations. At around 10:30 P.M. they left Columbus for the trip back. The sky was clear and moonless, and visibility extended for 15 miles.

Just before 11, as they passed near Mansfield in north-central Ohio, Sgt. John Healey, sitting in the left rear seat, noticed a red light off to the west and moving southward. Since it was far enough away to pose no problem, he said nothing. Three or four minutes later, however, the other backseat passenger, sitting to the right, Sgt. Robert Yanecsek, saw an unblinking red light to the east, apparently pacing the helicopter. After 60 seconds or so he mentioned it to the commander, Capt. Lawrence Coyne, who directed him to "keep an eye on it." Half a minute later, Yanacsek announced in alarm that the light seemed to be approaching them and closing the distance fast.

Coyne was now watching it, too, as was Healey, who got out of his seat and stooped in the aisle to get a clear view. Only copilot 1st Lt. Arrigo Jezzi, at the controls and sitting at the left front, had an obstructed view and thus did not see all that was about to befall the four. The object seemed to be moving at close to 700 mph, even though aircraft under 10,000 feet are legally enjoined to travel at no more than 285 mph.

Coyne quickly took over the controls and attempted to reach Mansfield Approach Control, to which he had spoken just minutes before to secure clearance to fly through the area. He knew that F-100s were stationed at Mansfield. Perhaps they were seeing one of them. "Mansfield, this is Army helicopter 15444," he said. "Do you have any high-performance aircraft in your area?" In response he heard, "This is Mansfield Approach. Go ahead, one-five-triple-four." Coyne repeated the question but heard nothing more. Now Jezzi tried and failed. He radioed Mansfield Tower. No response. He tried both UHF and VHF frequencies, and neither worked.

Healey had his undivided attention focused on the approaching light, which was now as brilliant as the approach lights of a 727 he and the others had seen a few minutes earlier. According to an account Healey gave a colleague in the Cleveland Police Department 18 hours later:

> This object cleared our aircraft by about 500 feet. It had a steady red light on the nose; it was cigar-shaped and had a green light shining down from the aft end. It was like a gunmetal gray, and it made no noise, nor were there any vibrations or air turbulences. It went from the eastern horizon to our point in a matter of about two minutes, and then from there it continued in a direction of about 270 degrees till it got near the horizon. Then it broke off and [executed a turn of] 340 degrees and was lost on the horizon, just like that . . .
>
> Now it's a funny thing, [the UFO] came from the horizon very quickly, but when it went over our aircraft, its speed was very slow until it passed over . . . and then it picked up speed again.

Fearing a collision as the object neared, Coyne pushed down the collective—the control stick—to send the helicopter on a 500-feet-per-minute descent. But when his eyes turned to the front, he was shocked to see a gray, cigar-shaped object filling the entire windshield. Fifty to 60 feet long, with a dome at the top center and running approximately half the length of the structure, it had a steady bright red light on the leading edge (to the witnesses' left) and, at the rear, a pyramid-shaped green beam which swept a 90-degree arc and shot into the cockpit, then covered the entire helicopter. Though not luminous itself, the structure reflected light from the lights it carried. The frightened and confused Coyne could only shout the obvious: "That's no F-100!"

It was apparent that the UFO had descended with the helicopter. Coyne could only conclude the worst: that this peculiar, unknown object, for whatever reason, meant to do him and his men harm. He pushed the collective all the way, for a 2000-feet-per-minute dive. By then the helicopter was at a dangerous 650 feet (1,700 feet above sea level) above the treetops below. Yanacsek told Center for UFO Studies (CUFOS) investigator Jennie Zeidman:

> The object may have hovered over us for 10 to 12 seconds. It seemed like a long time. . . . It was just stopped . . . and I mean *stopped*. It wasn't cruising, it was *stopped*. . . . It was coming at us, and then . . . it was there, just like that. No noise, no flaps. It reminded me very much of a submarine. I really didn't think we would really collide, because the object was obviously completely in control of the situation.

Then the UFO ascended, from its position in front of them and above them. At that point it started to accelerate toward the northwest. Only its white light was visible at this concluding phase of the sighting. It executed an abrupt 45-degree turn and, as Healey would put it, it "snapped out, and over the edge of the world it went."

Unsettling as all of this undoubtedly was, the strangest part was going undetected for a few moments as the crewmembers watched the departing light. On its vanishing, Coyne turned to deal with the collective so that he could stop the descent. His eye fell on the altimeter, which was attesting to the impossible: *the Huey was ascending*. It was now 3,500 feet above sea level and rising upward at 1,000 feet per minute. (At that rate of speed, 108 seconds had elapsed between the first awareness of the close encounter and the UFO's final disappearance.) Inexplicably, the collective was still all the way down.

Not knowing what else to do, Coyne pulled it upwards—not what one ordinarily would have done to stop a climb. But at 3,800 feet the crew felt a slight bump, and the ascent ceased. The bizarre incident was over. This time radio contact—now with Akron Approach—went off without a hitch. The rest of the trip went uneventfully.

On January 24, 1974, astronomer J. Allen Hynek, scientific director of CUFOS and Project Blue Book's longtime scientific advisor,[7] spent most of a day interviewing the witnesses. An old and trusted colleague, Jennie Zeidman, picked up the investigation at his request. Besides interviewing crewmembers separately and together, she reenacted the incident with Coyne, eventually concluding that the entire encounter, beginning with Yanacsek's initial sighting of the light, encompassed "270 to 300 seconds—or 300 seconds, plus or minus 10 percent." Eventually, and most remarkably, she was able to interview members of a family who had witnessed the incident from a car which had been traveling east-southeast of Mansfield just after 11 on the evening in question. Later, she found a family who heard a passing helicopter late on October 18, 1973—a date etched in memory because it was the birthday of a young family member—and observed a room covered in greenish light from a beam emanating from the sky. Unfortunately, nobody looked out the window to check its source.

"Magnetized" over Mexico City

Carlos Antonio de los Santos, 23, was a three-year flyer known as, according to a Mexico City newspaper, "a rather straightforward and prudent young man." On the early afternoon of May 3, 1975, he was at the controls of a Piper PA-24 south of his destination, Mexico City, flying at 15,000 feet. At 1:34, over Lake Tequesquitengo, the plane started shaking for no cause the pilot could determine.

De los Santos happened to glance to his right, where he saw a dark gray disc-shaped object, approximately 12 feet around and 4½ feet high. In the middle of the top there was a small dome with a single window. Then he spotted an identical UFO to his left, and now one heading straight for the plane. This last object hit the bottom fuselage, striking a "light blow." The aircraft registered the jolt. De los Santos for some reason tried to lower his landing gear—apparently hoping it would touch the disc—but the mechanism would not function. The plane seemed "magnetized," by which the pilot meant that the plane felt as if it were being lifted up.

He also attempted to slow the plane, but it kept going at the 120-mph speed at which it had been moving before the strange encounter unfolded. Fortunately, his radio worked, and he was in touch with Mexico City airport all the while, so shaken that he was weeping at times.

Mexico City newspapers quoted radar operators as saying the UFOs had registered on radar. They were last recorded moving away at more than 550 mph. A reporter for *Alerta* wrote that he had listened to tapes of the exchange between the pilot and air-traffic controllers. "All of this," he stated, "coincides with what was being declared by the pilot, which shows that he was not suffering from hypoxia, which also proves he was not the victim of a hallucination or invented the story in search of publicity."[8]

Eerie Effects, Dire Threats

On August 13, 1976, at about 5 P.M., a strange light out of the northeast approached a Piper Arrow PA-28 piloted by a man who requested that he be known only as D.W. He was flying between Diepholz and Petershagen, West Germany, and the object was at his 9 o'clock position in a clear, cloudless sky. It took the UFO—a bright yellow oval—three or four minutes to reach his position, at which time it fixed itself along his left wing. He was not sure how far away it was, but it seemed too close for comfort.

Without warning his plane rolled twice and rapidly descended. D.W. managed to keep his head and, operating manually, stabilized the Arrow after losing only 500 feet. That taken care of, he now had to deal with another worrying unexpected development: the magnetic compass on the instrument panel was spinning clockwise so fast that it was blurring the numbers in the square window as the needle passed. Glancing out his window, D.W. was disconcerted to see that the UFO was still with him, apparently having matched his descent.

Nonetheless, he pointed his aircraft upwards and headed toward his previous cruising altitude, the oval-shaped object still tagging alongside him. He called flight control at Hanover airport, to his east, and reported his ongoing experience. He was informed that radar had not only his plane but an unidentified second blip near it. Hanover told him that it was dispatching interceptors to investigate, and about four minutes later two U.S. Air Force F-4 Phantoms showed up, positioning themselves on either side of him.

When they arrived, the UFO shot forward, made a 30-degree turn upward, then passed to the right in front of D.W.'s Piper

Arrow. The F-4s tried to approach it, but it outdistanced them within seconds. Soon afterwards, the private plane's compass started working normally again.

Directed to land at Hanover, D.W. headed 45 miles to the south-southeast and landed at the airport in 20 minutes. Once there, he was instructed to taxi to a secure area. A military van drove up, and five taciturn men in business suits got out and took him into an underground room where a man sat behind a desk. At no time would the men identify themselves or name their employer. Two of the original five left, and the rest grilled D.W. for the next three hours, having him repeat the details of his sighting over and over. The pilot thought one of his interrogators was an American, but the entire exchange was conducted in German. Toward the end of the conversation, D.W. was handed a piece of paper. By signing it, he agreed never to discuss his UFO sighting. D.W. refused and stood his ground even after he was threatened with loss of his pilot's license. Apparently it was a bluff, because he suffered no such consequences.

He was finally let go. He spent the night in Hanover and flew home to Reichelsheim the next morning. In August 1999, in an interview with a visiting American, aviation psychologist/ufologist Richard F. Haines, he recalled that at some point not long after the encounter, he found that the engine crank shaft as well as parts of the landing gear was permanently magnetized and had to be replaced. He told Haines that he had "suffered greatly from this event," because he had not been "able to produce any definite proof" and had suffered ridicule. The interrogation in Hanover was also a source of continuing distress.

One Evening over Tehran

Late on September 18, 1976, anxious callers to the Mehrabad airport in Tehran, Iran, inquired about a strange aircraft with multicolored lights in the night sky over the city. After initial skepticism air traffic control chief Houssain Perouzi grew curious enough to scan the sky with binoculars until he spotted the object. It was no aircraft he recognized. An estimated 6,000 feet high and five miles away, it had blue lights on either side and a flashing red one in the middle. It was moving erratically, even seeming to change its shape.

To check his perceptions, he handed the glasses to a colleague, who saw exactly what he was seeing. Meantime, reports were coming in from passing aircraft; emergency beeper signals were inexplicably sounding on their radios.

Perouzi spoke with a military officer on duty at the airport, and he in turn phoned his commanding officer, Gen. Youssefi. Youssefi then saw the object from his porch. In alarm he contacted two radar stations, one at Shaharoki west-southwest of Tehran, the other at Babolsar to the northeast. These bases were 135 and 88 nautical miles, respectively, from the city, with the mountains that surround Tehran sometimes blocking radar signals and possibly explaining why the bases reported picking up nothing. The radar at Mehrabad was down while all of this was going on.

Responding to an order from Gen. Youssefi, an F-4 shot off from Shaharoki at 1:30 A.M. Twenty-five nautical miles from the UFO, the interceptor's instrumentation and communication shut down and did not resume functioning until the pilot had pulled away. The pilot gingerly followed the UFO to the Afghan border, then turned back, only to find the UFO in front of him.

Now at the airport, Youseffi ordered the pilot to close in on the UFO. The same dangerous avionics failure he had experienced earlier occurred every time he got within 20 miles, and eventually, as his F-4 grew low on fuel, he gave up. The UFO was still there, 14 miles away and at 15,000-feet altitude. A second jet took after it. When it got within 27 miles, the onboard radar picked up something, the second pilot reported, the size of a "707 tanker." This time the UFO moved away as the jet approached. According to a U.S. Air Force memo prepared by Lt. Col. Olin R. Mooy, based on an interview with the pilot the next day:

> The visual size of the object was difficult to discern because of its intense brilliance. The light that it gave off was that of flashing strobe lights arranged in a rectangular pattern and alternating blue, green, and orange in color. The sequence of the lights was so fast that all the colors could be seen at once. The object and the pursuing F-4 continued on a course to the south of Tehran when another brightly lighted object, estimated to be one-half to one-third the apparent size of the moon, came out of the original object. This second object headed straight toward the F-4 at a very fast rate of speed. The pilot attempted to fire an AIM-9 missile at the object but at that instant his weapons control panel went off and he lost all communications (UHF and interphone). At this point the pilot initiated a turn and negative G dive to get away. As he turned[,] the object fell in trail at what appeared to be 3–4 NM [nautical miles]. As he continued his turn away from the primary object[,] the second object went to the inside of his turn[,] then returned to the primary object for a perfect rejoin.
>
> Shortly after the second object joined up with the primary object[,] another object appeared to come out of the other side of the primary object going straight down at a great rate of speed. The F-4 crew had regained communications and the weapons control panel and watched the object approach the ground anticipating a large explosion. This object appeared to come to rest gently on the earth and cast a very bright light over an area of about 2–3 kilometers. The crew de-

scended from their altitude of 25,000 to 15,000 and continued to observe and mark the object's position. They had some difficulty in adjusting their night vision for landing, so after orbiting Mehrabad a few times they went out for a straight in landing. There was a lot of interference on the UHF and each time they passed through a mag. Bearing of 150 degrees from Mehrabad they lost their communications (UHF and interphone) and the INS fluctuated from 30 degrees to 50 degrees. The one civil airliner that was approaching Mehrabad during this same time experienced communications failure in the same vicinity (Kilo Zulu) but did not report seeing anything. While the F-4 was on a long final approach[,] the crew noticed another cylinder-shaped object (about the size of a T-bird [jet trainer aircraft] at 10 NM) with bright steady lights on each end and a flasher in the middle. When queried the tower stated there was no other known traffic in the area. During the time that the object passed over the F-4 the tower did not have a visual on it but picked it up after the pilot told them to look between the mountains and the refinery.

During daylight the F-4 crew was taken out to the area in a helicopter where the object apparently had landed. Nothing was noticed at the spot where they thought the object landed (a dry lake bed) but as they circled off to the west of the area[,] they picked up a very noticeable beeper signal. At the point where the return was the loudest was a small house with a garden. They landed and asked the people within if they had noticed anything strange last night. The people talked about a loud noise and a very bright light like lightning. The aircraft and area where the object is believed to have landed are being checked for possible radiation.

In the ensuing investigation conducted by the Iranian military, the principal witnesses—two pilots and two copilots, as well as two air traffic controllers—stated that radars on both aircraft were jammed when they locked onto the UFO. Bruce Maccabee, an American physicist and UFO researcher, learned from Gen. Abdulah Azerbarzin, who had sat in on the interviews, that at one point one jet flew under the object, which looked, the general said, "just like a saucer, and the shape of the cockpit was a ball . . . half a ball, and the color of the lighting of the cockpit was different with [sic] what it had on the outside. It was close to yellow. . . . It was unidentified. Definitely it was. Because we had six witnesses." Gen. Azerbarzin said that a fat file on the case had been turned over to the U.S. Air Force.

For its part the Air Force admits to possession only of the Mooy memo, which circulated widely through military, intelligence, and diplomatic offices and agencies. One copy even went as high as the White House. A Defense Intelligence Agency "Report Evaluation" rated the incident "High (Unique, Timely, and of Major Significance)." It went on:

> An outstanding report. This case is a classic which meets all the criteria necessary for a valid study of the UFO phenomenon.
>
> a) The object was seen by multiple witnesses from different locations (i.e., Shemiran, Mehrabad, and the dry lake bed) and viewpoints (both airborne and from the ground).
> b) The credibility of many of the witnesses was high (an Air Force general, qualified aircrews, and experienced tower operators).
> c) Visual sightings were confirmed by radar.
> d) Similar electromagnetic effects (EME) were reported by three separate aircraft.

e) There were physiological effects on some crew members (i.e., loss of night vision due to the brightness of the descent).

f) An inordinate amount of maneuverability was displayed by the UFOs.

Writing in a classified publication (*MIJI Quarterly,* Third Quarter, 1978) distributed among electronic-intelligence agencies in the U.S. government, Capt. Henry Shields reviewed the official documents and concluded, "No additional information or explanation of the strange events has been forthcoming; the story will be filed away and probably forgotten, but it makes interesting, and possibly disturbing, reading."

Terror over the Mountains

Manuel Jose Lopez Ojeda, a 22-year-old student pilot, left an airport at Bogota, Colombia, on a routine training flight. It was 9:15 A.M., May 5, 1977. He was to fly his small private plane, a Cessna 150, above the 8,500-foot mountains north of the city. An hour later, over the village of Tabio, while he was taking sharp turns as one of his practice exercises, he noticed with alarm that his instrument panel indicated that just about every function was not working. All read either zero or danger zone.

Lopez desperately looked for a place where he could land quickly. As his eyes fell down to his right, he experienced a fresh unpleasant surprise. A huge aerial object—resembling an inverted dish 50 to 65 feet long and 10 feet thick—was positioned only a few feet away. On its top was something that looked like a red and yellow lamp. "At times," he recalled, the UFO "would come right below the aircraft. And when I tried to straighten the steep turn in which I was, I found the controls of the aircraft would not obey. The whole aircraft seemed to be locked into this machine, or being controlled by somebody else."

He told a fellow pilot, "The UFO would not rotate—it was stationary. And when it would move, it would move in a straight and horizontal line in quick movements. Doing zigzag, but straight-line movements. [It] was white—snow white. I couldn't see any people, and I couldn't see any windows. . . . It was completely sealed."

Besides losing instrumental control of the aircraft, Lopez was facing an even more frightening development: he was rapidly losing his eyesight. "It was like being in a fog," he said. "I couldn't distinguish any objects too far, so I asked for guidance, to be able to return to my base. [Another] aircraft approached my aircraft. By this time, my vision was lost completely. I couldn't see anything. Not the dashboard. I couldn't see outside my airplane."

Just before he became completely blind, he saw the UFO departing. The approaching aircraft was a rescue plane responding to his distress signal. The pilot, a flight instructor, radioed him with directions on how to keep the Cessna in the air and headed in the right direction. As the two airplanes approached Bogota Airport, the flight instructor got in front and tried to get Lopez down safely. Lopez twice almost hit the control tower, but eventually just enough of his vision cleared to allow him to land without further drama. He was rushed to a hospital, where he recovered fully.

The incident was reported in the Bogota press. The daily *El Tiempo* quoted the testimony of a respected commercial pilot, Rudy Faccini: "The guy is a serious type of fellow. I spoke with his instructor, and during the few weeks that he has been at the school, he has shown [himself] to be a capable pilot . . . and he . . . has not made an impression on anybody as a charlatan. His story has been somewhat reluctantly told, but it has been accepted, and they believe that he did encounter something or other on that morning."

Sphere over Texas

At 5 P.M., on October 26, 1977, the pilot and passenger of a small aircraft at 19,000 feet between Abilene and Dallas, Texas, noticed an odd red sphere some distance ahead of them. It was at their 12 o'clock position. As they flew toward it, their navigation instruments registered erratic movements and the radio seemed not to work; at least the pilot could not communicate with anyone.

As the sphere changed color from red to white, it streaked upward and disappeared. The pilot recalled, "As soon as the sphere left, we got all of our radio gear back. Our navigation came back, and we were off course."

Two officers aboard a T-38, an Air Force jet trainer, also saw the sphere. The pilot reported, "The bright red glowing object was at our 12:30 position approximately 10–12,000 feet and seemed stationary." Fifteen seconds later the sphere began moving rapidly in their direction, leading the pilot to consider an evasive maneuver. That proved unnecessary, because "it appeared the closing had ceased. The size of the object at this time was about that of a dime." The headsets were filled with static all the while.

The UFO suddenly was gone.

"Mothership" over Alaska

On the afternoon of November 17, 1986, Capt. Kenju Terauchi was behind the controls of a Japanese Airlines Boeing 707 cargo plane, on a flight from Paris to Tokyo. The 707 was at 35,000 feet over northeastern Alaska. With him were his first officer and flight engineer. Nothing was out of the ordinary until 5:10 P.M., when Terauchi glimpsed lights to his left and 2,000 feet below his position. After studying them for a short time, he decided that they must be from a military aircraft.

A few minutes later, the lights had not altered their position. Concerned that they were pacing the 707, the crew started paying close attention. As Terauchi took a left turn, the lights appeared in front of the aircraft, and much closer. At this distance—one 500 feet away, the other a mere 100—they looked like two pairs of rectangular arrays of amber and white lights, with "jets" shooting fire out of a dark vertical panel at the center of each object. Seconds later, the fire ceased, revealing "small circles of light" like "numerous exhaust pipes." The objects themselves were, Terauchi would assert, "about the same size as the body of a DC-8 jet." After five minutes the two UFOs pulled abreast of one another.

Terauchi radioed Anchorage flight control and asked if it had anything on radar near the 707. The answer was negative, but it was hard to continue the conversation because the transmissions were garbled. According to Terauchi, "the VHF communications, both in transmitting and receiving, were extremely difficult for 10 to 15 minutes while the little ships came close to us and often interfered with communication from Anchorage." Meanwhile, Anchorage was in touch with the Air Force at Elmendorf Regional Operational Control Center (ROCC) and directing it to see if its radar could detect anything out of the ordinary. ROCC's radar controller reported back that he was picking up "surge primary return"—a radar signal with no corresponding transponder signal. (An airplane's transponder sends out a coded signal responding to a signal from a ground station. The absence of one was both extraordinary and illegal.) The ROCC operator speculated that the image was spurious, but Anchorage now was getting it, too. Anchorage's theory was that this was a military aircraft from ROCC, but that was not the case. All of ROCC's aircraft were accounted for, and none was anywhere near the 707.

Then a "primary return" appeared on ROCC's radar, showing an unidentified object in the general area where the UFO was said to be, until 5:28. Onboard the 707 the crew continued to monitor the lights, now below them and to the left, just above the horizon. As the sky grew darker, it was harder to distinguish them from the stars and planets coming into view. They were too far away to be picked up on the airplane's radar.

The plane proceeded on to a point 20 miles from Eielson AFB to its northeast and 30 miles from Fairbanks to its east-northeast. Something—a pale white light, presumably the one the crew had tracked earlier—was tailing them. They were able to get a particularly good look at it, as lights from the ground gave it increased visibility. Terauchi would call what they saw the "silhouette of a giant spaceship" or a "mothership"—an enormous Saturn-shaped machine the size of "two aircraft carriers." Terauchi believed that it had carried the two relatively smaller objects which had now, he thought, reentered it.

When alerted to this new development, Anchorage gave the pilot permission to take evasive measures. Whatever the aircraft did, the UFO matched it, maintaining its position in spite of turns and descents. ROCC was tracking it when it vanished at 5:39. Terauchi, fearing danger to the interceptor pilots, declined a suggestion that jet fighters be dispatched to the scene. Meantime, the UFO had reappeared, according both to visual observation and to ROCC radar.

A United Airlines passenger jet, which had just left Anchorage on its way north to Fairbanks, looked for the UFO when it reached 29,000 feet. (The JAL plane was at 31,00 feet.) Anchorage said it had an unknown on its radar behind the 707. The image disappeared before the airliner could get close enough to confirm it. By this time the "mothership" was gone for good.

The JAL sighting, as it became known, received massive publicity. It also generated an investigation by the Federal Aviation Administration, beginning with interviews with crewmembers almost as soon as they had landed in Anchorage (they were forced down because of a fuel shortage caused by their actions during the incident). The investigation continued into January 1987.

On March 5 the FAA announced its findings, which were that it "was unable to confirm the event," inasmuch as "a second radar target near the JAL flight at the time of the reported sighting was not another aircraft, but rather a split radar screen return from the JAL Boeing 707." In fact, this was less than certainly true, as Hank Elias, head of the FAA's Alaska air traffic division, subsequently acknowledged. Moreover, as Bruce Maccabee, who conducted his own investigation, would remark:

> The [FAA] press release did not mention that the "split return effect" was contradicted by the fact that the extra echo did not come back with every sweep of the radar and by a statement of an air traffic controller who said that they don't usually get a split image in the area that the JAL jet flew. The press release offered no explanation for the sighting, nor did it dispute the crew's claim that something unusual was seen.

Investigative journalist Marguerite Del Giudice's retrospective on the incident, published in the *Philadelphia Inquirer* on May 24, 1987, reviewed the various proposed explanations (including one that identified the ostensible UFOs as "the planet Jupiter, and possibly another—Mars"[9]) and concluded—as the title of the piece already attested—that this was "The UFO That Can't Be Explained."

AFTERWORD

In 1958, ASKED his assessment of the UFO phenomenon, the celebrated Swiss psychologist-philosopher Carl Gustav Jung pronounced, "Something is being seen, but it is not known what." Though he chose his words carefully, Jung's intention was to convey the conviction, which grew out of his reading of the relevant literature, that UFOs represented an authentic mystery. But when he also pointed to the obvious—that many people project their fantasies onto the images of flying saucers—newspapers around the world declared that this was *all* Jung thought the phenomenon amounted to. To this day, Jung, who died in 1961, is regularly cited as an authority figure who rejected UFO encounters as delusional.

In fact, Jung held the opposite view: that—aside from the subjective psychological, cultural, and folkloric aspects that interested him as a student and theorist of the mind—a core elusive, enigmatic UFO phenomenon existed. It was something that radar screens could track and photographs could record. Not even so determined a debunker as Donald Menzel, Jung wrote, had yet "succeeded in offering a scientific explanation of even one authentic UFO report. . . . By all human standards, it hardly seems possible to doubt [the reality of UFOs] any longer." Perhaps UFOs represent spacecraft that, though quietly present in human history, only now are being noticed, as human beings seek spiritual solace in a dangerous age. Conceivably, Jung reflected, "the appearance of real objects affords an opportunity for mythological projections."

These words appear in the last chapter of Jung's book *Flying Saucers: A Modern Myth of Things Seen in the Skies* (1959). Hardly any writer who has mentioned this book, which is not a long one and is quite readable, seems to have made it that far into the text, the rest of which highlights dreams, visions, and works of art that take direct or indirect inspiration from notions of flying saucers and otherworldly entities. The book is nearly always treated as a kind of definitive kiss-off of UFOs as objectively anomalous phenomena.

It is hard to explain why, contrary evidence notwithstanding, so many of us prefer to believe that UFO sightings are for crazy and gullible people only and thus nothing the sober in our number need to worry about. Why do scientists expend far more effort scoffing at the phenomenon than investigating it, or even forming some general knowledge of it via perusal of the more responsible literature?[1] Instead, we are asked to believe, in effect, that the long neglect of the UFO phenomenon is all the justification we need for that neglect to continue. When pressed, skeptical scientists demand to see "proof," as if such proof could ever be forthcoming without curiosity and effort (not to mention funding and scientific expertise) driving the search for it. A would-be science such as ufology can accomplish nothing if it is afforded neither resources nor respect—nor, for that matter, any real understanding of what it is about.

If UFOs do not exist as genuine anomalies, one would expect that high-strangeness reports of, for example, structured discs— the ostensible product of intelligent manufacture and control— would come overwhelmingly from unreliable—that is, naïve, dishonest, or emotionally disturbed—witnesses. More credible sighters would report ambiguous stimuli, such as nebulous light sources, which seem unusual only at the moment and whose true sources competent investigators could trace with relative ease. The more trained the witnesses, the less likely they would ever think they'd had a UFO experience to begin with. Over the years, a pattern like this would be readily documentable. It would amount to a falsifiable hypothesis for skeptics and debunkers, underscoring the cogency of the late astronomer Carl Sagan's famous quip that the interesting reports are not credible and the credible reports are not interesting.

The opposite happens to be true. As this book, for but one example, has shown, there are plenty of reports that are both credible and interesting. An impressive number have come from military and civilian pilots, whose very survival depends on their being able to make sound assessments of what they are seeing in their airspace. In the early 1950s, a study conducted for Project Blue Book by the civilian Battelle Institute revealed that the best reports came from the most qualified observers, the poorest from the least qualified. Moreover, the best sightings were the most difficult to explain and the ones of longest duration, affording observers a better chance of figuring out what they were or were not seeing. Battelle's analysis showed that reports of (in Blue Book's terminology) "knowns" and "unknowns" were fundamentally unalike. In other words, what we call unidentified flying objects are most unlikely to be identified flying objects in the waiting.[2]

Five and a half decades after Kenneth Arnold's 1947 sighting and Project Sign's 1948 Estimate of the Situation, a stubborn UFO phenomenon refuses to surrender to prosaic accounting, and the extraterrestrial hypothesis (ETH) remains an open question. We now know that the early sightings were not a simple fluke or a fad. We are also learning that our galaxy hosts planets in abundance and that some of them are bound to be earthlike. To every indication, scientists are close to documenting the reality of extraterrestrial life, in at least microscopic form, in even the most brutally inhospitable environments. In more friendly climes, life surely will evolve into more complex forms, some of them intelligent. One result could be beings who can imagine and create sophisticated tools and technologies. If life is everywhere, as many astronomers are convinced it is, and the galaxy is teeming with inhabited planets housing advanced civilizations, it would be more reasonable to expect visitors from elsewhere than not to.

If this proves to be so, perhaps future generations will see Alfred Loedding, the probable author of the pro-ETH Estimate of the Situation, as one of the great visionaries of the twentieth century—a prophet, like so many others, without honor in his time. Maybe the pilots and other credible observers who reported cigars, discs, and other ostensibly unearthly craft will get their due, their intelligence and good sense no longer dishonored by patently inadequate efforts to transform their experiences into trivial misidentifications. Perhaps one day we will know that Chiles and Whitted saw, as they insisted, a giant rocket with two rows of square portholes, and not, as the scoffers would have it, a meteor, and that Sign investigators were perfectly justified in reading the event as an enormously significant moment in human history.

All of this, of course, awaits future reckoning. For now, something is being seen, though we do not know what it is. It persists in strange skies.

NOTES

Introduction

1. Published in two editions, the first in three volumes between 1990 and 1996, the second in two volumes in 1998, by the reference house Omnigraphics.
2. From time to time, a theorist will propose that sightings are intended for witnesses. In recent years most such theories have come from the very small number of researchers who believe that public UFO phenomena exist only to cover the much smaller, private experience of UFO abduction. As the sentence to which this is a footnote indicates, I respectfully disagree.

Chapter 1: The Mystery Begins

1. The strip began in the *Chicago Tribune* in 1935 and continued until 1973. Smokey Stover, a comically inept fireman, was known as "The Foolish Foo Fighter." "Foo" derives from the French feu (fire).
2. This is surely the first printed reference to "foo fighters."
3. A U.S. Naval Intelligence attaché stationed in Paris, Lt. Cdr. C. A. Rocheleaua, filed a Top Secret, three-page report on August

13, 1946, summarizing what witnesses were describing: "A good number of these projectiles are of the V-1 type in the form of a torpedo with two small wings (of a spread of from 2.50 to three meters) and a system of jet propulsion (which allows the escape every two seconds of a jet of flame of about thirty meters often stated to be that [sic] of a blue-green color). . . . The altitude of flight varies greatly but certain passages have taken place at a very low altitude (300–400 meters). The speed is subsonic. . . . But there exists undoubtedly one or more other types of machines characterized by . . . a supersonic speed [and] . . . passages at very high altitude. . . . One report mentions 'an engine resembling a huge cigar. . . . ' On conclusion it would now seem possible to state that Sweden and Finland have been flown over by jet propelled projectiles whose general itineraries are fairly well known and whose range must clearly surpass those of the classic V-1 or V-2 (about 300 to 350 kilometers)."

Chapter 2: "There It Is"

1. The wreckage of the C-46 Marine Corps transport, which went down in a stormy sky one day in December 1946, was located on July 18 on the west slope of the South Tahoma Glacier. Some of the bodies were embedded in ice, but the attempt to recover them amid recurring rock falls proved too dangerous even to the trained military and civilian searchers who went to the site.

2. In a paper on the Arnold sighting, physicist and UFO investigator Bruce Maccabee writes, "Is it reasonable to assume that he could have made an error of several thousand feet in estimating [the UFOs'] altitude? . . . Arnold inferred the altitude by observing that the objects appeared to be almost exactly on his horizon (i.e., level with his airplane). In this case, the angle (the 'depression angle') between exact horizontal and his downward sighting line to the mountain peaks south of Mt. Rainier was very small. The depression angle from Ar-

nold's plane at 9,200 ft altitude to the top of a 5,500 ft high mountain at a distance of 20 miles (105,600 ft) was about 2 deg. Such a small angle would be difficult to detect from an airplane. So the answer is yes, he could easily have made an error of 4,000 ft in estimating the altitude of the objects."

3. As noted, Arnold was a privately employed seller of fire-fighting equipment.

4. Arnold told a United Press reporter that during his stay in Pendleton, he was eating in a restaurant when a woman burst in, stared at him, and dashed out the door screaming, "There's the man who saw the men from Mars!" She started sobbing and said something about protecting her children ("Harassed Saucer-Sighter Would Like to Escape Fuss," *Boise* [Idaho] *Statesman,* June 27).

5. Bruce Maccabee points to the central problem with Hynek's proposed identification. "[Arnold] said he was able to see a DC-4 at 15 miles (estimated distance). . . . By Hynek's criterion Arnold should not have been able to see the DC-4, and certainly he wouldn't have been able to see the engines and thereby to see the spacing of the engines. But Arnold said that he did see the airplane and its engines and Hynek did not dispute that statement."

6. Though we will never know for sure, it is at least possible that smaller, satellite objects entered a larger craft, anticipating the "mothership" phenomenon that would figure in a fair number of subsequent UFO reports worldwide

7. I have been unable to find any independent account of this supposed incident.

8. During Smith's stay, United Press reporter Ted Morello told of receiving phone calls from an anonymous man recounting "verbatim" the conversations going on in the hotel room. Smith and Arnold looked for bugging devices but found none. The calls, almost certainly made by Crisman, spooked the investigators and led them to wonder, even as Dahl and Cris-

man's claims seemed ever more dubious, if they had stumbled into something important, mysterious, and dangerous.

9. Crisman went on to lead a colorful, contentious, controversial life in Tacoma, some of it devoted to the perpetuation of the legend of Fred Lee Crisman. Periodically, he emerged to enlarge on the 1947 saucer story and to mystify it further. On at least one occasion he entered into correspondence with a ufologist under the name "F. Lee," pretending that Fred Crisman—"probably the most informed man in the United States on UFOs"—was somebody else. In the late 1960s, while hosting a right-wing radio call-in show under the stage name "Jon Lord," he briefly became a suspect in New Orleans District Attorney Jim Garrison's freewheeling, largely fact-untainted "investigation" of an alleged JFK-assassination conspiracy. Garrison identified him as one of three "tramps" found inside a rail car several blocks from Dealey Plaza, in Dallas. As participants in the assassination, the tramps—actually contract killers, it was speculated—would figure prominently in conspiracy literature until conclusively identified as actual hoboes in 1992 (see Gerald Posner's *Case Closed: Lee Harvey Oswald and the Assassination of JFK* [1993], pp. 272–73). Crisman was cleared when his employer, Rainier high school principal Stanley Peerboom, proved that Crisman was teaching at the school on November 22, 1963. To an inquirer Peerboom added that Crisman's certain innocence in the JFK murder aside, "I regard Mr. Crisman as a person lacking in truth." Writers Kalani Hanohano and Katiuska Hanohano, who interviewed persons who had known Crisman, observed, "If there is a term that continually characterizes Fred Crisman, that term would be con man." Charles Dahl, Harold's son and one of the purported witnesses to the flying doughnuts, called Crisman a "smooth-talking con artist" and the Maury Island episode a "hoax." Crisman died on December 10, 1975, at the age of 56.

10. To the incalculable distress of UFO historians, including this one, Arnold destroyed all but a handful of these letters in later years.

11. Surely there are worse names to be called. One supposes, however, that some accused him of starting another Martian panic not quite nine years after the Halloween 1938 *Mercury Theater* original.

Chapter 3: Killed by a Flying Saucer

1. Because of the size, the Air Force eventually decided that Armstrong had observed not flying discs but a balloon cluster. There apparently is no specific evidence beyond supposition to validate this interpretation. Pilots before and since, as this book documents, have reported seeing small discs which clearly are not balloons. In his memoirs Project Blue Book head Edward J. Ruppelt would remark that Armstrong's sighting was taken seriously and played a role in early military decisions concerning the seriousness of the flying-disc phenomenon.

2. Ufologist Kevin Randle, an authority on the Mantell case, believes this object—Pickering's description of its movement notwithstanding—was the planet Venus. In a private communication to me, he writes, "I know he said there was no overcast, but the weather records suggest the overcast had begun to break up at about dusk, and at the time of the sighting, the sky should have been completely dark. Venus was to the southwest of the field, and it was about at its brightest. It set about 1915 [7:15 P.M.]."

Chapter 4: Estimation Extraterrestrial

1. For a brief period the FBI entered UFO investigation for this reason. The Air Force Intelligence Chief Gen. George Schulgen was concerned, as an internal FBI memo (July 10, 1947) puts it in paraphrase, "that the first reported sightings might

have been by individuals of Communist sympathies with the view to causing hysteria and fear of a secret Russian weapon. . . . [Schulgen] desired the assistance of the Federal Bureau of Investigation in locating and questioning the individuals . . . to ascertain whether or not they are sincere . . . or whether their statements were prompted by personal desire for publicity or political reasons."

2. Reynolds would be the first and last FBI agent to devote his efforts to UFO investigation. In a September 25, 1947, memo to Hoover, FBI official D. M. Ladd reported, "The results of the investigation conducted by the Bureau Field Offices in this matter have failed to reveal any indication of subversive individuals being involved in any of the reported sightings." Two days later FBI director J. Edgar Hoover wrote Maj. Gen. George C. McDonald, at the Air Force office in the Pentagon, to complain of public statements which indicated that the FBI would not be interviewing responsible witnesses but "running down incidents which in many cases turned out to be 'ash can covers, toilet seats and whatnot'" portrayed by hoaxers and pranksters as disc remains. He went on, "I am advising the Field Divisions of the Federal Bureau of Investigation to discontinue all investigative activity regarding the reported sightings of flying discs, and am instructing them to refer all complaints received to the appropriate Air Force representative in their area."

3. According to UFO historians Michael D. Hall and Wendy A. Connors, authors of *Alfred Loedding and the Great Flying Saucer Wave of 1947* (1998), "Donald Loedding clearly remembers the controversy surrounding the rejection of his father's 'Estimate of the Situation' draft to General Vandenberg and the resulting deep disappointment by his father. Donald had the impression that Alfred Loedding, who had been a rising star at Wright Field, officially fell from favor as a result of his personal belief that many of the flying disc sightings could

represent craft of extraterrestrial origin. When he personally authored that carefully reached conclusion in the 'Estimate' draft, Loedding severely hurt his career. . . . Donald feels that officials at AMC [Air Materiel Command] attempted to phase his father out. . . . Records do show, in fact, that Alfred Loedding's efficiency rating reports went from excellent in 1948 to lower and lower grades until he resigned on February 16th, 1951." He returned to Wright Field (now Wright-Patterson AFB) in 1955 and resumed work, again in a civilian capacity. In 1960 he was assigned to Langley AFB, Virginia, where he served as the Air Force's liaison to NASA. "But from 1951 until his death in 1963," Hall and Connors write, "Loedding, according to Donald, never again worked on or talked about UFOs—so deep was his disappointment and disgust with being 'fired' from Project Sign for his views."

4. Also known as the Condon Committee, after its director, University of Colorado physicist Edward U. Condon. In 1966 the Air Force, which wanted out of the UFO business (a longstanding public-relations nightmare), entered into contract with the university to conduct an allegedly independent assessment of the UFO phenomenon. In fact, as subsequent events underscored, the Air Force and director Condon understood that the project would conclude that UFOs merit no further attention, thus allowing the Air Force to close down Project Blue Book. Col. Robert Hippler, one of the Air Force's chief scientists, delivered the message explicitly to Condon—who privately detested UFO reports—in a letter written from his Pentagon office on January 16, 1967. Almost from the outset, the project was beset with controversy and internal conflict. When two investigators uncovered an internal memo stating the project's true purpose and leaked it to critics, they were fired, amid much embarrassing publicity. The project completed its work on October 31, 1968, and in January 1969 released *Scientific Study of Unidentified Flying Objects*—known

informally as the Condon Report—whose introduction, written by Condon, urged that UFO investigation be discontinued because it had nothing to contribute to scientific knowledge. Those who got past the introduction and plowed through the book's nearly 1,000 pages found, however, that a third of the cases remained unexplained. Nonetheless, despite criticism by some scientists, the report was widely hailed as the definitive debunking. It allowed the Air Force, citing Condon's remarks, to close Blue Book the following December.

5. Though perhaps square windows seem a bit much to ask of such an effect.

6. Confusingly, however, Sperry told James E. McDonald in a February 1968 interview that the light was to the rear. In a television interview four years earlier, he referred to "a very bright bluish light in the nose of it."

Chapter 5: Grounding the Saucers

1. Nonetheless, the Air Force eventually came to the improbable conclusion that the object had been a meteor. In 1977, looking back on the case, longtime Blue Book scientific consultant and Northwestern University astronomer J. Allen Hynek expressed incredulity: "Meteors do not hover, do not move along with the aircraft, and then take off 'up and away.' The only way out of this one would have been for the evaluator to have claimed that *both* pilots were momentarily subject to a hallucination."

2. In the wake of his sighting, Nash, already a regular contributor to general-interest magazines on aviation and popular-science matters, would become an active UFO investigator and occasional participant in organized ufology. With Fortenberry he wrote an article about his sighting for the pro-UFO mass-circulation men's magazine *True* (October 1952). On his own he was an occasional contributor to small-scale periodicals such as Gray Barker's *The Saucerian,* in whose January 1955

number he added a curious footnote to his account of the Air Force interview. He wrote that just prior to the meeting he and Fortenberry agreed to ask if there was any substance to recurrent rumors—in circulation since the late 1940s—that the U.S. government had crashed discs in its possession. (The subject had been the topic of the best-selling, and subsequently discredited, *Behind the Flying Saucers* [1950], by entertainment columnist Frank Scully.) In the excitement Nash forgot to ask the question, but Fortenberry remembered and was told, according to Nash, that the story was true. When the two were interviewed together, Nash thought to raise the issue. He claimed that the officers "all opened their mouths to answer the question, whereupon Maj. Sharp[e] looked at them, not me, and said very quickly, 'No!' It appeared as if he were telling them to shut up rather than addressing the answer to me." Nash earlier had related the same story in an April 18, 1954, letter to a friend, fellow airline pilot and UFO witness W. J. Hull. The relevant portion of the letter is reprinted on page 11 of *International UFO Reporter,* Spring 2002.

3. In 1969 the Air Force Environmental Technical Applications Center analyzed the Washington sighting and rejected the temperature-inversion theory as essentially a physical impossibility.

Chapter 6: Discs in Daylight

1. Hynek separated UFO reports into six categories: (1) nocturnal lights; (2) daylight discs; (3) radar/visuals; (4) close encounters of the first kind—"sighting reports . . . of objects or very brilliant lights . . . less than 500 feet away"; (5) close encounters of the second kind—"the reported UFO . . . leaves a visible record" or "physical effect of some sort"; and (6) close encounters of the third kind—"in which the presence of animated creatures is reported" (i.e., sightings of UFO occupants).

Chapter 7: The New War of the Worlds

1. In a later book, *Aliens from Space* (1973), Keyhoe wrote that someone at Air Force Headquarters told him, "That F-94 pilot said there was a separate effect besides the heat. Something made his mind black out—he couldn't even remember bailing out. He did recall the sudden heat and he saw the radar observer eject himself. But everything was a blank from then on until his parachute opened. . . . The pilot begged the AF to let him talk privately with the relatives of that family and the people who got hurt, so they'd know what really happened. But [the Air Force] wouldn't let him. Both of those men were really muzzled."

2. "C.R.I.F.O." stood for Civilian Research, Interplanetary Flying Objects.

3. Renamed Kincheloe Air Force Base in September 1959, it was closed down in September 1977.

4. An October 30, 1968, article in the *Sault Daily Star* states, referring to this incident, "Sometime later [that evening], Algoma Central Railway workers reported hearing a crash that could have been caused by the F-89. . . . The railway workers heard the sound only about 100 miles from the Sault."

5. In *The UFO Casebook* (1989) Kevin D. Randle, a well-regarded UFO investigator and former Air Force pilot, cites the testimony of an unnamed "lieutenant colonel who was there" at Truax when the incident happened: "One group thought that the plane had gone straight into the lake. If it didn't break up, there would have been no oil slick or wreckage. It is entirely possible. However, the other school, supported by the majority of the pilots, was that Moncla had been 'taken' by the UFO." Subsequently, according to the informant, a large, luminous UFO paced a jet aircraft, frightening the pilots, who feared they would suffer Moncla's fate.

6. One of the few undisputed aspects of the case is that just

prior to the disappearance, Moncla asked for and received permission to drop down to 7,000 feet from 30,000 in the identification attempt. In other words, whatever happened to it, the F-89 was descending when it met its fate.

7. The other also resembles it in significant ways. Smith's notes paraphrase Hill thus: "A transport plane with 26 persons aboard was rapidly approaching its air base some 10 miles from shore. Back on land at the radar station the operator was carefully tracking the transport plane and was in constant radar communication with the plane. Suddenly the radar operator spied a second blip on his radarscope. He immediately radioed the transport and advised the pilot to beware of the alien object. The UFO was traveling at a high rate of speed, about 2,500 mph. All of a sudden the mysterious blip headed straight for the transport plane, and before the radar operator could warn it, the two objects had united into one on the radar screen. The one remaining blip sped straight up at a terrific rate of speed. A surface search of the water in the vicinity revealed no oil slick, although a general's briefcase was found floating. The plane had completely disappeared." If such an incident happened, it has so far managed to evade documentation by ufologists.

8. By then he was director of a prominent civilian UFO group, National Investigations Committee on Aerial Phenomena (NICAP), based in Washington, D.C.

9. The same writer, Willy Smith, author of *On Pilots and UFOs* (1997), stresses the point, typically overlooked by those attempting to explain the Kinross incident as a tragic misunderstanding between an F-89C and a Canadian transport plane, that the two blips disappeared *at the same time.* If this was indeed an encounter between two earthly airplanes, the only possible inference is that they collided and both fell into Lake Superior. Yet no one has ever alleged such a dual disaster.

10. Baker, for example, claimed that on one occasion he and Hunrath saw something that "closely resembled a skeleton for a saucer mock-up." They suspected it was the model for the "Venusian scoutcraft" which figures in some of Adamski's most often reproduced photographs.

11. Lemuria is the Pacific counterpart to Atlantis, coming into prominence in occultist circles through Helene Petrovna Blavatsky's metaphysical text *The Secret Doctrine* (1889). Its popularity on the speculative fringes notwithstanding, there is no reason to believe that such a place ever existed.

12. Bailey would subsequently retract his testimony. Interviewed by Moseley in 1954, he acknowledged that he saw neither spaceman nor spaceship.

13. "Several experienced pilots believe Karl cracked up on the side of Big Bear—a rugged, mountainous area of California," Williamson wrote in *Other Tongues—Other Flesh* (1957). "The plane didn't carry much fuel, and Big Bear is deceiving to those who have not flown over it before. Hunrath hadn't flown in a long time, and he had never flown near Big Bear before. The down-draft and illusive qualities of the mountain could have doomed the small plane." Others speculated at the time that Hunrath and Wilkinson had gone into hiding, but those who were acquainted with them, and especially with Hunrath's manifest need for attention and stimulation, discounted the idea.

Chapter 8: High Strangeness

1. During the 18th and 19th centuries sea serpents were as controversial as UFOs would be in the 20th and the 21st. On June 16, 1826, off St. Georgia's Bank south of Nova Scotia, the captain and an English passenger on the American ship *Silas Richards* reportedly observed an immense snakelike creature making its way toward them on the water. The Englishman hurried to inform other passengers, who were below deck, but

only a few took the trouble to see what the excitement was about. The captain would recall, "The remainder refused to come up, saying there had been too many hoaxes of that kind already."

2. In his official report, written soon after the airplane had landed, Jones recorded that when he first saw it, the UFO "resembled a huge fiery orange disc on its edge. As it went further away, the center became darker, but the edge still threw off a fiery hue. When it went over the horizon, it seemed to go from a vertical position to a horizontal position, with only the trailing edge showing in a half-moon effect. Since I was not the first to see it, it was going away from the plane when I was notified."

3. "Encounter" would not be used as a way of describing a UFO experience until the 1970s.

4. Nothing in the undisputed history of government and military handling of the UFO phenomenon speaks to this alleged group. In the early 1980s alleged classified government documents surfaced claiming the existence of a high-level group called Majestic-12, or MJ-12, said to consist of a dozen leading scientists, military officers, and intelligence specialists (including, bizarrely, the vehement UFO debunker Donald H. Menzel). The most notorious of these, dated November 18, 1952, is a supposed briefing given to President-elect Dwight D. Eisenhower informing him of the group's existence and its mission to investigate visitors from outer space. The document asserts that the evidence includes the remains of two crashed UFOs and their dead occupants, called "extraterrestrial biological entities." Though for many good reasons this and related documents—many others would circulate in the next decade and a half—are regarded as forgeries, at least the Eisenhower briefing document still has a few hard-core defenders, notably the well-known ufologist Stanton T. Friedman, who argues the case in *Top Secret/Majic* (1996). Though I regard MJ-12 as fiction, Bethune's anecdote is certainly intriguing—assuming, of course, that his memory is not playing tricks on him.

5. Bethune would write, "I finally met Klass at the 1996 [Mutual UFO Network] Symposium in Greensboro, North Carolina. He noticed my name tag and eventually connected me with the North Atlantic UFO case. Then he proceeded to lecture me about what we had *really* seen! . . . I have often thought that he could use an hour or two in the cockpit of an airplane over the North Atlantic, watching the real Moon and stars, instead of those he conjures up in the warm safety of his office."

6. The official Blue Book explanation, apparently believed by nobody, had been "inversion reflection of the planet Mars."

7. Project Blue Book closed in December 1969. Hynek had served Blue Book and its predecessors since 1948 but by the mid-1960s had grown outspokenly out of sympathy with the Air Force's negative views and, in his opinion, unscientific approach to UFO investigation and analysis. He outlined his views in the well-received *The UFO Experience* (1972). In 1973 he co-founded, with Sherman J. Larsen, the Center for UFO Studies. He died on April 27, 1986, but CUFOS, now under the direction of sociologist and Hynek associate Mark Rodeghier, continues to operate out of an office in Chicago.

8. I interviewed De los Santos personally in Mexico in April 1977. He gave every impression of being sane, sincere, and thoughtful. Nonetheless, he related a bizarre sequel which makes the aerial encounter seem almost mundane by comparison. A week after the sighting, he said, he was driving to a Mexico City television station, where he was to participate in a talk show discussion of his experience. On the freeway a large, black, brand-new-looking Galaxie limousine pulled up very close in front of his car, and a similar vehicle did the same behind it. Together they forced him to the side of the road. Four dark-suited men with broad shoulders and oddly pale skin got out and approached him as the young man, who was still behind the steering wheel, sat paralyzed with fright. They warned him to stop talking about his sighting "if you value your life and

your family's, too." He drove straight home. A month later, however, when visiting American astronomer/ufologist J. Allen Hynek asked him to breakfast at a downtown hotel, De los Santos agreed to meet with him. Walking up the hotel steps, he was confronted by the same menacing strangers. One of them shoved him and warned that his movements were being monitored. The young pilot broke this appointment, too. (Hynek confirmed that much of the incident to me later.) Stories like these, reported from time to time, come out of ufology's murky "men in black" tradition.

9. A theory rushed into print by a debunking organization six weeks before the FAA released documents providing vital information, essential to any meaningful analysis, about the incident. Among other criticisms Maccabee disputes the identification of the "mothership" with Jupiter on the grounds that the FAA documents reveal that "just before the end of the sighting, when Jupiter was ahead of the plane and to the left (about at the 10 o'clock position), the UFO 'mothership' was behind and to the left (at the seven-to-eight o'clock position)."

Afterword

1. For instance, Hynek's *The UFO Experience* and Peter A. Sturrock's more recent *The UFO Enigma*, both written by scientists with long track records in UFO research.

2. For more details, see "Project Blue Book Special Report No. 14" in my *The UFO Encyclopedia: The Phenomenon from the Beginning*, pages 742 to 745, or Bruce Maccabee, ed., *Project Blue Book Special Report No. 14*, which consists of the original text with annotations and analysis. The study is also discussed in J. Allen Hynek's *The Hynek UFO Report*.

BIBLIOGRAPHY

Adamski, George. *Inside the Space Ships.* New York: Abelard-Schuman, 1955.

Aldrich, Jan L. "Investigating the Ghost Rockets." *International UFO Reporter* , vol. 23, no. 4 (Winter 1998): pp. 9–14.

———. *Project 1947: A Preliminary Report on the 1947 UFO Sighting Wave.* N.p.: UFO Research Coalition, 1997.

Andrus, Walter H., Jr. "Strange Alaskan Encounter." *MUFON UFO Journal,* vol. 226 (February 1987): pp. 3–8.

Angelucci, Orfeo. *The Secret of the Saucers.* Amherst, WI: Amherst Press, 1955.

Arnold, Kenneth. *The Flying Saucer as I Saw It.* Boise, ID: N.p., 1950.

———. "I *Did* See the Flying Disks!" *Fate,* vol. 1, no. 1 (Spring 1948): pp. 4–10.

———. "The Maury Island Episode." In Curtis G. Fuller, ed., *Proceedings of the First International UFO Congress.* New York: Warner Books, 1980.

———. "What Happened on June 24, 1947." In Hilary Evans and Dennis Stacy, eds., *UFOs 1947–1997: From Arnold to the*

Abductees: Fifty Years of Flying Saucers. London: John Brown Publishing, 1997.

Arnold, Kenneth, and Ray Palmer. *The Coming of the Saucers: A Documentary Report on Sky Objects That Have Mystified the World.* Boise, ID, and Amherst, WI: N.p., 1952.

Barnes, Harry G. "Washington Radar Observer Relates Watching Stunts by Flying Saucers." *New York World-Telegram,* July 29, 1952.

Begg, Paul. *Into Thin Air: People Who Disappear.* North Pomfret, VT: David and Charles, 1979.

Behr, Howard S. *Sighting of Howard S. Behr, USAF (Retired).* Statement in files of National Investigations Committee on Aerial Phenomena, n.d.

Berliner, Don. "Aircraft Pilot Spots Object Over Colombia." *MUFON UFO Journal,* vol. 115 (June 1977): pp. 4, 7.

Berlitz, Charles, with J. Manson Valentine. *The Bermuda Triangle.* Garden City, NY: Doubleday and Company, 1974.

Bethune, Graham E. *UFO in the North Atlantic, February 10, 1951.* Toms River, NJ: N.p., 1999.

Bloecher, Ted. *Report on the UFO Wave of 1947.* Washington, DC: N.p., 1967.

Buckle, Eileen. *The Scoriton Mystery.* London: Neville Spearman, 1967.

"Captain Tom Mantell's Last Words." *C.R.I.F.O. Newsletter,* vol. 1, no. 9 (December 3, 1954): p. 4.

"Chichester Made a UFO Sighting Over Tasman in 1931." *Wellington* [New Zealand] *Evening Post* (March 1968).

Chiles, C. S. Letter to S. L. Shannon, Eastern Airlines (August 3, 1948).

Clark, Jerome. "Carlos de los Santos and the Men in Black." *Flying Saucer Review,* vol. 24, no. 4 (January 1979): pp. 8–9.

———. *The UFO Encyclopedia: The Phenomenon from the Beginning,* Second Edition. Two volumes. Detroit, MI: Omnigraphics, 1998.

Clarke, David, and Andy Roberts. *Out of the Shadows: UFOs, The Establishment and the Official Cover-up.* London: Piatkus, 2002.

Comella, Thomas M. "Have UFOs 'Swallowed' Our Aircraft?" *Fate,* vol. 14, no. 5 (May 1961): pp. 32–37.

Cowgill, Warner. "Curious Phenomenon in Venezuela." *Scientific American,* vol. 55 (December 18, 1886): p. 389.

Cox, Billy. "Have We Lost Our Curiosity?" *Florida Today* (July 30, 2002).

Creighton, Gordon. "Healing from UFOs." *Flying Saucer Review,* vol. 15, no. 5 (September/October 1969): pp. 20–23.

Cumber, Jim. "The Case of the Disappearing Air Force Jet Interceptor." *MUFON UFO Journal,* vol. 392 (December 2000): pp. 12–13.

Del Giudice, Marguerite. "The UFO That Can't Be Explained." *Philadelphia Inquirer* (May 24, 1987).

Department of Defense Minutes of Press Conference Held by Major General John A. Samford, Director of Intelligence, U.S. Air Force. Washington, DC: Department of Defense, 1952.

Durant, F. C. *Report of Meetings of Scientific Advisory Panel on Unidentified Flying Objects Convened by Office of Scientific Intelligence, CIA: January 14–18, 1953.* Washington, DC: Central Intelligence Agency, 1953.

Eckert, Allan W. "The Mystery of the Lost Patrol." *The American Legion Magazine* (April 1962): pp. 12–23, 39–41.

Edwards, Frank. *Flying Saucers—Serious Business.* New York: Lyle Stuart, 1966.

Extraterrestrial Object Involved in Japan Air Line Pilot's UFO Sighting, According to Leading UFO Investigator. Buffalo, NY: Committee for the Scientific Investigation of Claims of the Paranormal, 1987.

Fawcett, Lawrence, and Barry J. Greenwood. *Clear Intent: The Government Coverup of the UFO Experience.* Englewood Cliffs, NJ: Prentice-Hall, 1984.

"Flying Saucers in 1931?" *The Aeroplane* (November 24, 1950): p. 448.

Fort, Charles. *The Books of Charles Fort.* New York: Henry Holt and Company, 1941.

Fowler, Raymond E. "Commercial Pilot Reports Daylight Disc." *Skylook,* vol. 98 (January 1976): pp. 16–18.

Friedman, Stanton T. *Top Secret/Majic.* New York: Marlowe and Company, 1996.

Fuller, Curtis. "The Flying Saucers—Fact or Fiction?" *Flying* (July 1950): pp. 16–17, 59–61.

Gaddis, Vincent H. "The Deadly Bermuda Triangle." *Argosy* (February 1964): pp. 28–29, 116–18.

———. *Invisible Horizons: True Mysteries of the Sea.* Philadelphia, PA: Chilton Books, 1965.

Gillmor, Daniel S., ed. *Scientific Study of Unidentified Flying Objects.* New York: Bantam Books, 1969.

Gross, Loren E. *Charles Fort, the Fortean Society, and Unidentified Flying Objects.* Fremont, CA: N.p., 1976.

———. *UFOs: A History—July 1947–December 1948.* Fremont, CA: N.p., 1980.

———. *UFOs: A History—1949.* Fremont, CA: N.p., 1982.

———. *UFOs: A History—1950: April–July.* Fremont, CA: N.p., 1982.

———. *UFOs: A History—1951.* Fremont, CA: N.p., 1983.

———. *UFOs: A History—1952: January–May.* Fremont, CA: N.p., 1982.

———. *UFOs: A History—1952: June–July 20th.* Fremont, CA: N.p., 1986.

———. *UFOs: A History—1952: July 21st–July 31st.* Fremont, CA: N.p., 1986.

———. *UFOs: A History—1952: September–October.* Fremont, CA: N.p., 1986.

———. *UFOs: A History—1953: January–February.* Fremont, CA: N.p., 1988.

———. *UFOs: A History—1953: August–December,* Second edition. Fremont, CA: N.p., 1994.

———. *UFOs: A History—1954: June–August.* Fremont, CA: N.p., 1990.

———. *UFOs: A History—1956: January–April.* Fremont, CA: N.p., 1993.

Haines, Gerald K. "CIA's Role in the Study of UFOs, 1947–90." *Studies in Intelligence: Semiannual Unclassified Edition,* vol. 1 (1997): pp. 67–84.

Haines, Richard F. "An Aircraft/UFO Encounter Over Germany in 1976." *International UFO Reporter* (Winter 1999): pp. 30–6.

———. *Melbourne Episode: Case Study of a Missing Pilot.* Los Altos, CA: L.D.A. Press, 1987.

———. *Project Delta: A Study of Multiple UFOs.* Los Altos, CA: L.D.A. Press, 1994.

———. "A Review of Selected Aerial Phenomenon Sightings from Aircraft from 1942 to 1952." In Walter H. Andrus, Jr., and Dennis W. Stacy, eds., *MUFON 1983 UFO Symposium Proceedings.* Seguin, TX: Mutual UFO Network, 1983.

Hall, Michael David. *UFOs: A Century of Sightings.* Lakeville, MN: Galde Press, 1999.

———. "Was There a Second Estimate of the Situation?" *International UFO Reporter,* vol. 27, no. 1 (Spring 2002): pp. 10–14, 32.

———, and Wendy Ann Connors. "Alfred Loedding: New Insight on the Man Behind Project Sign." *International UFO Reporter,* vol. 23, no. 4 (Winter 1998): pp. 3–8, 24–28.

———. *Alfred Loedding and the Great Flying Saucer Wave of 1947.* Albuquerque, NM: Rose Press, 1998.

———. *Captain Edward J. Ruppelt: Summer of the Saucers—1952.* Albuquerque, NM: Rose Press International, 2000.

Hall, Richard H. *The UFO Evidence.* Washington: National Investigations Committee on Aerial Phenomena, 1964.

———. *The UFO Evidence II: A Thirty-Year Report.* Lanham, MD: Scarecrow Press, 2000.

Harris, Waldo J. Letter to Zan Overall (December 7, 1961).

Hynek, J. Allen. *The Hynek UFO Report.* New York: Dell, 1977.

———. *The UFO Experience: A Scientific Inquiry.* Chicago: Henry Regnery Company, 1972.

Hynek, J. Allen, and Jacques Vallee. *The Edge of Reality: A Progress Report on Unidentified Flying Objects.* Chicago: Henry Regnery Company, 1975.

Jacobs, David M. *The UFO Controversy in America.* Bloomington: Indiana University Press, 1975.

———, ed. *UFOs and Abductions: Challenging the Borders of Knowledge.* Lawrence: University Press of Kansas, 2000.

"Japan: Planes Chased by Flying Saucer Over Inland Sea." *Flying Saucer Review,* vol. 11, no. 4 (July/August 1965): p. iii.

Jessup, M. K. *The Case for the UFO.* New York: Citadel Press, 1955.

Jones, William E. "Historical Notes: Thomas Mantell." *MUFON UFO Journal,* vol. 264 (April 1990): pp. 18–19.

Jung, C. G. *Flying Saucers: A Modern Myth of Things Seen in the Skies.* New York: Harcourt, Brace and Company, 1959.

Keyhoe, Donald E. *Aliens from Space: The Real Story of Unidentified Flying Objects.* Garden City, NY: Doubleday and Company, 1973.

———. *The Flying Saucer Conspiracy.* New York: Henry Holt and Company, 1955.

———. *Flying Saucers: Top Secret.* New York: G. P. Putnam's Sons, 1960.

———. *The Flying Saucers Are Real.* New York: Fawcett Publications, 1950.

———. "The Flying Saucers Are Real." *True* (January 1950): pp. 11–13, 83–87.

———. *Flying Saucers from Outer Space.* New York: Henry Holt and Company, 1953.

Klass, Philip J. *UFOs Explained.* New York: Random House, 1974.

Kusche, Larry. *The Bermuda Triangle Mystery Solved*. Buffalo, NY: Prometheus Books, 1986.

———. *The Disappearance of Flight 19*. New York: Harper and Row, Publishers, 1980.

Leslie, Desmond. "Captain Mantell—No Further Doubts About Interception." *Flying Saucer Review*, vol. 1, no. 5 (November/December 1955): pp. 7, 30.

Long, Greg. "Kenneth Arnold: UFO 'Pioneer.'" *MUFON UFO Journal*, vol. 165 (November 1981): pp. 7–10.

Maccabee, Bruce. "The Arnold Phenomenon." *International UFO Reporter*. Part I: vol. 20, no. 1 (January/February 1995): pp. 14–17. Part II: vol. 20, no. 2 (March/April 1995): pp. 10–13, 24. Part III: vol. 20, no. 3 (May/June 1995): pp. 6–7.

———. "The Fantastic Flight of JAL1628." *International UFO Reporter*, vol. 12, no. 2 (March/April 1987): pp. 4–23.

———. "The Muroc Discs." *Fate*, vol. 37, no. 9 (September 1984): pp. 79–82.

———. *UFO/FBI Connection: The Secret History of the Government's Cover-up*. St. Paul, MN: Llewellyn Publications, 2000.

———, ed. *Project Blue Book Special Report No. 14*. Evanston, IL: Center for UFO Studies, 1979.

Martin, Jorge. "Did Huge Triangle Shaped UFO Abduct Two U.S. Jet Fighters in Puerto Rico?" *MUFON UFO Journal*, vol. 261 (January 1990): pp. 20–23.

Martin, William J. Letter to Richard Hall (February 11, 1990).

McCage, Gladys. Letter to Albert Baller (September 30, 1965).

McDonald, James E. *Science, Technology, and UFOs*. Tucson, AZ: N.p., 1968.

Menzel, Donald H., and Lyle G. Boyd. *The World of Flying Saucers: A Scientific Examination of a Major Myth of the Space Age*. Garden City, NY: Doubleday and Company, 1963.

Michel, Aimé. *The Truth About Flying Saucers*. New York: Criterion Books, 1956.

Moseley, James W. "The Mysterious Disappearance of Hunrath and Wilkinson." *Saucer News,* vol. 5, no. 3 (1958): pp. 10–13.

Moseley, James W., and Karl T. Pflock. *Shockingly Close to the Truth! Confessions of a Grave-Robbing Ufologist.* Amherst, NY: Prometheus Books, 2002.

Nash, William B. "Does the Air Force Have 'Hardware from Outer Space'?" *The Saucerian,* vol. 3, no. 1 (January 1955): pp. 29–31.

Nash, William B., and William H. Fortenberry. "We Flew Above Flying Saucers." *True* (October 1952): pp. 65, 110–12.

"Nazis' Newest Trick, 'Fire Balls,' Follow or Precede Planes." *Washington Evening Star* (January 2, 1945).

Oliver, Norman. *Sequel to Scoriton.* London: N.p., 1968.

Page, Thornton. "Robertson Panel." In Ronald D. Story, ed., *The Encyclopedia of UFOs.* Garden City, NY: Doubleday and Company, 1980.

"Pilot, Ground Crew Observe Disc." *The A.P.R.O. Bulletin* (January 1962): pp. 1, 3.

"Pilot Says Compass Affected." *Skylook,* vol. 89 (April 1975): p. 5.

Powell, Rolan D., Byron D. Varner, and Walter Andrus. "UFO Sighting Over Hanford Nuclear Reactor in 1945." *MUFON UFO Journal,* vol. 344 (December 1996): pp. 13–14.

Project "Saucer." Washington, DC: National Military Establishment Office of Publication Information, 1949.

"Radar and the Saucers." *Washington Post* (July 25, 1952).

Randle, Kevin D. *Invasion Washington: UFOs Over the Capitol.* New York: Harper Mass Market Paperbacks, 2001.

———. *The UFO Casebook.* New York: Warner Books, 1989.

———. "Walesville Revisited." *International UFO Reporter,* vol. 25, no. 3 (Fall 2000): pp. 3–6.

Randles, Jenny. *UFO! Danger in the Air.* New York: Sterling Publishing Company, 1998.

Reid, Frank J. "Keyhoe's Context." *International UFO Reporter,* vol. 25, no. 3 (Fall 2000): pp. 6–7, 28–29.

"Rocket Craft Encounter Revealed by World War 2 Pilot." *The U.F.O. Investigator,* vol. 1, 2 (August/September 1957): p. 15.

Rodeghier, Mark. *UFO Reports Involving Vehicle Interference: A Catalogue and Data Analysis.* Evanston, IL: Center for UFO Studies, 1981.

Ruppelt, Edward J. *The Report on Unidentified Flying Objects.* Garden City, NY: Doubleday and Company, 1956.

Sagan, Carl, and Thornton Page, eds. *UFOs—A Scientific Debate.* Ithaca, NY: Cornell University Press, 1972.

Saunders, David R., and R. Roger Harkins. *UFOs? Yes! Where the Condon Committee Went Wrong.* New York: World Publishing Company, 1968.

Shallett, Sidney. "What You Can Believe About Flying Saucers." *Saturday Evening Post.* Part I (April 30, 1949): pp. 20–21, 136–39. Part II (May 7, 1949): pp. 36, 184–86.

Smith, Willy. *On Pilots and UFOs: A Collection of Interesting Cases from the Blue Book Files and the Spanish Air Force Records.* Miami, FL: UNICAT Project, 1997.

Stacy, Dennis. "1983 MUFON UFO Symposium: 'UFOs—A Scientific Challenge.'" *MUFON UFO Journal,* vol. 185 (July 1983): pp. 3–8.

Steiger, Brad, ed. *Project Blue Book: The Top Secret UFO Findings Revealed.* New York: Ballantine Books, 1976.

Story, Ronald D., with J. Richard Greenwell. *UFOs and the Limits of Science.* New York: William Morrow and Company, 1981.

Strentz, Herbert J. *A Survey of Press Coverage of Unidentified Flying Objects, 1947–1966.* Ph.D. dissertation, Northwestern University, Evanston, Illinois, 1970.

Stringfield, Leonard H. "The Case for Interplanetary 'War.'" *C.R.I.F.O. Orbit,* vol. 2, no. 8 (November 4, 1955): pp. 1–4.

———. *Situation Red, The UFO Siege!* Garden City, NY: Doubleday and Company, 1977.

———. "World's Air Forces, in Joint Operations, Challenge Incursion of UFO's. Mysterious Jet Disasters Mount. G.O.C.

Alerted—to Coordinate in Skywatch with Radar." *C.R.I.F.O. Orbit,* vol. 2, no. 4 (July 1, 1955): pp. 1–4.

Sturrock, Peter A. *The UFO Enigma: A New Review of the Physical Evidence.* New York: Warner Books, 1999.

Svahn, Clas, and Anders Liljegren. "Close Encounters with Unknown Missiles." http://www.project1947.com/afumiss.htm, n.d.

Swords, Michael D. "Classic Cases from the APRO Files." *International UFO Reporter,* vol. 24, no. 2 (Summer 1999): pp. 21–22, 31.

———. "Dr. Robertson Requests the Honor of Your Attendance." *International UFO Reporter,* vol. 20, no. 2 (March/April 1995): pp. 16–20.

———. "The Summer of 1947: UFOs and the U.S. Government at the Beginning." In George M. Eberhart, ed., *The Roswell Report: A Historical Perspective.* Chicago: J. Allen Hynek Center for UFO Studies, 1991.

Tacker, Lawrence J. *Flying Saucers and the U.S. Air Force.* Princeton, NJ: Van Nostrand Company, 1960.

Tulien, Thomas. "The 1952 Nash/Fortenberry Sighting Revisited." *International UFO Reporter,* vol. 27, no. 1 (Spring 2002): pp. 20–23, 27–28.

"UFOs Pace, Disrupt Airplane." *Skylook,* vol. 93 (August 1975): pp. 3–4.

Vaughan, Valerie, ed. *UFOs and Science: The Collected Writings of Dr. James E. McDonald.* Mount Rainier, MD: Fund for UFO Research, 1995.

Velasco, Jean-Jacques. "Report on the Analysis of Anomalous Physical Traces: The 1981 Trans-en-Provence UFO Case." *Journal of Scientific Exploration,* vol. 4, no. 1 (1990): pp. 27–48.

Wilkins, Harold T. *Flying Saucers on the Attack.* New York: Citadel Press, 1954.

Williamson, George Hunt. *Other Tongues—Other Flesh.* Amherst, WI: Amherst Press, 1957.

Zeidman, Jennie. "Green Light Over Mansfield." *International UFO Reporter,* vol. 13, no. 6 (November/December 1988): pp. 13–14.

———. *A Helicopter-UFO Encounter Over Ohio.* Evanston, IL: Center for UFO Studies, 1979.

———. "The Mansfield Helicopter Case: Anatomy of an Investigation." In Walter H. Andrus, Jr., ed., *MUFON 1989 International UFO Symposium Proceedings.* Seguin, TX: Mutual UFO Network, 1989.

INDEX